The VIKINGS
and AMERICA

Erik Wahlgren

The VIKINGS and AMERICA

WITH 103 ILLUSTRATIONS

THAMES AND HUDSON

THIS IS VOLUME ONE HUNDRED AND TWO IN THE SERIES
Ancient Peoples and Places
GENERAL EDITOR: GLYN DANIEL

Frontispiece
Viking ships under sail in Sognefjord by Hans Gude (1889).
This conception of the Vikings and their long ship is clearly a product of
19th-century Romanticism, though Gude's painting also reflects the
growing historical awareness of his time. The Gokstad ship had been
discovered only nine years previously.

© 1986 Thames and Hudson Ltd, London

First published in the United States in 1986 by
Thames and Hudson Inc., 500 Fifth Avenue,
New York, New York 10110

Library of Congress Catalog Card Number 85-51467

Printed and bound in Hungary

Contents

Preface

Since the spring of 1933, emboldened by my then new-found if sketchy acquaintance with the Old Norse/Icelandic language, I have pursued the Icelandic sagas. In 1950 I began in earnest to inquire into what they might tell us about the discovery of America. Except on Greenland, archaeological evidence at that time was slight, misidentifications and romantic or frivolous 'evidence' abounded, and literary or historical interpretations were often mutually contradictory. The situation is better now. With the warming of the Arctic and sub-Arctic climate, new archaeological sites have been discovered and older ones have become more productive. Marine architects have conducted practical experiments, presumed Viking Age voyages have been retraced, ethnologists have contributed valuable insights and enjoyed some success in countering popular myths. Historians have become more constructively critical, and philologists have attempted to look realistically at their data, while readers in general are learning that ethnic pride does not require the crutch of spurious or doubtful achievement. What were once vague possibilities have become probabilities, probabilities have become stronger and in some cases facts. And a few one-time 'facts' have been shed in the process.

An ancient text does not yield all its information to him who runs. It is quite unlike a newspaper, which is supposed to do exactly that. As a person of linguistic training I have attempted to draw reasonable conclusions from the sagas and from whatever else is currently known about the early exploration of North America and in particular the 'problem of Vínland.' For reasons that will become clear as the book progresses, I spell that place-name in the Icelandic way, with an acute accent over the *i*. In somewhat regretfully using the word 'Eskimo' I am aware that it is a name conferred on them by American Indians, and that the Eskimos themselves far prefer to be known as *Inuit* ('The People').

My personal gratitude embraces first and foremost those ancients whose vision encourages ours and whose daring intimates what might yet become ours. Secondly, it reaches back to the sagawriters, some portion of whose literary product survived to put us latecomers on the trail. Thirdly, it is extended to all who have written about Viking exploration, for those whose works I have not encountered may in one way or another have influenced those I have read. For special favors I must thank the following institutions and individuals: The Simon H. Guggenheim Memorial Foundation and the American Philosophical Society for invaluable financial assistance during early stages of this project; Professor Glyn Daniel of Cambridge for insisting that I write this book; Professor Peter Schledermann and the Arctic Institute of North America and Editor Robert E. Lee of the *Canadian Journal of Anthropology* for Canadian materials; and the staff of Thames and Hudson for invaluable advice and suggestions.

My gratitude is extended likewise to the Skraelings whom, to my knowledge, nobody has previously bothered to thank; to Chester N. Gould (1872–1957) who introduced me to the Icelandic sagas and spoke winningly – though not omitting the frustrations – of an academic career in the humanities; to my forbears, whose respective clusters of Swedish and Anglo-Saxon idiosyncracies are so unmistakably imprinted on my own genetic code; to my son Arvid, for his interest in the antics of humankind; lastly and never least, to dear Helen Jean, whose wifely solicitude can cope with even an author's abstracted gaze and random replies.

Unless otherwise credited, all translations or adaptations from foreign languages have been made by the author, who alone bears full responsibility for all statements of fact or interpretation in the following pages.

Seattle, Washington   Erik Wahlgren
May 1985

70°

FINLAND

SWEDEN

NORWAY

L.Ladoga

Novgorod

Volga

BALTIC

Birka

GOTLAND

ÖLAND

40°

Dnjepr

Kiev

Oslo

Bergen

Oseberg

Gokstad

Kaupang

Copenhagen

Vistula

Dnjestr

BLACK SEA

Byzantium

SHETLAND IS.

DENMARK

DE IS.

ORKNEY IS.

Hedeby

Elbe

Danube

SCOTLAND

HEBRIDES

LINDISFARNE

IONA

ENGLAND

York

Rhine

ITALY

IRELAND

Dublin

FRANCE

20°

rcle

B

SPAIN

0°

20°

20°

1 The western world of the Vikings.

1

The uttermost reach

It was cold up there, then as now. Making their way past numerous islands and – at last – out of the accursed Arctic fog, the ship's crew sighted a shore dominated by glaciers, with seals and polar bears all about. Now returning southward past a row of those tall *nunatakks*, or solitary rocky humps that poke hundreds of feet above the surrounding land-ice, past Nugssuak Peninsula which, whether they knew it or not, bears west Greenland's highest mountain, they believed themselves – though mistakenly – to have sailed farther north along Greenland's western coast than any white man had done before.[1] As one checks such things on a modern map, they must have reached Melville Bay, were perhaps above 76°N. latitude and a good 600–700 miles north of the Arctic Circle, measured in a straight line. But in those difficult waters, or in any waters, a sailing ship does not proceed in anything like a straight line. Deeming it wise now to return home with his report, the expedition leader noted that the temperature had fallen below freezing during the night. It was 25 July, the year was 1267, and passengers and crew were chiefly Norse Greenlanders. Among them were at least some who could be accounted 10th-generation residents of the vast island whose ice cap is the Northern hemisphere's largest remnant of the great quaternary freeze.

Voyages to the *úbygdir* ('unpeopled tracts'), however hazardous, were no novelty to a hardy race of farmer-hunters and fishermen of chiefly Norse-Icelandic stock who, even in their settled abodes along Greenland's southwest coast, were regarded as living 'at the end of the world.' The activities of sealing, whaling and the gathering of driftwood had for generations lured these descendants of Scandinavia's Vikings past islands, fjords and ice floes to hunting grounds ever farther north of their fragile civilization at the edge of the inland ice. A degree of systematization had long since taken place. Hunting stations had been established, even tiny 'factories' set up for the melting of blubber into train oil, the precious fluid transported homeward in leather sacks at the end of each hunting season. But

2 Iron Viking helmet from Valsgärde; the crest and eye-guards are of bronze, the lower half of chain mail.

this expedition was a bit special in that it had been commissioned by the Church. And to the Church, as represented by Greenland's episcopal see at Gardar (modern Igliko) the expedition made its report. For even in this remote outpost of European civilization, distant from Iceland, farther still from ancestral Norway and incredibly far from Rome, one senses the high Middle Ages. No malodorous heathens, these outdwelling Scandinavians of the 13th century were pious, indeed anxious Christians. Long gone was the time of Erik the Red and the other founding fathers of well on to three centuries before, who knew no external authority, paid no taxes. Many of them were Christian by the turn of the millennium, at their own request provided with a resident bishop since 1126. Submitting to the nominal authority of Norway's King Hakon the Old in 1261, the Greenlanders were now the subject of special clerical concern.[2]

Records show that a large part of the best land owned by the Greenlanders had gradually come into the possession of the Church. As elsewhere, such property had been donated by living parishioners or bequeathed in their wills, chiefly to ensure the celebration of requiems for their souls. Heathendom there may have been in remote corners of the settlement and, surely enough, among such Norse colonists as lived a life of apostasy and outlawry beyond the borders, but basically the Christian faith was strong. It needed to be tenacious in a land where life was fraught with heavy uncertainty and where trolls abounded on land and sea. It required as well the guidance of a trained clerisy, the support of dignified places of worship and the inspiration of bell, book and candle. The religious establishment had in turn to be supported. That support comprised land ownership and gifts *in natura*, for there was neither gold nor coinage among the Greenlanders. And now Church officials in Norway, pressed by the Papal curia, were concerned not merely with the immortal souls of their distant parishioners, but with their tithes as well. The authority and the Greenlandic revenues of the King of Norway were slight in comparison with the influence and the property of the Church: the moral authority and the services performed by the latter were tangibly omnipresent, whereas the dignity of the Crown was a theory and that *quid pro quo*, its promised services, destined to be unreliable.[3]

Greenland had been sighted, and once landed upon but never properly explored, by Norsemen well before Erik the Red's famous tour of exploration in the years 982–5. After returning to his home in western Iceland, Erik had assembled twenty-five shiploads of eager colonists and made, in the year 986, his westward sailing that planted the Norse tongue and republican institutions on the northern hemisphere's largest island.

It is not too early to remind the reader that no real understanding of the settlement of Greenland or the problem of early American history is possible without a perusal of the so-called Vínland sagas. Nowadays usually referred to in English as *The Saga of the Greenlanders* and *The Saga of Erik the Red*, these two short works – peripheral products of a major prose tradition in Old Icelandic – will hereafter be cited as *Greenlanders' Saga* (O. Icel. *Groenlendinga saga*) and *Erik's Saga* (*Eiríks saga rauda*).[4]

To return to the reconnaissance of 1267: it was conducted as a survey of the colony's, and hence of the Church's, prospects in the northern region, and undertaken in the wake of the previous year's reports by hunters who had ventured farther than was then usual into the *Nordrsetur* ('northern seats'), those hunting grounds that were never reached without effort. It cannot now be determined whether it was that 'official' journey of 1267 or some later voyage unknown to fame which resulted, directly or indirectly, in the world's most northerly inscription in a Scandinavian language. The word-forms of the inscription as well as the shapes of the characters – runes – in which it was quite competently carved comport with any date from the second half of the 13th century to the first half of the 14th. This was late runic, the only form of writing preserved to us from the Norse habitation of Greenland. At all events, the rune stone from Kingigtorsoaq gave major impetus to the modern discussion of that early settlement along with the discovery of the North American continent and the effort to establish a colony on its eastern fringe.[5] By virtue of political events in which the Greenlanders had small interest and over which they had no control, their country was by *c.* 1400 a remote and poorly known protectorate of the Danish–Norwegian Crown, a source of mixed fact, legend and misinformation. The recolonization of Greenland from Denmark[6] started with the distinguished Norwegian-born Lutheran clergyman and colonizer Hans Egede (1686–1758) who, sent out from Copenhagen in 1721, established the Greenland Mission. Through the labors and writings of Egede, Greenland re-entered European consciousness as a real place, if as yet little more than the primitive territorial annex of a culturally backslidden Scandinavian

3 Location of the
Kingiqtorsoaq stone in
Greenland.

4 The rune-inscribed
stone from Kingiqtorsoaq.

monarchy. It was thus under Danish auspices that the Kingiqtorsoaq stone was discovered – perhaps we should say rediscovered.

For hundreds of years the Eskimos – or as they themselves prefer to be called, Inuit, 'the People' (*Eskimo* is an Indian word meaning 'eater of raw flesh') – had been aware of traces left by the race of tall, blond strangers who at one time had regularly visited the *Nordrsetur* hunting grounds. Among the remains that had survived the vicissitudes of weather, the curiosity of animals and the collecting proclivities of the Inuit themselves, were three small cairns, or piles of rock, arranged by human hands on the island of Kingiqtorsoaq, north of Upernavik at 72°58′ N. lat. The cairns had been called to the attention of visiting Danes, including, of course, government administrators and religious missionaries to the Upernavik district. Half a millennium after the original piling of the cairns, the distinguished cartographer and naval officer Lieutenant, later Commander, W. A. Graah (1793–1863), who on a subsequent voyage nearly died of hardship and starvation while exploring Greenland, was reconnoitering the Upernavik area on his first voyage to Greenland in 1823–4. In the latter year he was shown a small stone, no more than 10 cm by 3.5 cm, discovered by the Eskimo Pelimut. Found beside the three cairns in one of which it must once have been placed, the stone is of a black–gray or dark green quartz slate. The 'front' surface bearing the inscription is smooth. The three cairns were so arranged as to form an equilateral triangle that may have some directional significance. Though one of the smallest rune stones known, it is among the most pivotal. Most of the inscription can be easily interpreted:

Erling Sighvatsson and Bjarni Thordarson and Endridi
Oddsson on the Saturday before Rogation Day raised these
cairns and cleared . . . (alternatively 'and runed', i.e.,
composed a runic charm for apotropaic purposes).

The inscription ends in six secret runes that have never been
satisfactorily interpreted, though they may indicate the year.
The probable date is 24 April (Gregorian 2 May) 1333. We may
ask ourselves whether the ambiguously spelled word
'cleared/runed' designated the laborious but prosaic task of
clearing something – stones, ice? – or the to us more exotic effort
at banishing the obstructive pack-ice through some vestigial
runic magic. Three men, three cairns. The three authors took
pains to identify themselves. Was this a formal property claim?
Was it an ordinary 'Kilroy was here' inscription, an exultant
expression of achievement? Or was it the final monument of a
solitary trio facing an early death? The men could not have
reached these parts that same year, and were consequently hold-
overs from the year before. Unless they were accustomed to
wintering at this latitude, their ice-bound plight must have been
a desperate one throughout the ghastly winter. Did they die of
starvation or amid the ice and waves during a last frantic effort at
flight? Or did they hold out until rescued during high summer, to
return in triumph and edify kinfolk and friends with tales of
walruses and trolls? It may be that the practice of wintering over
was not so rare, after all. That possibility reduces the drama, but
not our curiosity. Illustrating the fragmentary nature of ancient
data, the question remains.[7]

Since the Pelimut–Graah discovery another sixteen decades
have passed. Archaeological expeditions have been probing the
identifiable sites of Norse habitation in Greenland, and about
three hundred farmsites have been recognized. What has been
found in the way of material goods confirms and amplifies the
little that the Icelandic sagas and annals have bothered to tell us
about existence in Greenland. But many puzzles remain,
including, as we shall see, the ultimate mystery of what caused
the Norse Greenlandic colonies as a whole to fade from history.

Several things are known to us from manuscript sources as
well as from the most recent digging investigations. The
Greenlanders sailed north, they sailed south, they crossed Davis
Strait and searched the shores facing them. How far south, how
far north, is not as yet known, but the picture has become clearer.
These western Norsemen encountered here and there the native

5 Eskimo with seal; 19th-century illustration from Greenland.

peoples – of various tribes and cultures, but Skraelings all – who had preceded them as visitors or settlers. The word *skraeling* signified in Old Norse something like 'pitiful wretch.' And indeed, one of Hans Egede's sons, himself brought up in Greenland, wrote in later life of how dreadful they had appeared to him as a new arrival from Europe.[8] It took some time for the shock to wear off. The medieval encounters were alternately casual or intense, characterized by peaceful trading or by hostility to the point of bloodshed. The similarity of these contacts to those recorded throughout history everywhere on the globe need surprise no one. The Norse were scarcely noted for gentleness, the natives were either helpful or fearful and suspicious, eager for contact or prepared for battle, and as we shall note later, ignorance and bad luck often tipped the odds simultaneously against both sides. Peace calls for greater exertions than war.

In the opinion of the Arctic ethnologist Dr Robert McGhee, the Norsemen encountered both Indians and Eskimos.[9] The Indians were probably Beothuk, related to the Algonkians who occupied the coastal regions of Newfoundland during the summer, fishing and hunting sea mammals and birds – these would be puffins, gannets and related species – from birchbark canoes. In winter the tribesmen retreated to the interior forest. By the 16th century they were described as being extremely hostile to intrusion by Europeans, who had not been above kidnapping them for the slave trade. Implements of the Dorset Eskimos had been found by the Norse when they explored southern Greenland beginning in 982. But the Dorset themselves had apparently withdrawn, though they remained in northern Greenland, northern Labrador and the Ungava Bay region.[10]

Eskimos of the Thule culture had migrated eastward from Alaska during the 11th century, reaching northwestern Greenland by the 12th. During the 13th century the Thule had come to Ungava Bay and northern Labrador, where they coexisted for two centuries with the Dorset, having then, also, reached Disko Bay. During the following century Thule Eskimos colonized the outer fjord areas of the Norse settlements. The Norse, living by preference at the heads of the fjords, were compelled now to conquer, be conquered by, or coexist with the natives. The Norse clung to Greenland from 986 to possibly 1480, and there is some shaky evidence of their tenure past 1500. But a comparable Norse presence on the mainland was not to be.

Nevertheless, the extent of Norse exploration is now seen to have been wider, and its effects somewhat greater, than once believed. Our enhanced understanding of this we owe to archaeology. Let us first gaze northward.

6–8 Norse implements from Greenland: spade of reindeer horn, knife with wooden handle, wooden spade.

Norse traces in the Arctic

The intractable Arctic climate, with its long winters, cuts the digging season to a minimum, and the process of orderly retrieval and preliminary labeling and classification of data proceeds almost round the clock during the brief northern summer. The climate has softened somewhat in recent decades. But where winter relaxes its grasp, the mosquitoes take over to plague both man and beast. The cryptic descriptions by medieval commentators convey no hint of this, and we can only surmise as to how they coped with the problem. At sea, of course, and on land when the wind blew, one was free of the menace. And possibly whale oil helped. The rest is fortitude. Modern scholars rely upon netting, ointments, tobacco smoke and at times such brilliant inventions as the electrical bug exterminator, commonly known in the US and Canada as an electrical zapper. These may or may not be effective. I shall refer later to the discoveries in the known settlement areas, the so-termed Eastern (actually, southern) and Western (northern) Settlements in Greenland, as well as to the now famous diggings near L'Anse aux Meadows at the northern tip of Newfoundland. In this chapter attention is called only to objects believed to be of Norse manufacture and usually found in connection with old Eskimo encampments.

More than fifty years ago the Danish archaeologist Erik Holtved was the first modern scholar to find and identify such articles in the high Arctic regions of Greenland. Including a comb, fragments of a cooking pot, chessmen, fragments of a shirt of mail and other items, these were located in Eskimo winter houses on Ruin Island in Inglefield Land.[11] A dozen or so years later Count Eigil Knuth found, on the Arctic coast of Perry Land, the remains of an *umiak* or sizeable Eskimo boat, from which a section of gunwale molding made of oak could be C-14 dated to *c.* 1220. This gives us merely an approximate *terminus a quo*, inasmuch as the oak may have seen some years of service before falling into Eskimo hands. But acquired one way or another, whether through trade or following a shipwreck, the oaken piece had been Norse before it became Eskimo.[12] Since the late 1970s, a number of ancient Norse finds have been reported from Arctic Canada, not least from the east coast of Ellesmere Island facing across Kane Basin towards Greenland's slanting 'top'. Professor Peter Schledermann, Director of the Arctic Institute of North America, has reported such finds between

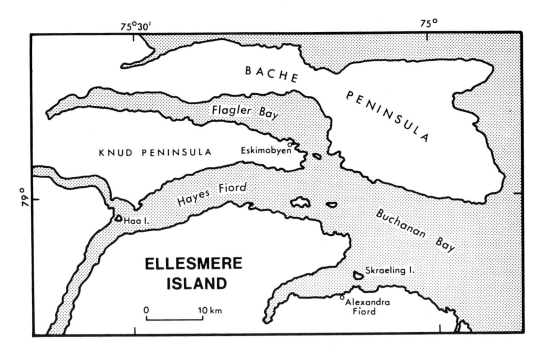

9 Arctic areas where Norse artifacts have been discovered.

1977 and 1981 from various localities in the areas of Bache Peninsula. Most are from Knud Peninsula and Skraeling Island, in Thule culture Eskimo winter houses, dating from various periods but all in phase with the previously mentioned Ruin Island culture. By 1982 Schledermann could report more than twenty-five objects of Norse provenience from Thule houses of that type on tiny Skraeling Island just north of Alexandra Fjord (79° N. lat.), at the south side of Buchanan Bay. There are a number of pieces of non-Eskimo (i.e., smelted) copper and iron, two pieces of woollen cloth that can be C-14 dated to *c.* 1280, a knife-blade, a section of ring byrnie similar to what Holtved had found earlier at the corresponding latitude in Greenland, a carpenter's plane, ship rivets and several iron chisels and blades.[13]

Schledermann's general conclusions based on a score of C-14 dates, obtained from various materials lying about the ruined house-sites, make reasonable an assumption of one or more forms of contact between Eskimos and Northmen in the period 1250–1350. Norse artifacts from a somewhat later period in the Bache Peninsula area include part of an oaken box (from *c.* 1390), several bottom sections of wooden casks, bits of iron and copper and, finally, a small piece of carved ivory that appears to be an Eskimo artist's impression of a Norseman. Found in the ruin of a large community house dated to about 1650, these items very

10 Piece of woollen cloth
from Skraeling Island.

11–14 Items from
Skraeling Island: iron
blade; iron rivet; a section
of chain mail, C-14 dated
to c.1280; iron point
manufactured by altering
a ship rivet section.

15 Barrel bottom from
Eskimobyen on Knud
Peninsula.

16 Ivory figurine, thought to be an Eskimo's representation of a Norseman, from Haa Island.

likely reflect the extent to which Norse articles by way of commerce had ultimately penetrated the general Greenlandic, Thule Eskimo material culture.[14]

The discovery of a small figure carved out of wood and representing a human face is surprising for its apparent date. A C-14 evaluation would place it in the range of 1100 ± 50. The carved figure shows a pointed chin, 'straight' eyes and the front rim of a Norse hood, details not to be expected in an Eskimo's representation of a fellow Eskimo. Schledermann finds Dorset elements in the carving. Remarking that Dorset dwellings were influenced by contemporary Thule culture, he launches a fascinating suggestion: could the carving have resulted from an early meeting between exploring Norsemen in the Thule/Smith Sound area and a mixed group of Dorset and Thule Eskimo sealers or whalers?[15] That question is of special interest for Arctic ethnology but has interest for the Scandinavianist as well. During the centuries of their tenure, did the Northmen acquire any knowledge, develop any criteria for distinguishing between cultural variants among their Eskimo co-inhabitants? Particularly during the later centuries, before the whites disappeared, and when, at least according to late-recorded Eskimo legends, the two races may occasionally have helped one another, did each acquire a few words of the other's vocabulary? There is absolutely nothing recorded as to that. Resorting to surmise, it is likely that such things took place on a local and occasional basis and with no enduring effects in either direction. The Eskimo villages were widely dispersed, and the Norse ultimately vanished.

Remembering the exploratory expedition sent out by the Church in 1267, we may begin to suspect that the assumption on the part of those 13th-century Norse clerics, that they were 'the first' to have reached such northerly parts, was an honest error. We recall that the first shiploads of colonists from Iceland had settled in southwestern Greenland in 986. Soon they were followed by others, some of them people of wealth and consequence, in the grip of the expansionist urge that, as we shall see in the next chapter, characterized the Age of the Vikings. By shortly after 1000 the newcomers to Greenland had not only spied the great islands that lay opposite them to the west, but had landed, explored and even tried to colonize the more habitable of these regions. The explorers were impressed by, among other things, the ample supplies of growing timber to be found on these farther shores, a supply that they are known to have exploited for centuries. There is absurdity in supposing that they could not, or would not, have exerted themselves, while in the youth of the colony's ambition and strength, to satisfy their curiosity about their nearest shoreline by following it continuously, for as far as conditions permitted. And this they would have done not merely once or twice during the generations immediately following on their landtaking. Was there a subsequent discontinuity of tradition among them so that, for whatever reason, by 1267 the memory of earlier pushes in this particular direction were lost? We cannot say.

17 (*top left*) Medieval Norse representation of a walrus, carved from the back tooth of a walrus; found at Umiviarssuk, Greenland.

18 (*top right*) Norse representation of a polar bear, carved from a walrus tusk, Sandnes, Greenland.

19 Flint arrowhead, Sandnes, thought to be of American Indian origin.

20 Bone chequer-board piece, Brattahlid.

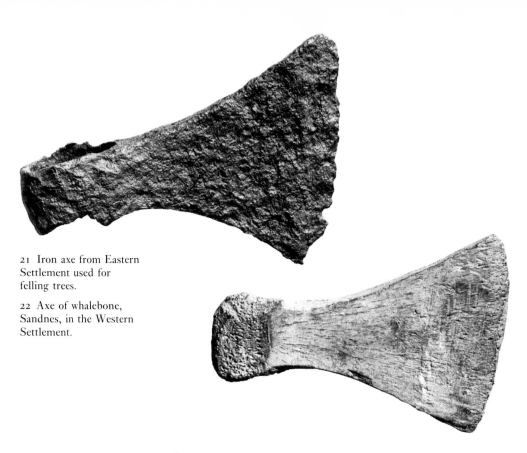

21 Iron axe from Eastern Settlement used for felling trees.

22 Axe of whalebone, Sandnes, in the Western Settlement.

Conditions of pack-ice varied, as they vary now, from year to year. Air conditions vary strongly, as everyone can observe. Less well known to the average landlubber are the constant struggles between various ocean currents. A relatively warm, northward-moving branch of the Gulf Stream flows along Greenland's west coast, largely to dissipate in the colder waters of Davis Strait, though traces of it, at a depth of 500 m, are found in Baffin Bay. Icy currents flow from the Polar region. As the currents compete, not only the pack-ice but the flora and fauna as well are influenced by the conjunction of factors.[16] If one were able to penetrate the pack-ice sufficiently to reach the open waters of Smith Sound, further navigation was possible, and from northwest Greenland it is barely 16 miles to the nearest Canadian island. Interestingly enough, the most prolific source of floating ice is a fjord south of Jacobshavn, just below 68° N. lat., and considerably below Upernavik.

During the 13th century the climate appears to have deteriorated, though the facts regarding this are not fully agreed upon. Increasing cold would have influenced routes and sailing methods. Climatic tables indicate, after a level, comparatively ice-free period 860–1200, a sharply rising level of marine ice in the years around 1260, declining thereafter only to rise again after 1300.[17] The drop in temperature caused the Greenlanders to change the arrangement of their houses in the interests of heat conservation.[18] Geological and botanical studies conjoined have confirmed and refined our understanding of the phenomenon. For example, ice-borings have revealed the rate of growth of the central ice mass as well as its contents, physically and chemically. There are air bubbles, atmospheric dust in which the effects of major volcanic eruptions throughout the world are conspicuous, and such factors as the percentage of lead absorbed – not until our day a matter of concern – and the two isotopes of oxygen, 16 and 18, whose shifting proportions relative to one another vary with air temperature. An ice-boring undertaken in the vicinity of the Norse settlements in Greenland not only confirms the climatic rhythms revealed in studies of ocean ice, but is in turn confirmed by parallel investigations undertaken in the European high Alps as well as by the study of tree rings.[19] However: annual averages are merely that. They do not of themselves tell us much about fluctuations *within* a given year. The effects upon plant and animal life and, in consequence, on human economic and social activity need not be identical for (a) a period of hot summers and cold winters and (b) a time of warm winters and cool summers, nor for (c) a set of average summers and winters, even though the annual average of temperatures might well in each case be the same or close to it.

Similarly, borings in the sea-floor reveal fluctuations in the pollen count that indicate what has taken place on shore. We

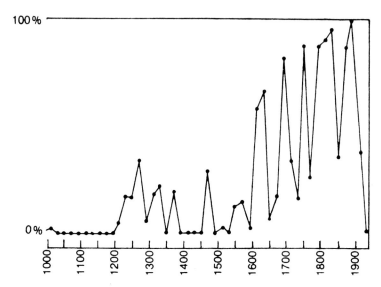

23 Relative thickness of ocean ice around Iceland from the year 1000 onward.

should not be astonished to note the extent to which the Norse Greenlanders, tiny part though they were of the whole, influenced for a few centuries the ecology of their environment.[20] The pollen count at Brattahlid, famous as Erik the Red's manorial establishment, reveals the sudden disappearance of birch, willow and elder, chopped with Viking Age axes, cleared to make way for pasturage, consumed in the continually stoked fire-pits of a population that may never have exceeded four thousand bodies.[21] The smallish trees were replaced, as the pollen record shows, with meadow plants casually brought in by the colonists, such as sorrel, yarrow, wild tansy and shepherd's pouch. That they made some attempt at grain cultivation is shown in the addition by them of *Elymus arenarius*, a type of wild rye, to augment the types native to the area. The immigrant plants took hold and survived the disappearance of the humans who had originally imported them in their hay bundles and grain sacks and deck sweepings. But in time the cleared meadows and grazing grounds yielded once again to the elder, willow and birch. A 'Little Ice Age' sometimes blamed for the disappearance of the Greenland colonists did not *per se* destroy their tiny civilization, despite a cold period in mid-15th century. Not until 1600 did a precipitous, intensive chill take place, and before then the Norsemen had vanished. Various Danish expeditions during the 17th and later centuries sought them in vain. The manner of their going, and the reasons for it, have been debated for the past five hundred years. In a later chapter there will be occasion to scrutinize the case anew.

One problem with much of our historical evidence is that the manuscripts in which it is recorded are so seldom contemporary with the events narrated. That is the case, for example, with the impressive Family Sagas of the Icelanders that tell us so much, not merely about life in Iceland but about other lands as well, including even Greenland and the so elusive Land of the Grapevine somewhere to the southwest. Events of the 10th and 11th centuries come down to us inscribed on parchments of the 13th and 14th centuries. Comparative studies can often work out their degree of probability, which on occasion is surprisingly high. Extant manuscripts are invariably copies of older ones, the earliest – in the case of those not in themselves mere compilations of other documents – in turn based on inherited oral accounts or even personal observation.[22] The Icelanders to whom we owe the accounts, both oral and written, were remarkably disciplined and responsible narrators. The great corpus of medieval Icelandic literature is testimony to a people who were, and are still, anything but wishy-washy in their aesthetic standards, their actions or their opinions.

The finds of today's ethnologists and archaeologists have triumphantly confirmed the principal indications of the so-called Vínland sagas. It can equally be said that the excavated artifacts would be tragically enigmatic without the medieval literary accounts that flesh them out. Uncorroborated by physical finds, on the other hand, the Vínland sagas would remain the rousing fiction that many persons, including the great Fridtjof Nansen, have always thought they were. Nansen, who himself almost a century ago braved the interior Greenland ice to cross from the East coast to Godthaab on the West, did not credit his collateral ancestors with having performed actions of comparable valor farther to the west. The Vínland sagas, he opined, were tales of the fictional *Insulae Fortunatae*, Isles of Bliss.[23]

Hundreds of years before, the distinguished Arab geographer Muhammed al-Idrīsi (1100–1166) had evidently heard of Eskimos and their habits. Writing in Sicily in 1154, he knew of a people in the 'inner islands' of the North Atlantic who hunt sea animals so huge that their bones and vertebrae are used instead of wood for the construction of their houses.[24] This is strikingly accurate as reflecting certain Eskimo structures, even though that eminent Arab, if not the Norse or Eskimos, might have been startled to know that eight centuries later and some thousands of miles west of Greenland, one would be able to attend Christian services in a small church whose roof is supported by the ribs of a whale.[25] After studies in Córdoba and much travel, al-Idrīsi had settled down at the court of the Norman King Roger II at Palermo, where he proceeded to construct a map of the world in silver. His work *Nu'zhat al-Muschtā*k ('The Satisfaction of the Yearning One') is a commentary on the map. Whence did al-Idrīsi's information derive? Probably by way of the royal Norman connection. Allowing an interval for the transfer, the report may amount to confirmation of rather early direct contact between Norse Greenlanders and the Eskimos.

We have far from exhausted the subject of early European references, of recent archaeological finds in the high Arctic, or of the historical, cultural and technological facts to which such finds must be related. Before returning to these matters, we must consider the ultimate background of migration from the 'black beaches and white mountains of Iceland to the forefront of Greenland and the vestibule of America.'[26]

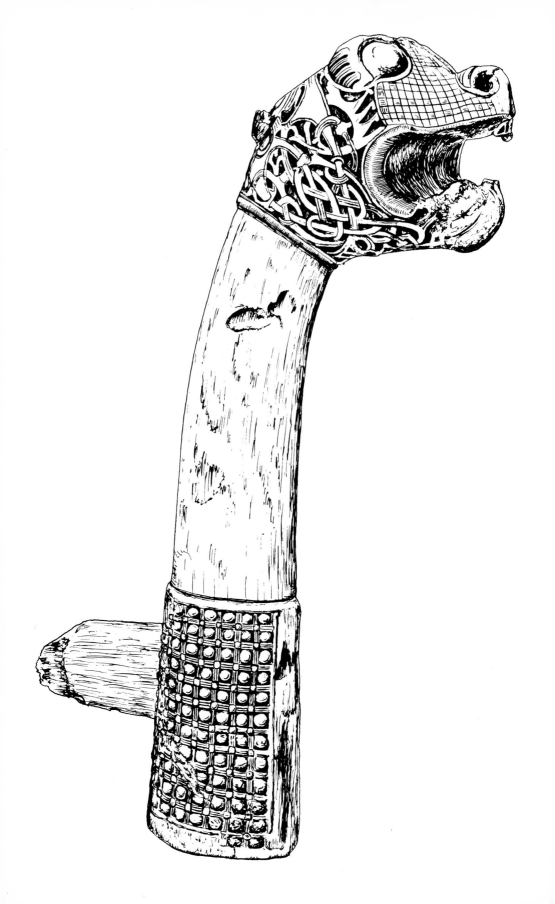

2

An expanding universe

Tiny specks swayed on the watery horizon, gained rapidly in size, revealed themselves, frighteningly, as low-slung, lap-straked ships' hulls, each with its complement of formidably accoutered men. With appalling speed the vessels were beached and their freight of yelling warriors discharged on shore for pillage and slaughter. So it had been on undefended Lindisfarne, St Cuthbert's Holy Island off the Northumbrian coast, in the year 793. And so it went at Monkwearmouth the following year, at famous Iona the year after that. Within a decade or so, Northern Vikings had fallen upon Scotland's Kintyre, Ireland's Rechru, the Isle of Man and, twice again, St Columba's monastery on Iona. The pattern was in each case the same: organized ferocity by skillful hit-and-run predators from the sea. Under canny and resolute captains the marauding foreigners operated with brutal efficiency to seize their plunder, withdrawing as they had come before resistance could be organized. Clergy and laity suffered alike, but the most profitable and hence most obvious targets were those repositories of wealth, the churches and monasteries. Growing decade by decade, the menace ultimately encompassed much of Europe and beyond and persisted, in one form or another, for almost three centuries. Who were the predators, where did they come from and what brought them so unexpectedly?[1]

The earliest recorded raids which introduced what is now termed the Viking Age were conducted in the main by Norwegians. It was not long before Danes and Swedes participated in the forays. At times the three nationalities conducted joint ventures, at other times they clashed in an opportunistic pattern of frequently shifting alliances. The nature of the Viking expeditions as well as their impelling forces and their results varied from generation to generation, but the bloody incident at Lindisfarne was a spectacular introduction to the menace from the north. Terrifying omens, we are told in the *Anglo-Saxon Chronicle*, had heralded the event shortly before.

24 Wooden animal head, carved *c.*800, found with the Oseberg ship burial.

29

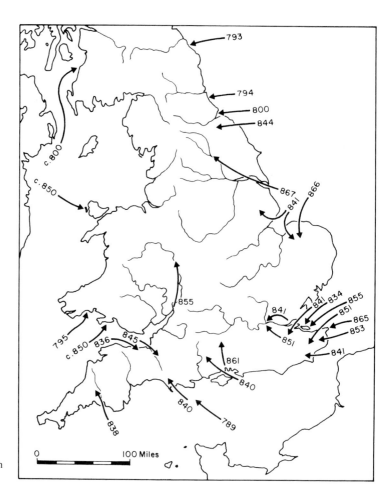

25 Early Norse attacks on Britain.

These included famine, untoward lightning and drops of blood that fell from the roof of St Peter's Church in York. Of these portents of human wickedness the lightning, at least, is still with us, for as this is being written a British clergyman is reported in the world press as interpreting the recent lightning damage to York Minster – in spite of its array of lightning rods – as a specific instance of God's displeasure. Alcuin[2] would have approved, but the Vikings who once ruled York can no longer be singled out for blame. They have long since been assimilated.

With the inevitable exception, Viking raids were purposeful enough for us to conclude that the lie of the land had been sized up in advance. The shores of Britain were not totally unfamiliar to Scandinavian fishermen, traders and adventurers, or fine craftsmen and purveyors of heroic lore, not too distantly related, after all, to the Angles and Jutes who had preceded them a few centuries before. Scandinavian trade with other countries via Frisian intermediaries had certainly given the Northerners some conception of what lay outside their own territories. Indeed, the first firm date in Scandinavian history is an attack by the Gautar (southern Swedes) on Frisia in 516. The Vandili, the Cimbri, the Teutoni had all flowed onto the Continent from the Jutland Peninsula, just as the Goths had come from Sweden. Lindisfarne need not literally have been the first English locality to suffer. We know at least that three shiploads of Norsemen had put ashore at Portland in 789 and, simply through hotheadedness and misunderstanding, killed the king's reeve from Dorchester who had come to interrogate them. Human activity in most spheres being spottily recorded, events of which we have reasonably precise knowledge may be likened to infrequent and often defaced signposts along a welter of poorly kept back lanes. The task of connecting the murky lanes with recognizable highways is toilsome and imperfect. Our picture of so-called Viking activities across a tumultuous period spanning ten generations has repeatedly been modified through the testimony of the spade. In equal measure, a modern examination profits by studies in comparative culture as well as by the clarity that time and relative disinterest often afford. Before sketching the Viking raids in greater detail, let us examine the question of their definition, background, and motivation.

Viking groups

The term Viking (O. N. *víkingr*, a masculine noun denoting 'sea-raider,' cf the feminine word *víking*, 'freebooting voyage, piracy') has through extension to the Viking Age in general become a loose and inaccurate designation for the inhabitants of Denmark, Norway, Sweden and ultimately Iceland, from shortly before the year 800 to the Norman subjugation of England in 1066 and the years immediately following. Many of the intervening events may of course be considered under the heading of inter-dynastic rivalry. Indeed, a pair of Scandinavian monarchs, Knut Sveinsson of Denmark (St Knut!) and Olaf (the Peaceful!) of Norway, following in the footsteps of their energetic predecessors, made elaborate if unsuccessful plans as late as 1085 to conquer England. More surprising than this were the anachronistic Viking exploits throughout many decades of the Orkney chieftain Sveinn Ásleifarson, terminated only by his violent death at Dublin in 1171. Not for nothing is he the hero of Eric Linklater's *The Ultimate Viking*.[3]

Viking expeditions ranged from random forays by one or half a dozen shiploads of booty-bent, more or less anonymous pirates to undertakings by leaders of note. It became the fashion for young men of quality, including the sons of Scandinavian princes and jarls, to gain experience and leadership stature during one or two and perhaps a whole series of summer forays. Many a younger son got his 'start in life' with the aid of plunder acquired on such voyages; many a dispossessed man repaired his fortunes thus and, if he were wise enough not to go too often to the well, lived to enjoy his gains. Many a Viking, too, left his bones on a foreign beach or perished in the waves, while some, cut off and captured, had to suffer the indignity of slavery, tempered only by some faint hope of escape or ransom by their countrymen. It was a hazardous occupation, but the temptations were immense. Aside from ornaments of gold and silver, caches of which frequently turn up in Scandinavia, the raiders acquired brocades, precious stones, wine and slaves for domestic use or barter. Grain, cattle and horses were commonplace items, for the raiders lived off the land during increasingly lengthy sojourns on foreign soil. Ultimately, great hordes of the unwelcome visitors established themselves in winter quarters on islands conveniently located off the coast or in major rivers. The British Isles, France, Frisia, the Baltic regions inhabited chiefly by Slavic, Finnish or Estonian tribes, were constantly beset by Scandinavians of one nationality or another or by combinations of these. Norwegian raids on Ireland, Scotland and the north of England were launched from Orkney, Shetland, the Hebrides and the Isle of Man. There, Norse settlers had filled a vacuum or replaced an earlier population, presumably of Picts, who in their turn had driven out or assimilated the megalithic builders of the near half a thousand brochs whose well or poorly preserved remains have been uncovered.[4]

For modern speakers and readers of English and French, the Danes bulk largest in the received accounts of Viking malevolence, and for good reason. The Northmen themselves, speaking slight variants of a common language, called it *dönsk tunga* ('the Danish tongue') or *norroent mál* ('Northern speech'), cf the Norn language on Shetland and Orkney. Particularly during the second half of the 9th century, Denmark's energies seem to have been applied abroad, with England and France bearing the brunt of their effort. King Alfred's struggles against the Danes are proverbial. And in France around 860, King Charles the Bold, after trying for seven years to expel a Danish–Norwegian force from the vicinity of Paris, finally commissioned a rival Viking force, in return for a couple of tons of silver plus 'expenses' – provender for man and horse – to get rid of them. Alfred's great victory over the Danes in 886 deflected the Danish host towards the Continent, and Flanders, Belgium, France and Germany, as we would call them today, suffered the agonies of a thirteen-year devastation at Viking hands. On the theory that 'money talks,' the strangers were several times, but unsuccessfully, bribed to desist. In the end it was neither military force nor cartloads of silver that brought a temporary respite from the Viking plague. Ironically, it was *plague* of a different category. Desolated by these pitiless human locusts, the countryside fell prey to famine and disease, and the Northerners retired for the nonce, ultimately to regroup in England. Many of the Vikings who survived warfare chose, in fact, not to leave England. Their descendants are normal citizens in England today. To that topic we shall return below.

Sneaking up rivers and skulking along the coasts of Britain and northern Europe, the Norsemen eventually fell upon Spain in two waves, one in the 9th century, one in the 10th. Italy and what is now Portugal, Pamplona of the bulls where in 859 the captured emir of the Basques had to be ransomed for 70,000 pieces of gold, La Coruña, sacred Santiago de Compostela, Lisbon, Seville, Algarve, Algeciras, Narbonne, Toulouse, Navarre, for whose Moorish prince a ransom of 90,000 *denarie* was received, Arles, Nîmes and Pisa all came to know their swords and their extortions. The Vikings even assailed Morocco where, striking a bit of bad luck, they were compelled to retreat from Nakur with nothing for their pains. Through brilliant guile they besieged and captured Italian Luna (no longer in existence), allegedly thinking in their equally impressive ignorance that this walled town of five thousand was fabled Rome. Other Vikings meanwhile harried Hamburg, Cologne and Trier.

During these decades of turmoil the northerly Swedes were not sitting on their cabbage patches. Many Swedes (*Svíar*, Latin *Suiones*) joined with their Danish and Norwegian brethren in the looting of western Europe, and many a runic inscription on Swedish memorial stones records their participation in such exploits. Swedes accompanied Rollo – Rolf the Ganger (O. N. Hrólfr), the first Duke of Normandy – to his duchy, and their remote heirs continue to live there as domesticated Norman

26 This Swedish runestone from Yttergärde, Uppland, tells of the warrior Ulv who made three expeditions to England in the early 11th century.

French. Sweden's southernmost provinces, most conspicuously Skåne (Scania), had most of the time been part of the Danish realm (until 1658, in fact), in consequence of which the Viking ancestor of many a modern Swede passed muster as a Dane. To complicate matters Sweden, socially stronger and better organized in the early 10th century and long before, actually occupied and ruled portions of Denmark until, after four decades of governance, the Swedes were expelled from Hedeby *c.* 936. However, Sweden's external pushes were directed largely east and southeast, into the Baltic regions.

The Rus

As an ancient, established kingdom, the Swedes had pre-Viking commercial and colonial ventures in Estonia, Lithuania, Latvia, and before long in Finland, Poland and Russia. Despite controversy it is almost certain that the very name Russia (R. *Russija*) is ultimately Swedish in origin. The word *Rus*, as the Swedes came to be known by the Slavs with whom they alternately fought and traded, derives from the Old Swedish word *rothsmathr* ('rower, sea-farer'), cf Finnish *Ruotsi* ('Swede'). Along with other Viking Age Scandinavians the Swedes were also termed Varangians (Slavic *Varjag* and variants thereof) in Russian, eastern Arabic and Byzantine sources, as reported in *Nestor's Chronicle* and the *Annales Bertiniani*.[5] That re-Scandinavianized Slavic term deriving from a Scandinavian word denoting faithfulness to one's companions became associated with Swedish merchant activities by way, it appears, of the traveling merchant guilds. The Germans called them, less poetically, *Ascmenni* ('Ash men'), from their ships made of ash. Seemingly unaware of the term *Rus*, the western Muslim centred on Córdoba called the invading Vikings *Madjus* (approximately 'heathen wizards'). Ironically, that is more or less the conception that the Vikings themselves had of the Lapps who lived north of them, as well as of the natives of North America, the *skraelingar* 'wretches' with whom they traded and clashed. Everything is relative.

In the west, Irish slaves were a favorite catch. The Swedes, including the inhabitants of Gotland, specialized more conveniently in rounding up unwary individuals from the Baltic areas and freighting them, along with wax, honey, hides, walrus ivory, oil and precious furs from the Baltic up the Volga, the Dvina and the Dnjepr to various commercial centers. They traversed the Black and Caspian Seas, reached Byzantium (today's Istanbul) and beyond. The trade route extended to Baghdad, seat of the Eastern Caliphate, as Córdoba was of the Western. Trade goods received by the Rus included silver – at least until after 970, when nomadic tribes cut off the Caliphate's silver mines – precious stones, spices, silks, fruit, wine. The Rus are picturesquely described by several Arab observers, who with a measure of hyperbole thought them 'tall as trees.'[6] Swedes served along with Danes and Norwegians in the so-called Varangian Guard of the Eastern Emperor at Byzantium, and were handsomely rewarded for it.

Russian scholars are not as a rule enthusiastic in their interpretation of Swedish influence on the establishment of Russian governmental institutions. Legend and semi-history aside, it is archaeologically evident that the Swedish Rus, moving eastward into the regions of Lake Ladoga and Lake Onega, established a large settlement called by them Aldeigjuborg (Staraya Ladoga), 6 miles from the Volkhov River's debouch into Lake Ladoga. The river route leads to Novgorod, the Holmgard of the Rus, and comprises a natural pathway of rivers and lakes to the east, the south, or north to the White Sea. In the south, they entered the very territories that may have been the original home of the Indo-Europeans. In northern Russia the Swedish Rus, according to a message sent in 839 by the Eastern Emperor Theophilus to the Frankish Emperor Louis the Pious, had established a principality or 'Khaganate of Rus.' From its capital Novgorod this Khaganate had sent its ambassadors to Theophilus, and the ambassadors acknowledged their Swedish descent. After capturing Kiev, the Rus formed a second Khaganate there, and in 860 they actually made an ill-considered attack on Byzantium itself, but were repulsed.

By 980 the two Khaganates were combined into a larger Rus kingdom extending from Kiev to Ladoga, and until mid-11th century it was powerful enough to stave off the nomad Kurgans from Asia. Inevitably, it became Christian under the Eastern Church. Just as inevitably, despite steady connections including dynastic intermarriages with the Scandinavian homeland, it became Slavic in language, sentiment and, through simple biological proportioning, genes. Swedish names had become Russicized. Yngvarr and Ívarr turned into Igor, Valdemar underwent a metathesis to Vladimir, Helgi became Oleg, Helga turned into Olga, etc. In many Russian place names, particularly

27 Small pair of scales used by Viking traders for weighing silver. When folded, they would fit in a small box.

28 Some of the tens of thousands of Arabic coins found in Viking Age Scandinavia. Date and place of issue are usually recorded.

along river courses, one can trace Old Swedish nomenclature. Besides Kiev and Novgorod, the Rus established Byelosersk, Chernigov, Izborsk, Murom, Polotsk, Rostov. Their burial grounds, mixed in varying proportions with Baltic and Slavic graves, are found at Gnezdova near Smolensk. At Bjelimer near Bulgar, capital of the 'Black' or Volga Bulgarians, there are graves of strongly Nordic character, and at Jaroslavl on the Upper Volga, the Rus are buried among Finns.

The many thousands of Arab silver coins, Kufic *dirhems*, excavated in Sweden undoubtedly came from Baghdad, the

Serkland ('Saracen-land') of Swedish runic inscriptions, during the 9th and 10th centuries. With the decline of the Caliphate, western European coins gained in importance, and thousands of buried Anglo-Saxon coins are testimony to Sweden's share in the English Danegeld.

Characterization

Various aspects of the Viking expansion have become evident in the foregoing discussion. If there is a single, all-encompassing pattern to be discerned in the propellants behind social phenomena so diverse, so widely spread in a geographical sense and so persistent, historians have yet to agree on it, but some things are obvious. Described early on as *Vagina gentium* ('Womb of nations'), the chilly north had yielded up tribe after tribe that wandered forth in search of a more bounteous life. Thus, some of the early Swiss, in the canton of Schwyz, whether reliably or not, claimed Sweden as their pristine homeland. The Cimbri, so troublesome to the Romans until Marius gave them a thorough whipping in AD 101, seem to have emigrated from Himmerland on the Jutland Peninsula long before anyone thought to consider them Danes (the O. Scan. name *Danmörkr*, O.E. *Denemearc* probably means 'forested border land' and thus could only have spread to the northern parts of the country from the southern marches in Slesvig on the borders of the Frankish empire). It is even considered possible that the Danes themselves came from Sweden.

Forty-odd years ago the Swedish philologist Fritz Askeberg divided the Viking raids into four types:[7]

1. Private undertakings by individuals.
2. Political expeditions.
3. Colonizing ventures.
4. Commercial penetration.

Having now witnessed examples of all four types, one perceives that Askeberg's proposed arrangement is not a chronological one. The raid on Lindisfarne and the anachronistic exploits of the Orkneyman Sveinn Ásleifarson give an extreme span of 378 years, with raids at either end of that preposterous spectrum coming under the heading of *individual* piratic activity. Out and out political expeditions were conducted against the Baltic Slavs (Wends and Obotrites) and against Charlemagne – in short, against the Frankish empire. For example, with two hundred ships Danish King Godfred fell upon the empire's Frisia (the Low Countries) in 810, partly to secure useful territories while in equal measure seeking vengeance for the Emperor's overt and ever-threatening hostility towards 'heathen custom,' that is, the Scandinavian religion.

We have seen that commercial penetration was conspicuous in the case of the eastward-forging Swedes, but as we shall note in the following chapter, it was no less important in the west. Dublin, essentially founded by the Norsemen, and York, taken over and run by them, flourished commercially in their hands. Scandinavian colonizing efforts affected the social organization and governance of provinces and entire nations – England, Ireland, France, Russia – as well as resulting in the founding, or attempted founding, of tiny new nations, of which Iceland became the most influential, Greenland the most valiant, and colonial Vínland the most elusive.

What lay behind those centuries of centrifugal maneuvering? Ever-waxing populations, large in relation to the available agricultural and economic technology – in brief, the 'impatience of younger sons,' perhaps along with cyclical disturbances in the climate. Political upheavals on the home turf, as tribal chieftains and petty princes – *smákonungar* ('small kings') – saw their properties and their authority threatened or submerged in larger political configurations. A burst of biological and cultural energy, as witnessed by the Scandinavian decorative art forms of the age. A phenomenal advance in the art of shipbuilding. A huge expansion in international trade during the 8th century. The dawning realization that rich plunder was to be had virtually for the taking, along with a measure of contempt for the weaklings who could not defend it. However obstinate the Viking might be in his private feuds, however heroic in 'principled' combat, when searching out foreign victims he was quick to size up weakness, but equally adept at counting the percentages and subduing his greed in the face of competent counter-force. Inevitably, there was a need perceived by the Northmen to extend their territorial sway. We have noted such stimuli as the romance and challenging hazards of international commerce, handled, not in some office, but in the field. These factors of push and pull involve, likewise, certain demographic details. England and the Continent were neither so heavily populated nor so efficiently organized as to render preposterous their victimization by numerically inferior but resolute, highly motivated, well equipped and militarily adept predators.

The term *víkingr* (pl. *víkingar*) itself has been the subject of protracted researches.[8] Among half a dozen principal suggestions, two theories as to the word's derivation have won a respectable following. One refers the word to a specific place name, the *Vík* or coastal area adjoining the Oslo fjord. Vikings, then, would be nautical marauders from the Skagerrak. No Pirates of Penzance (though recently celebrated in a Muppet Show), they have nevertheless received their share of literary notice, from the bitter litanies of medieval monks to the animadversions of a modern British prime minister and historian. The second, and not unrelated, etymological proposal would connect Vikings to the word for bay itself, any bay or *vík*. These sea-robbers had learned, perhaps in the course of domestic squabbles that now in the face of sterner policing were diverted into foreign channels, to lurk in bays and hide behind islands – Norway alone has 150,000 – while waiting for targets of

29 Head of man carved on cart found as part of grave goods in Oseberg burial ship.

opportunity. As a rule they avoided engagements on the open sea. Nor did the pillagers invariably come off best, inasmuch as the admirals and shipbuilders of afflicted countries gradually learned methods of coping with the menace. The ultimate counter-measure proved to be the outclassing of the sleek Viking ships by larger and taller vessels, against which they could not compete in naval engagements.

European population growth, improved defense on land and sea, the decline of the slave trade and the spread of Christianity, the technique adopted by the victims of hiring Viking mercenaries to protect them against Vikings, the bribery, as in England and France, of landed possessions that bred collective responsibility in lieu of alien status and quickly dissipated danegelds paid out in silver, and finally – who can say? – perhaps a certain social and biological fatigue, were bound to bring the Viking Age to a close. In the end, 'their boys' became 'our boys' and part of the social fabric. Any rascality they might thereafter engage in was simply an aspect of domestic history.

Having considered who the Vikings were, what prompted them to go a'viking and what ultimately slowed them down, we shall take a look at their material and spiritual culture, including the technological development that facilitated their troublesome descent upon the 'civilized' world.

3
Ships and helmets, poets and kings

Towards the end of his long life, King Harald Fairhair of Norway (860–940?) despatched an embassy to his admired contemporary, King Athelstane of Wessex (r. 924–939), with the magnificent gift of a Viking ship. Whether the English were able to utilize its full capabilities is a matter of speculation. There is at all events well-nigh universal agreement that the single most important weapon in the Viking arsenal was the skillfully maneuvered ship.

> The ships of the Vikings were the supreme achievement of their technical skill, the pinnacle of their material culture; they were the foundation of their power, their delight, and their most treasured possession. What the temple was to the Greeks, the ship was to the Vikings: the complete and harmonious expression of a rare ability.[1]

Professors Brøgger and Shetelig (1951) have given us a comprehensive account of the origin and development from its early predecessors of the Viking ship proper, of which there were several types.[2] Their examples were principally Norwegian and largely based on the fortunate discovery and excavations of Viking ships at Tune (1867), Gokstad (1880) and Oseberg (1904). Reclaimed from the preserving clay, reconstructed and interpreted as required, these ships not only brought on a wave of Norwegian, Pan-Nordic and even international enthusiasm but introduced into the much-debated subject of trans-Atlantic voyaging a solid *additamentum* of factual observation to correlate with frustratingly casual saga notices regarding Norse voyaging in general. *Grau ist alle Theorie.* Here at last were some facts. Under Captain Magnus Andersen a replica of the Gokstad vessel sailed across the Atlantic and to the Columbian Exposition at Chicago in 1893, triumphantly exceeding every expectation as to its seaworthiness and performance,[3] concerning which last-named qualities the otherwise admirable treatise by Brøgger and Shetelig is now somewhat dated. Danish finds, reconstruction

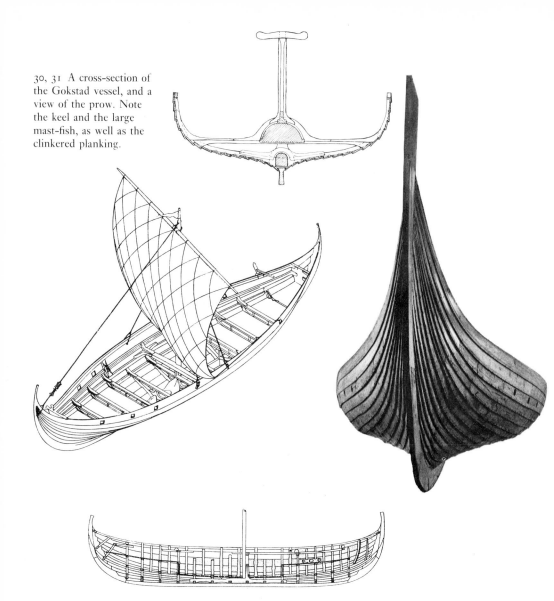

30, 31 A cross-section of the Gokstad vessel, and a view of the prow. Note the keel and the large mast-fish, as well as the clinkered planking.

32, 33 Two of the reconstructed cargo ships from Skuldelev.

and experiments during the past quarter century with the so-called Skuldelev ships now on exhibit at Roskilde Ship Museum, have added much to our understanding of Viking navigation.[4] Wave tanks, wind tunnels and manipulations that never troubled a Viking's dreams, and new voyages that certainly would have, are transforming the subject. Replicated Viking ships have sailed both east and west between Scandinavia and North America, and as recently as 1979, a beautiful Viking ship was dug up at Hedeby in Denmark.[5]

It was, however, not the trans-Atlantic capabilities of northern shipping that made it so effective an instrument of

34 The decorated Oseberg ship, which had served as the coffin of a Norwegian queen (for detail, see ill. 92).

35 Scene from the Bayeux Tapestry illustrating the accessibility of a Viking-type ship.

marauding warfare. Low-slung, with single, steppable masts, clinker-built, i.e. lapstrake or formed of overlying rows of thin horizontal planks, withy-tied and hence flexible rather than rigid, light enough to be portaged if need be, the early Viking ships were as a rule smaller than the renowned $76\frac{1}{2}$-foot vessel from Gokstad and Chicago. Riding as gracefully as swans upon the wave, these marine vehicles could be sailed or rowed with great maneuverability because of their low draught, and easily beached, requiring no docks for the loading or unloading of man or beast. The Bayeux tapestry[6] actually depicts how effortlessly a horse could clamber in or out of such a ship. Slipping noiselessly even into shallow rivers, the ships could be placed on rollers and dragged by crewmen or horses past Europe's defensive log jams, or Russia's rapids and waterfalls.

However traumatically the entry of Viking navigation onto the larger scene may have affected its early victims, the art of shipbuilding in the Northland had not sprung fullblown from the head of Odin. Boats of skin and bark had once been used. Such finds as the Nydam ship from Slesvig (preserved at Schloss Gottorp), the Kvalsund ship from Norway – both from around the year 400 – and the ship traces at Sutton Hoo in southeastern England, from *c.* 625, indicate that the Viking ship had its early native precursors, for the Sutton Hoo ship must have been constructed on behalf of an English chieftain by an imported Scandinavian shipbuilder, as the burial goods interred with it seem Swedish-related.[7] Several tolerably distinct types developed, in obvious accommodation to a severality of purposes: the small fishing vessel, which has descendants in Norway virtually to our time; the fully-decked ship of war with its rowing benches and steppable mast; the broader, semi-decked merchant vessel or *knörr* (pl. *knerrir*), with its emphasis on cargo capacity. The line of brightly painted war shields that so firmly identify the Viking ship to modern eyes made a brave display in harbor, but were not allowed to hamper navigation on the high seas. So characteristic of ancient Scandinavian thinking was the ship that the concept very early transcended the actualities of marine navigation on planks of oak or pine. The so-called *skeppssätt-ningar*, or arrangements of boulders so laid as to form the pattern of a ship, and far antedating the Viking Age, are common sights in the fields of Scandinavia. Clearly, they have philosophical and religious significance.[8]

Behind the Viking ship was the shipbuilder, the man of sure eye and steady hand who, product of a long line of forbears handy with the axe and the adze, precise with the augur, the chisel and the saw, did not work from a set of specifications, but built the ship from keel to masthead with the design and measurements in his head. Sculptor in wood, navigator and visionary, he incorporated the particular genius of an age.

Navigation will occupy us further in Chapters 8 and 9. But the Vikings were not merely expert with ships. Canny horse-breeders, they had developed excellent cavalry skills as well. Bringing some horses with them, they would round up the rest from the targeted countryside. The Danish conquest of England by Sveinn Forkbeard and Knut the Great in the early 11th

36 Impression in the sand, with iron nails, of the 7th-century royal burial ship excavated at Sutton Hoo, England, in 1939. Clinker-built, it is clearly a forerunner of the Viking Ship. Grave goods recovered from the excavation are on exhibit in the British Museum.

37 Stone ship-setting from the late Iron Age, Skåne, Sweden. It contained five fire hearths and a number of pits containing burnt bone.

38 Golden horns of Gallehus from c.425. Note the figure carrying a spear and wearing ritual horns.

century was in fact made possible by the Danish Cavalry, which dashed past the fortified Five Boroughs (Nottingham, Derby, Leicester, Stamford and Lincoln) with such speed that they could not be stopped at any one location. And in terms of weaponry for offence or defense, the *Dani–Normani–Varangi–Madjús–Ascmenni–Rus* possessed equipment that well matched their needs.

Weapons and clothing

Our traditional representation of the Viking in horned helmet, today so trivialized by comic strips and advertisements for air travel or aquavit, is fully as absurd, if less slanderous, than 19th-century imaginings that the Vikings skoaled each other from the emptied skulls of fallen enemies. In that case, of course, a faulty conclusion was drawn from etymology (cf O.N. *skál*, 'bowl', and Eng. 'skull'). As to the horned helmet: if there was anything in the days of hand-to-hand combat that a pragmatic Viking would *not* have encumbered his head with, it was a pair of handy levers by which any foe within spear's reach could unhelm him in a trice. Of various pictorial sources for the amusing misconception, all are pre-Viking, from the so-called Age of Gold in Scandinavia (400–800), and even earlier. The Golden Horns of Gallehus (Tønder, south Jutland), one found in 1639, the other in 1734, and both stolen from the Royal Treasury in 1802 and melted down for bullion – our consolation being that the offender spent the following thirty years in prison – are famous for the brief runic inscription on one of them, and a depiction of men and animals along with unidentifiable symbols. Fortunately, tracings had been made before the theft, and the models now on display at the Nationalmuseum in Copenhagen were patterned on the tracings.[10] Dating from *c.* 425, one horn depicts two of the men as armed and wearing long, outwardly curving horns. They are presumably participants in an ancient cult ceremony, and their headdress, useless for either combat or the less spectacular purposes of everyday life, is probably an animal symbol of a type known from many cultures (as with the bison headdress of American Indians). The alliterative formula of the runic inscription is no guide to an interpretation of the figures, though we may grant it historical significance as perhaps the oldest line of poetry in a Germanic language. It reads EK HLEWAGASTIR HOLTIJAR HORNA TAWIDO: 'I, Hlewagastir, son of Holti, made the horn.' In a woman's grave in the Swedish province of Uppland was found an amulet shaped as a horned warrior, presumably a figure in a ritual dance. In the man's right hand is a sword, held high and upside down, in the left a bundle of javelins. The horns on the man's head are curved, not to face outward, but circularly so as to join, and each horn ends in a bird's head. A similar depiction is found on a die from Öland.

39 Pre-Viking Age bronze amulet found in a woman's grave in the Swedish province of Uppland. The dancing man is presumably a priest of the cult of Odin.

But helmets of a practical kind the Vikings and their ancestors certainly did have. We know this from preserved fragments (one closely related Anglo-Saxon helmet is preserved at Viking York), such as the splendid example from Sweden's Valsgärde, as well as from numerous contemporary pictorial records which include both rune stone ornamentation and carvings into wood, elk horn, etc. The average Viking probably wore a protective skull cap of heavy bull's hide, but conical or ridged metal helmets were certainly known, sometimes provided with guards for eyes and nose. The helmets of chieftains were often elaborately carved and ornamented.

More than a score of sword types have been identified. No rapier but usually a long and broad two-edged affair with a straight or curved guard or hilt, grip and pommel, the latter usually a triangle or semi-globe. Though Scandinavian weapon-smiths were skilled, the best blades were imported from the Franks and then fitted with hilts by experts at home. The very finest were pattern-welded or damascened, of a type that the Emperors Charlemagne and Charles the Bald tried in vain to prohibit as export to Viking centers. Men of wealth would acquire swords richly inlaid with silver or gold. Both in legend and in fact, exceptionally good swords were given names and, if they survived both use and non-use, handed down from father to son. Prose and verse celebrate the gleaming blade with its wavy damascening, its blood-questing edge, 'Odin's Gleaming Fire-Flame,' 'Helm's Hurt,' 'The Ice of the Red Rims' (rims = shields), or simply 'Golden-hilt.'[11] Preserved spearheads exhibit incrustations of silver and copper wires. The Rus custom of interring fine weapons with their dead warriors is said to have led to grave-robbing by the Arabs, though their own weaponry ought to have been at least as good. The battle-axe, use of which down in Europe had already waned, was a characteristic weapon of the Vikings, who used both the broad-axe and the so-called beard-axe characterized by the lower extension that gave it the appearance of a bearded chin.

40 Helmeted Swedish Vikings carved on the rune-stone from Ledberg, Östergötland.

The all-purpose knife was carried by both sexes, women wearing it on a chain at the breast, men at the belt. Archery was practised expertly by the Northerners, and the whine of arrows, those 'angry bees,' is often mentioned in skaldic verse.[12] If burial goods are a reliable indication, the bow and arrow were wielded for hunting and for sport by women as well as men. The targe or shield, frequently covered in leather, sometimes painted, often had a round iron boss in the center, with which many an enemy was bashed, many a weapon deflected. Coats of mail were rare and late, a stout leather jerkin sufficing for most men. Our knowledge of their clothing derives largely from depictions on rune stones and various tapestries, augmented by fragments found in graves, together with scattered literary descriptions by Scandinavian and foreign observers. Clothing for men comprised breeches, shirt and shaggy woollen or fur cloak, with leather shoes and, for inclement weather, gloves and hat of wool or leather. Prosperous men of the Viking Age often wore brightly colored and sometimes expensively braided clothes, and both silken garments imported from China (centuries before Marco Polo), and gold thread have been found in graves from that period.[13]

A woman wore a long linen chemise, and over that a short-sleeved or sleeveless woollen dress, then a shawl or jacket. Aprons were also known as were, of course, hats, shoes and gloves. Clasps and brooches in their endless variety of patterns, often derived from foreign sources, have given archaeology much grist for its mill. Bracelets and finger rings were common, stamped or plaited in a wide variety of ways. Spiral bracelets were sometimes marked for division, that is, to facilitate the

41 Elk-horn carving of a Viking in typically conical helmet (no horns), with neatly trimmed beard and mustache. This was dug up among Viking Age finds at Sigtuna, south of Stockholm, an important medieval trading center and focal point for the introduction of Christianity into Sweden.

42 Cross from Middleton, Yorkshire, late 9th century, shows a Viking laid out in his grave with shield, helmet, sword, knife and spear, revealing a mixture of paganism and Christianity.

43 Swords from a 9th-century Viking grave outside Dublin.

44 10th-century spearheads from Valsgärde, Sweden, encrusted with silver and copper wires.

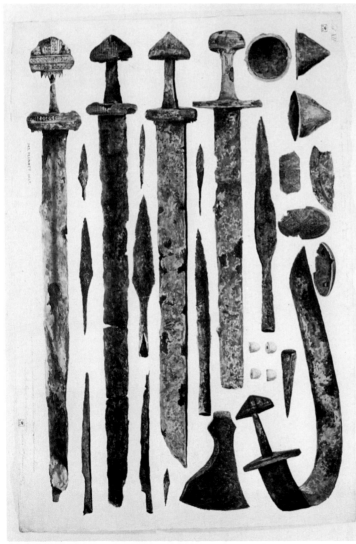

45 Silver arm rings from Sweden, late Viking.

breaking off of pieces in lieu of coins. By around 900 Scandinavian goldsmiths and silversmiths had perfected their craft and shaken off foreign models. Thousands of foreign coins have been found in Sweden, for example 80,000 Arab, 40,000 English, with thousands more lost or melted down to create jewelry and other items of conspicuous consumption. Coins and similarly precious objects were buried in times of crisis (and sometimes, according to the sagas, even out of pure spite), but frequently they were interred with the wealthy deceased as well, presumably as a passport to ease and comfort in Valhalla (*Valhöll*, 'abode of the slain,' esp. those who had died in combat). A type of artifact worth mentioning are the beads of amber or colored glass, or of imported cornelian and crystal, worn as festoons or as regular necklaces. Viking Age earrings, these chiefly of foreign manufacture, often turn up.

Runes

Though the common Indo-European ancestor of the modern Scandinavian languages, Danish, Swedish, Norwegian and the latter's daughter languages Icelandic and Faeroic (Finnish is not a Scandinavian language) may have been spoken in Scandinavia for thousands of years, the art of writing developed late among the Scandinavian tribes, taking by perhaps the 2nd century AD the form of runic carvings on pieces of wood, most of which naturally have perished, on metal and bone, and ultimately on stone.[14] Of preserved inscriptions we have for the early period about 125, the oldest being from around AD 200. The word 'rune' (O.N. *rún*, pl. *rúnar*) is closely related in the Germanic languages, of which Scandinavian is the most northerly representative, to ideas of secrecy, mystery, whispering and confidentiality. And the silent and confidential nature of writing and reading was obvious, not least to those, the majority, who, lacking such skills, considered them magical. Though the runes were easily adapted to religious purposes and were used for invocation, malediction and protection, they were created, perhaps in southern Denmark, as an indigenous form of written communication to rival those of the Classical languages. Obviously inspired by the example of the Latin and Greek alphabets but with differing phonetic values in some cases, the twenty-four characters of the Nordic runerow were arranged in an utterly original order comprised of three sets of eight. Based on the sounds of the first six runic characters, transcribed as F–U–TH–A–R–K, it has come to be known as the futhark (sometimes written as futhork). From Denmark the runes spread almost immediately to Norway and Sweden, then traveled with migratory tribes to the Continent.

For a while during the 5th and 6th centuries the Danes stamped runes rather indiscriminately on golden bracteates, those ornaments imitated from Roman coins. Then runes, at least on relatively permanent materials, fell out of use in Denmark during the period 600–800, at a time when the practice of carving them on stone gained in Norway and Sweden, spreading in due time back to Denmark. After a period of linguistic transition, a new and materially shortened runic futhork, comprising sixteen symbols, was devised by 800. It was less satisfactory from a phonological point of view but easily learned and quite adequate to the expression of the

46 Late silver brooch from Lindholm Höje, Denmark.

47 Earliest forms of the runic alphabet. With variations, the runes continued to be used for over a thousand years.

f u þ a r k g w   h n i j p e R s   t b e m l ng d o

circumscribed, often formulaic nature of Viking Age inscriptions. Though the Swedes thereafter experimented with a form of runic 'shorthand,' the Danish type proved to be the most satisfactory for Swedish inscriptions, of which several thousand have been preserved. Frequently carved in serpentine patterns on memorial stones, often illustrated with mythological scenes and even painted in different colors, these stones were placed along public highways to inform travelers, and posterity, of the power and wealth of prestigious families and the exploits of their individual members. In measured prose, or occasionally in alliterative verse, we are taught to associate those who participated in Viking expeditions, who perhaps fell on foreign soil, with heroic traditions that already at that time were ancient. In Denmark a great king composed his own epitaph along with that of his royal parents. More modest inscriptions commemorated such exploits as those of highway construction and bridge-building. During the 11th century, while the Viking Age was still in flower, the majority of inscriptions took on a Christian tinge.

Though runes were little suitable for the art of writing on parchment,[15] they developed and ultimately penetrated all layers of Scandinavian society, persisting for calendrical and local purposes in an occasional rural district down to modern times.[16] The Vikings took them to the British Isles, where of a hundred or so that remain, Orkney and the Isle of Man have thirty-two each. The thirty inscriptions from Greenland are the only form of writing preserved on that western island.[17] From west of Greenland there is, unfortunately, nothing.[18]

Dublin and York

The great trading centers of the Viking Age, such as Hedeby in Denmark, Kaupang in Norway, Birka in Sweden, make up a large archaeological chapter in themselves. Dublin and York, too, have now been the objects of archaeological investigation of their Viking artifacts that has hugely enriched our comprehension of ancient Scandinavian activity in foreign lands. Dublin was founded as a trading center by the Norsemen, and with an occasional interruption it was governed by them for two centuries. It is even reported that the Irish city was still Norse-speaking when conquered by the Anglo-Normans in 1170. All the fortified harbors established by the Norse in Ireland, such as Cork, Limerick, Waterford, Wexford, Wicklow and Larne,

48 11th-century runic stones at Spelvik, Södermanland, in Sweden.

49 These two stones are from the Danish royal Cemetery at Jelling, Jutland. The larger stone, bearing an inscription on one side, an animal on the second, and this earliest recorded Scandinavian depiction of the Crucifixion on the side facing forward, was raised by King Harald Blue-Tooth in honor of his parents and himself, shortly before 985.

prospered on trade, but greatest, and to the Irish most useful of all, was Dublin. Despite pillage and slaughter, harshness and injustice at times, the Norse occupation brought great prosperity to Ireland, and it would appear that depredations by the Northerners, acting sometimes merely as mercenaries in Irish employ, were in the long haul no greater than those caused by inner dissension among the Celts themselves. The Irish vocabulary relating to ships and trade borrowed much from the Norse who, in return, as it were, adopted Christianity. The two dissimilar temperaments and cultures, if they did not fuse, owed much to one another. The disruptions brought about by the recent digging have become the subject of hot, and one can suggest anachronistic, dispute in Ireland. There, archaeology finds itself as usual in a nip and tuck race with 'progress,' a race in which progress will win and archaeology will make advances. At York (O.N. Jórvík), the process of excavation and preservation by the York Archaeological Trust is far advanced, and the whole must be regarded as an educational project of international significance.[19]

One of the high points in world literature is found in the section of the Old Icelandic saga of Egil Skallagrímsson that depicts the heathen hero's forced meeting at Jórvík with his equally heathen, implacable ancestral enemy Erik Blood-Axe and the latter's malevolent queen, Gunhild.[20] The unpeaceable son of the famous Harald Fairhair, Erik has been dispossessed by his half-brothers of his throne in Norway and now (947–8, 952–4) holds uneasy tenure as resident Norse king at Jórvík. Gunhild, reputedly concupiscent and a sorceress who drew Egil hither, may or may not have been maligned by history. Known as the mother of kings, she has had with Erik a number of sons, no fewer than five of whom are kings or about to become kings in their own right. Shipwrecked on the Northumbrian coast and thus within Erik's royal reach, Egil unhesitatingly mounts a horse, fully armed but with a hood over his helmet, and rides straight to Jórvík where he has a powerful friend at court. This is the influential baron Arinbjörn, who alone of the great Norwegian nobles has followed the restless Erik into banishment. Inquiring his way to Arinbjörn's house and learning that the baron is at his evening meal with his men, Egil takes the precaution of asking a manservant to announce him.

The saga account could not be improved upon. 'That's easy,' replies the fellow, who thereupon goes in and roars at the top of his voice, 'There's a man outside, huge as a troll, and he bade me

50 Craftsman's house of wattle and daub in Norse-founded Dublin, consisting of a single entrance surrounded by small rooms and with a central hearth in living room.

go in and ask whether you would rather talk outside or inside with Egil Skallagrímsson.' The vastly startled Arinbjörn puts in a hasty appearance and inquires right off whether Egil has met anybody in the town who might have recognized him. Egil has not.

'Let men take their weapons, then,' says Arinbjörn, and with his retainers trooping after, the two repair to the royal compound, and are admitted. On being greeted by King Erik, the shrewd Arinbjörn delivers a little speech, a *chef d'oeuvre* of priceless hocum. Its burden is that he has brought with him a warrior who has fared vast distances over dry paths and wet, solely in order to seek reconciliation with his royal enemy.

'Then the king looked and saw above the row of heads where Egil stood, and whetted his eyes on him.' After some colloquy, during which Arinbjörn defies the vengeful Queen and points out that 'night slayings are murder' – that was indeed Norse law – Egil is remanded to Arinbjorn's custody, to be brought back for sentencing in the morning.

In the course of a restless night, Egil, not merely a Viking warrior but one of Iceland's greatest poets, composes on Arinbjörn's advice a twenty-stanza encomium on King Erik. More than a thousand years later, it is preserved under the title of *Höfudlausn* ('Head Ransom'). One stanza of the twenty will convey something of the spirit of the original:

Rang clatt'ring sword   gainst rim of board (= shield),
Around him strife,   he risked his life.
Midst battle's flow   harsh blades did glow,
Fate's fury sent,   were foe's ranks rent.[21]

In the morning, Egil is allowed to recite his poem in the presence of the court. Arinbjörn has taken the precaution of entering the hall with only half his force, the remainder being left outside to guard the exit (and heighten reader suspense). The mood is uneasy. Egil recites the poem, the gleaming eyes of King and Queen upon him the while. Torn between hatred and royal generosity, between his consort's vengeful urgings and recognition of the honor being done him in a poem that might last a thousand years ('while mankind survives' is Arinbjörn's prediction), and hustled no little by a bit of plain speaking from his baron, Erik announces his decision. Like any chieftain worthy of the name, Erik is a judge of poetry and recognizes the forced nature of Egil's tribute. His terse comment is a prime example of grim Nordic humor: 'The *recitation* of the poem was excellent.' He then gives Egil a week to 'forth himself,' 'but come never before my sight again.'

The saga atmosphere and the contents of Egil's poem are stern and heathen. But we are in the 10th century. More than three centuries previously, in 627, King Edwin had been baptized by Paulinus as the first Christian, Anglo-Saxon king of Northumbria. The archbishopric of York was established in 735. Scandinavians were in control there most of the next eighty years. Despite the see-saw of dynastic alternation, York throve. England's second city, it was also the second richest. One would not know from our saga that it was the site of several prosperous churches, of which one, St Olave's, was later rebuilt and dedicated to the Norwegian King Olaf Haraldsson (slain 1030).

But St Olaf was, so to speak, old hat. When York's Anglo-Saxon archbishop Woldhaere was driven out of his see in an upheaval in 872, who but the Viking army restored him to power? About 905 the Scandinavians of York minted and issued coins bearing the name of St Peter, patron saint of York's cathedral church. But to the Latin mottoes D(OMI)N(US) D(EU)S REX and MIRABILIA FECIT ('He performed miracles') were added a sword and the hammer of the pagan god Thor. Whether we call this cultural syncretism or merely a cautious campaign donation to both parties, is irrelevant. The coinage of Viking Jórvík had a stricter standard of silver purity than the smaller and debased

Anglo-Saxon coins, which enjoyed no high rating internationally. These several ambiguities, now ancient history, illustrate not merely the vigor of Viking Age creativity but also the coalescent nature of early British cultural institutions. Three-quarters of the names found in Viking Age Jórvík are Scandinavian and especially Norwegian. Scandinavian styles, taste and patterns are reflected in the thousands of personal items excavated in modern York, extending from jewelry and combs to the 'hogback' type of tombstone in the cemetery of York Minster, which depicts scenes from Northern mythology.[22]

To guarantee the permanency of their rule, the Normans burnt down most of York in 1069, and a period of decline followed. The extraordinary archaeological undertaking of recent years goes far towards compensating us for a certain historical amnesia, or at best, a skewed representation of the ancient Viking. Alfred fought the Danes, his sons learned from them organization and military technology. What we moderns can learn is now up to us. Thanks to the York Archaeological Trust, we know exactly how the ordinary population lived, chiefly in small houses of planking. The royal palace of Erik and the other Norse kings has not yet been located, nor have the certainly (for that age) comfortable residences of the gentry and wealthier merchants. We know exactly what the Jórvíkings ate, for – stand by! – their very excrement has been retrieved, microscopically examined and expertly evaluated. Beans, carrots, celery, apples and stone fruits were common. The large amount of bran excavated from their latrines is indication of the prominence of whole grains in their diet, which naturally included lots of both fresh and dried fish, an element that would leave few remains, oysters and mussels, chicken, geese and red meat, the flesh of cattle being favored. We gain insights also, through research in archaeopathology, into what intestinal parasites infected them. Cleverly constructed dummies represent men, women and children at work, at play and in the loo. Ancient Jórvík had what might charitably be described as an open sewer system, a situation faithfully reflected in the dozen or so smells – petroleum fumes and the stench of chewing gum mercifully excepted – concocted at York by modern chemists and wafted to the startled nostrils of visiting scholars and tourists. That triumph of archaeological verisimilitude deserves classification as *le dernier odeur*.

Finally, we know that the banks of the rivers Ouse and Foss must once have been lined with warehouses in keeping with

York's great importance to international trade. 'The recovery of these waterside facilities is one of the major challenges still facing the archaeologist at York.'[23]

Religion

The story, no short one, of the Christian missions to the Northland naturally relates to the heathen religion, or asserted lack of it. While the worst of the Viking raids were in progress, rival missionaries from Germany and England struggled to convert the heathen, with mixed success. Denmark and Sweden were visited in 830, but the effort had constantly to be repeated. When a respected monarch was for personal or public reasons sympathetic to the 'new custom,' progress was facilitated, perhaps only to be undone by his successor. Norway was harshly converted by the swords of its two famous kings, the ex-Viking Olaf Tryggvason (995–1000) and Olaf Haraldsson the Fat (1016–1030), whose Christianizing savagery the aggrandizing Church cleverly exploited by proclaiming him a saint. The powerful rulers of central Sweden, prospering under their heathen gods, sensed no urgency to convert, and the new faith was not well established there before the mid-11th century. By 1060 there were two bishoprics in still Danish Skåne and seven in the rest of Denmark, in Norway and Sweden three each. By 1104 Lund had under English clerical influence outmaneuvered Hamburg–Bremen to become the administrative see for all of Scandinavia, although within two generations national arch-episcopates were established in Uppsala, Sweden, and Nidaros (now Trondheim), Norway. One is skeptical of Adam of Bremen's claim that Skåne alone had 300 churches. In any event, most churches were small, built of wood, and have left no recoverable traces, whereas some of the stone-built churches have survived and are in use today.

The term 'heathen' need not signify an absence of religious belief. The picture of the Norse gods presented to us in literature, such as the retroactive descriptions in the *Prose Edda* of Snorri Sturluson (1178–1241), allows us, without excessive reverence, to reconstruct the divine hierarchy in loosely the following set of analogies:

The gods had originally carried on business as two separate corporations, the Aesir and the Vanir. Through a semi-hostile corporate take-over by the Aesir, the amalgamated corporation now went under the name of Aesir, though the corporate officers

of the Vanir still had their perks and pensions. Corporate headquarters was in the town of Asgard, a sort of mountain resort high in the mountains. One-eyed Odin, sinister, fickle, depraved, fomenter of strife, god of runic wisdom and hanged men and exponent of the berserk ecstasy of combat, was Asgard's chairman of the board. Carrying his spear Gungnir, Odin rode an eight-legged horse, Sleipnir, was constantly accompanied by the two ravens, Mind and Memory, and employed Valkyries as his messenger girls. Warriors who died in combat were privileged to join his country club, Valhalla, where Ullr served as director of athletics. Red-bearded Thor with his faithful hammer Mjölnir was door-keeper and bouncer, doubling as hit-man and enforcer. The fair Freyja was everybody's bedmate. That well-endowed fertility symbol, Frey (regularly described as *deus cum ingente priapo*), was the envy of all roving males. Balder, the god of Goodness and Light, was an easy-going fellow, a born loser doomed to an early death. The mixed-breed Loki, messenger and gossip, represented malice and betrayal.

Historically speaking, however, this Nordic pantheon, like that of the Greeks, was a gradual creation, for the gods were

51 (*left*) This carved picture-stone from Tjängvide on the Swedish island of Gotland probably portrays Odin on his eight-legged horse, Sleipnir, receiving a drinking-horn from a female figure, perhaps a Valkyrie. Below is a ship with its load of armed warriors.

52 (*top*) Silver amulet in the shape of the hammer of Thor, from Öland, Sweden.

53 Bronze figure from Södermanland, Sweden, probably representing the god Frey.

59

numerous, had developed individually in different areas and at different times, represented different aspects of life and had different constituencies. When Christianity was making itself felt, many of the gods were still young and vigorous, while the emeriti among them were remembered only by scholars and poets. Cultural attrition rendered unnecessary any decrees of desanctification. The gods had their pecking order and their squabbles and none, not even Odin, was all-powerful. Their hereditary enemies were the giants, of whom there were many categories and degrees, and against whom the final battle, Ragnarök, must one day be fought – and lost. Behind men, gods and giants was Fate, stern, immutable. The 'somber magnificence'[24] of the gods and of the Norse conception of life and its ultimate law was not a facile or cheery one, but perhaps it is worth a passing thought by lateborn generations to whom whimpering and complaining have become second nature. At all events, it served its purpose until undermined by a bewildering monotheistic religion that preached the twin poles of Hellfire and Hope, Salvation versus Eternal Damnation.

With no religious hierarchy, each chieftain and indeed each paterfamilias being his own priest, and few or no temples (Gamla Uppsala was a prominent exception, and temples are described for Iceland, though these may have been no more than the residences of the *godar* or chieftain-priests), no bells or books, possibly no sacred music (Adam's secondhand reference to *carmina obscoena* indicates some sort of chanting not pleasing to Christian ears), no special clerical garb and no single god guaranteed to be superior to all others, heathendom as a religious fellowship was not organized to compete with the Christian way. Those who resisted the orders of a proselytizing monarch, as in Norway or in the Frankish Empire under Charlemagne, learned soon enough through bloodshed and torture that the new faith would brook 'no false gods.' Scandinavian merchants traveling in Christian lands, as well as heathens in the employ of Christian princes, frequently adopted prime-signing (L. *prima signatio*, 'the first marking with the sign of the Cross') as a half-way station on the way to Christianity. This made them acceptable to both camps. Of those who returned home, many relapsed into heathendom, others ultimately accepted baptism, characteristically on their deathbeds, as a final precaution. Excavated graves often indicate a mixture of the two faiths; thus at York, Scandinavians buried in a Christian churchyard might take a coin with them in death. Since the Scandinavians were not

monotheists their gods, some of whom merely had a local
following perhaps analogously to the saints and sub-saints found
in other religions, were in the main tolerant of each other and of
foreign divinities. For perhaps similar reasons the Northmen
appear to have been largely tolerant towards other races and
nationalities, and even their attacks on monasteries aimed at loot
rather than destruction. Sadly enough, as we shall see later, it
was in the New World that conspicuous exceptions must be
recorded.

Even in his home territory, above all in times of 'unpeace,' the
Viking of consequence seldom put foot outside the door without
weapon in hand. He who breached this rule might well have
short time to regret it. As a consequence of the blood feuds that
so often became self-perpetuating among Icelandic families of
note, as they had in Norway before the emigration, totally
innocent men might on occasion be victimized in retaliation for
the malfeasance of a friend, relative or employer. For the ancient
Scandinavian, religion and custom were one, the principal word
for it being *sidr*, 'custom, moral life, faith' (cf Ger. *Sitte*, Sw. *sed*
etc), not to be confused with *sejdr* ('wizardry, magic'). Heathen
faith had a stern and pessimistic cast to it, for the northern view
of life was fatalistic. This comported with the so-called heroic
ethic, which made great demands on the physical and mental
constitution of its followers. Hardihood and violence went hand
in hand, death on the battlefield was not to be feared, death in

54 The so-called Kings'
Mounds at Gamla (Old)
Uppsala, from the 5th
century. The modern
parish church in the
background reputedly
stands on the site of the
old heathen temple whose
fossilized remains can be
seen underneath the floor
of the church.

vindication of personal honor or in support of one's leader was commendable:

> Cattle die, kinsmen die,
> One dies oneself the same.
> One thing I know that never dies,
> The doom over each man dead.[25]

'Doom' in this quotation from that great compendium of heathen lore and legend *The Poetic Edda* means, not destruction, but judgment, report, reputation. A man's fate was his reputation – the Greeks knew it – and it was his fame to boot. Bravery was mandatory among free men, cowardice being attributed, often unjustly, to slaves. Loyalty to a leader, faithfulness to a friend, solidarity with the blood relation and clan, were pre-eminent virtues. The loss of an individual was a loss to the clan, a breach in the common defense, to be warded off, and to be avenged if it nevertheless occurred. The status of women was high, a situation that survived the introduction of Christianity. Generosity was esteemed and its opposite, greed, though of course well known, looked down upon. The pillaging of foreign countries was not evil, and there was usually something impersonal about it. The question of right and wrong was subjected to an esthetic standard. Morality *was* in fact esthetic and included the satisfaction obtainable from actions that could result in no material profit. There were bullies and asocial types among the Vikings, an occasional one a psychotic killer, perhaps given to indulgence in poisonous mushrooms or some relative of the American jimson weed. The sagas refer to them as berserks – perhaps useful as kings' henchmen in battle but a scourge domestically – and a passport to social credit in the community would be the killing of one or two such pests on the home front.[26]

The negative view

'History has seldom cared to remember what songs the sirens sang; it has much preferred to relate what ships they wrecked', writes Eric Linklater.[27] A cultured lady of my acquaintance, on catching a chance reference to Vikings, exclaimed: 'Oh, they were *vicious* people, were they not?' That was the sum of her knowledge and the limit of her interest. The day to day activities of hewers of wood and drawers of water, of farmers, fishermen, housewives and children in 9th, 10th, or 11th-century

Scandinavia do not form a large part of our modern world picture. The excitement and the horror of a Viking raid fill the vacuum nicely. The Vikings did wreak harm to many, did cause upheavals of note, did effect seldom appreciated changes in social development. Those who suffered most from their depredations were precisely those who could tell us about it: the scholars. And these were the Christian clergy. Some of the best energies of bishops, abbots and ordinary priests were devoted to eloquent lamentations in Latin, occasionally preserved to us. How many of the clergy may have deplored the massacre, on 13 November 1002, ordered by Ethelred the Unready to encompass 'every Dane in England' is not known, and that this political *bêtise* would result in reprisals was quite to be expected. Among the murdered was Gunhild,[28] sister of Sveinn Forkbeard, King of Denmark and ultimately King of England. But our traditional conception of Viking influence is aptly summarized in the oft-quoted plea *A furore Normannorum libera nos, Domine*! The English scholar Alcuin had written:

> . . . never previously has such terror appeared in Britain as we now have suffered from a pagan race, nor has it been thought that such an inroad could be made from the sea. Behold, the Church of St Cuthbert spattered with the blood of God's priests, despoiled of all its ornaments, a place more venerable than all in Britain fallen prey to heathen tribes.[29]

Some time after 860 a French monk wrote:

> The number of ships grows: the endless stream of Vikings never ceases to increase. Everywhere the Christians are victims of massacres, burnings, plunderings: the Vikings conquer all in their path, and no one resists them: they seize Bordeaux, Périgueux, Limoges, Angoulême and Toulouse. Anger, Tours and Orléans are annihilated and an innumerable fleet sails up the Seine and the evil grows in the whole region . . .[30]

Continuing at length, the monk spoke for all his brethren, and he spoke well. And yet, some comparisons are in order. The Vikings may have had special characteristics, but they were by no means alone in their depredations.

The scholarly digging at *Dubh Linn* ('Black Pool') on the Liffey is sometimes opposed by modern Irishmen resentful of the trouble that those outrageous 'foreigners' (frequently their own ancestors!) can cause while still in their graves. But before and after the start of Norse Viking operations, Frisian pirates plied their craft. The Frisians had become prominent as merchant traders, and piracy seems inevitably to follow trade. There are accounts of pirate forays by the Picts, and Welsh raiders were well known. In the regions of the eastern Baltic the Estonians, the Finns, the Wends and other Slavic tribes were frequently active in piracy, being just as frequently the object of retaliatory chastisement by their neighbors. Rather on land than by ship, the Mongols and the Magyars (Hungarians) conducted lightning-like and massive operations against the west. Before 900 the Magyars had established themselves in the Carpathian Basin and Pannonia. Noted cavalrymen, they were during the 10th century a fearsome plague with their quick advances on Italy, France, Burgundy, Spain and even Byzantium. Later came the Tartars. Writers such as Simon of Saint-Quentin, in his *Historia Tartorum*, describes them as eating human flesh (the Vikings, after all, are merely charged with impracticably guzzling beer out of human skulls, and even that allegation is a very late invention). The famous Matthew Paris wrote that the Tartars were rather monsters than men, and Henry Raspe, Landgrave of Thuringia, described them as 'terrible of body, furious of countenance, with wrathful eyes, rapacious hands and blood-dripping teeth.'[31]

The 7th century had witnessed the sudden eruption of the Arabs, followed by their savage onslaught on southern Europe early in the 8th. Crossing the Jordan in 634 they had within three years taken Damascus, Syria and Jerusalem. Egypt fell in 641. By 711 the Arabs could cross the Straits of Gibraltar. Soon all Spain, Sicily and southern Italy were in their power, and France stood threatened until Charles Martel was able to defeat them at Poitiers in 732. Their appearance on the European scene induced economic and social changes in Europe as a whole. Unlike the religiously tolerant Norsemen, the northward pushing, monotheistic Muslim developed no acceptance of Christianity and did not convert. The Vikings had no prophet and no *Koran* to keep them on track. Theirs was a different mentality, and their clash with the Arabs was in the end something of a draw. The Norse did not colonize in the south, and the Arabs remained in possession for hundreds of years thereafter.

4

The stepping stones

Studying a map of the North Sea southwest of Norway, one inclines to count the islands clockwise, first Shetland, well out to sea. Some 50 miles south of Shetland, Orkney, a mere 20 miles off Scotland's northern coast. Down in the Irish Sea, the Isle of Man. Northwesterly then, to the Hebrides that parallel the Scottish mainland. More northerly yet, the Faeroes, half way to Iceland. Every one of these foggy, windswept aggregates once sheltered a miniature Norse civilization, and the Faeroes do still.

Shetland, with its 117 islands, of which a quarter are inhabited, is today a Scottish county. The Vikings, who probably by 800 had muscled in on the Picts and Celts, called its 551 square miles of slate and sandstone, heath and moss, *Hjaltland* ('Shelfland'), and the highest shelf reaches 1475 feet above sea level. Birds, hares, rabbits and sea otters abound there, and humans brought sheep and the shelty to share the rain. Christianity, introduced by St Columba in the 6th century, remains; the Gaelic and Norse languages do not, but a few Norse customs have survived.

Orkney, 'Seal Island', is a Scottish county, too. Its ninety islands, a third of them inhabited, extend for nearly 60 miles along Scotland's coast. They are comprised of old red sandstone, the highest point of its 375.5 square miles rising 1562 feet above the sea. The Norsemen who maneuvered amid its dangerous storms and tides recognized its naval importance (Scapa Flow) and established a powerful earldom there. The old Norn language that it shared with Shetland is now found only in dictionaries.

The Isles of the Hebrides, Inner and Outer, some 500 of them on a foundation of gneiss rock, form two of Scotland's counties. Pliny called them *Hebudes*, the invading Norsemen named them *Sudreyjar* ('Southern Islands'). Norwegian rule lasted until 1266, but the Norse language yielded in the end to Gaelic, the power of the clan chieftains was broken in 1748, and the sheep have survived all administrations.

55 Animal ornaments on a cross at Kirk Andreas, Isle of Man.

The highest point of Man's 221 square miles of slate and graywacke is Snaefell ('Snow Mountain'), which pokes skyward for upwards of 2000 feet. Its inhabitants have been chiefly Celts, but the Isle of Man was once Scandinavian and ruled by the Viking kings of Dublin, then by the mighty earls of Orkney. Known for its uniquely decorated rune stones, it retains a certain degree of freedom, with its tiny assembly the Tynwald (O.N. Thingvöllr, 'Parliamentary Plain') as a memorial to Viking independence under the protection of the British Crown.

The Faeroes ('Sheep Islands') have their own capital, Thorshavn ('Thor's Harbor', though they are no less Christian for all that). They fly their own flag and speak their own Scandinavian language, which has a baffling pronunciation but a grammar and vocabulary seemingly half way between those of Norwegian and Icelandic. The total area is 551 square miles, the highest mountain Slaettaratinden 2894 feet. Rain and wind blow fitfully over a high plateau that ranges from *c.* 1650 to 2400 feet in elevation. The hay crop is excellent: cod-fishing, whaling and the harvesting of sea-bird eggs and down have been the economic backbone of this tiny country which was independent until 1035, Norwegian until establishment of the joint Danish–Norwegian monarchy in 1380, and Danish after the separation of the joint monarchy in 1814. The Faeroes have enjoyed self-government in local affairs since 1948 and are known for their rich store of Scandinavian folklore. To such ballads as *Sjurdar kvaedi*, the Ballad of Sigurd (the Dragon-Slayer), the Faeroese, often in national costume, have from the Middle Ages until today assembled to dance the Long Dance, an unforgettable event for eye and ear.

Among these five sets of islands, great anomalies abound. In Orkney the place names are chiefly Norse; in the Hebrides, where Celtic has survived, the place names are mixed. Orkney retained the ancient Norse system of land tenure, *odal* ('allodial right'), in the Hebrides there was no such system. On Orkney Christianity was soon extinguished by the Norse, only to be re-established forcibly by Norwegian King Olaf Tryggvason in 995. In the Hebrides, conversion among the Norse took place easily and early. Orkney was a Norse earldom, whereas the history of governance in the Hebrides is most uneven, the southern portions remaining part of Irish civilization, the northern areas ever beyond its grasp. In one measure or another the imprint of the Norseman is on these islands, and they were his stepping stones to the republics of the New World.

The North Sea is no blue Aegean. Irish anchorites, their meditations shaken by Northern fists, embarked in their bull's hide *curraghs* and dangerously discovered a larger island, 250 miles west of the Faeroes, a volcanic region of smoke-plumes and snow set down among sea monsters, and sufficiently large that its northern edge grazed the Arctic Circle. By the year 800 at least, an undetermined number of these pious meditants had settled in. They called the place Tyle or Thule, presumably echoing Classical tradition regarding Ultima Thule. The early Norsemen, ignorant of Classical lore, called it, practically enough, *Ísland* ('Land of Ice'), and that unflattering and semi-justified name has stuck. When the Norse, some of whom were of mixed ancestry and had even been born on the once Pictish–Celtic islands we have enumerated above, began their landtaking (*landnám*) on the periphery of this roomier island, the monks and anchorites withdrew to escape the curse of heathendom, doubtless not all at once, leaving traces behind. Bells, croziers and Latin manuscripts in Irish script clearly identified the fugitives. Some may have starved in the desolate interior, others must have perished at sea, while an occasional *deórad* may have reversed his pilgrimage and returned to his former home and the world that is too much with us. Information concerning them comes from both Irish and Scandinavian sources, such as Dicuil, *Íslendingabók*, *Landnám-abók*.[1] The Norsemen called these Irishmen *papi*, pl. *papar*, cf Ir. *pabba*, L. *papa*, and several Icelandic place names reflect this. What neither the *papar* nor the Norsemen knew, or could know, was how distinguished a civilization was destined to rise out of this volcanic soil.

Iceland

Next to Great Britain Iceland, with its 39,709 square miles is the largest island of Europe, somewhat over 600 miles from Norway, 500 miles from Scotland. Fjord sites are steep, curved spits (*eyri*, pl. *eyrar*) often project from shore with good natural harbors inside them. Since Viking times, thirty volcanoes have been active, some grossly destructive, while others, in small-scale replication of Iceland's primal birth act fifty million years ago, have actually added new territory. Since 1975 there has been much volcanic activity, the ninth and most serious of which convulsions caused a six-mile 'unzipping' of the earth near Lake Mývatn, famed for its bird life and scenic beauty.

Iceland was thrice discovered by Scandinavians. The first discovery was by the Swede Gardar Svavarsson, who circumnavigated the island in about 860. Pleased with the island and his own achievement, Gardar modestly named it after himself: Gardarsholm. Gardar did not remain, but some years later his son Uni became one of the early settlers. The second discoverer, several years after Gardar's trip, was the Viking Naddod, who was off course and found the place by mistake. He gave it a name, but not the favor of his tarrying, and the name, *Snæland* ('Snow-Land') bestowed by this chance visitor ought to have introduced an element of caution into the enthusiasm for the new territory. But not so. The third discoverer, following Naddod by a couple of years, was Floki Vilgerdarson, and the elaborate preparations he made for colonizing the island included no care for winter's cold. Two harsh winters later the sadder but wiser Floki was back in Norway, badmouthing the place that he had decided to call Iceland. The Past was Prologue. The foster-brothers Ingolf and Hjörleif settled Iceland in 874, and within a few short years people from Norway and the British Isles were beginning to pour into the island.[2] *Landnámabók* records, in sometimes tantalizingly compressed terms, the landtaking of the first four hundred settlers, who came usually with family, often with slaves or freedmen servants, to make an average, it is assumed, of ten persons per family unit. Within sixty years – by 930, say – most of the arable land had been taken by these four thousand pioneers, who then bequeathed, sold or lost it to their successors.[3]

This Land of Ice was far from lacking desirable features. Ample pasturage for livestock made it practicable for a dairying people to prepare their curds and whey, their leather hides and their sheep's wool for spinning. There were some forests in the beginning, salmon abounded in the streams, fish and sea mammals splashed the island's margins. Roughness there might be, bloodletting feuds developed among the surly or the ambitious, but no stern king or jarl held the reins of power, not for nearly four centuries – not that attempts were not made.[4] Harald Fairhair of Norway, dangling the bribe of an earldom, attempted through Uni Gardarsson to secure renewed sovereignty over some of the citizens he had lost. But the Icelanders – for as such they thought themselves now – would have none of that. They developed their institutions, built fine mansions, established a code of law and the world's oldest parliament, and created a literature that ranks among time's

greatest. They served as highly prized poets at foreign courts (including the pragmatic Norwegian!), wrote their country's history and that of their lands of origin, traveled to distant places as Viking harriers and skillful merchants, observant tourists or humble penitents, built churches and established monasteries, squabbled and depleted their creative energies, and submitted in the end to foreign domination.[5] But: not before they had pushed west, colonized Greenland, and explored America.

56 Kirkjubaer, in the south of Iceland. The land's south coasts remain ice-free in winter on account of the North Atlantic Drift.

The nation-to-be was spectacularly fortunate in its founding families. They had ambition, independence, energy and aristocratic tradition, and an aesthetic appreciation of character and conduct, and the dominant Norse strain was generously leavened with Celtic blood. The literary and historical sources play down the Swedish and Danish share in the settlement, whereas the grave-findings tend to exaggerate it, particularly the high proportion of chapes (which may point to Sweden) and the absence of any evidence for cremation (which may point to Denmark); and it is reasonable to think that there was a bigger infiltration of Swedes and Danes into Iceland by way of south-west Norway than native writings allow. Still, the Icelandic homeland was Norway, more particularly the south-west, Sogn, Hordaland, and Rogaland . . .[6]

The language, too, from which their own dialect came within a few centuries to differentiate itself, was Norwegian.[7] Not least,

69

their antipathies sprang from Norwegian sources, though not every immigrant squire could claim to have been a mortal enemy of Harald Fairhair, 'first to make himself king over all of Norway,' whose tyranny, real and imagined, Icelandic sagawriters have transmitted to posterity. The chieftains who had fought Harald at the Battle of Hafrsfirth (890?), and lost,

> . . . resented the loss of their titles, saw no reason why they should hold their estates of the king, regarded taxes as robbery and oaths of allegiance as the diminution of a free man's dignity.[8]

Harald was thoroughgoing, and those who would not bend the ever so stubborn knee in Norway could look forward to losing their possessions and perhaps their lives, or to seeking their fortunes in another place. Many dispossessed Norwegians, settled on the islands, vented their spleen on Harald by raiding the coasts of their former homeland. In response, Harald mounted expeditions to put down the western raiders, as a result of which many of them moved out to Iceland. The efficiency with which King Harald rid himself of major enemies and minor malcontents is matched only by the zeal with which his later successors, the two Olafs, enforced Christianity upon the enemies of themselves and God. To *that* enforcement free Iceland was the exception, for after much hesitation and a lengthy debate, the Icelanders agreed not to slaughter one another for the glory of God. Power-seeking political malcontents were demanding that the law be changed. And in the year 1000, in Parliament (Althing) assembled, it was decided to adopt the new faith, this, be it added, by the advice of a wise heathen. The account of the affair is not without its quotient of wry Nordic humor. While the matter was being considered at Thingvellir (twenty miles from modern Reykjavík), there was an earthquake and flaming lava began running out of crevices in the earth. 'The heathen gods are angry', protested a member of the heathen phalanx. 'At whom then were the gods angry when this land we stand on was created?' retorted another heathen, a skeptic and vulcanologist before his time. For a while, at least, Christianity in Iceland, being largely nominal and superficial, was tolerant of heathen deviancy (such as the eating of horse flesh) so long as religious misdemeanors were kept out of the public eye.[9] And one Christian Icelander was actually banished from the island for slandering the goddess Freyja in the ditty:

> I like it ill that gods should bark,
> That bitch Freyja's barking, hark!

Legal custom, historical tradition and pride of ancestry were powerful components in Icelandic culture, precisely because of their immigrant status. To the Vikings as scheming strategians or swashbuckling swingers of axe and sword must be added the skilled creators of intricate verse and the disciplined spinners of oral tales and entire novels which improved upon history by elucidating human character. In large measure, history and literature among the Icelanders were one. Enlisting all the resources of modern scholarship, we can sometimes improve on their history. On their 'novels' we can never improve because they represent the pinnacle of their particular genre. In due time the oral novelists, or *sagnamenn*, became writers as well, and the body of letters thus transmitted to us amounts to an imposing shelf's burden of sometimes thrilling, often puzzling, but ever forthright and instructive comment on the human condition. Because of the conservatism of Icelandic society – the conservatism of the perimeter – the sagas yield insights into events and folkways anterior to their own time. That fact has at times led Pan-Germanic enthusiasts to claim the Icelandic sagas, lock, stock and barrel as common Germanic intellectual property, with consequences not invariably pleasant to remember. It is not extravagant, however, to position the character delineations of the best Icelandic Family Sagas among the glories of world literature.

Unlike the Greeks, the Icelanders have left us not a single epic poem, yet the best of their sagas have epic proportions. Unlike the Greeks again, they have bequeathed to us not a single drama, yet their dialogue, woven into prose narrative, was above all dramatic. Unlike the Irish, they did not indulge in the intricate flights of fancy that charm the emotions and put carping criticism to sleep. The Norse scene is no faerie wonderland, no realm of marvels and magic and endless improvisation.[10] Ultimately the Norse translated and adapted Celtic and Continental romances, but never could they have produced an Arthurian cycle on their own. The genius of Old Scandinavian literature was its arrangements of the factual, or at least the believable. Witchcraft was not unknown to them, but intellectual discipline kept its literary manifestation to a minimum. During the long period of natural disasters coupled with economic and social deprivation that afflicted the Icelanders during the centuries following their loss of independence (1262–4), they found in the sagas the strength to continue a national culture grounded in individual strength of character amid conflict and adversity. Of pertinence to our present study is the fact that two of the shorter sagas give us our first view of the New World.

In Chapter 3 we beheld the spinetingling meeting between the two mighty heathens, Egil Skallagrímsson and King Erik Blood-Axe. Saga literature, in a few terse sentences, knows how to make the most of an irresistible force in its clash with an immovable object. The essence of the force, and the resistance to it, is not physical, but moral. 'Where there is no choice, there is no problem,' the Icelander might have quipped. So it was in the case of the famous Icelandic leader Njál and his wife Bergthora, who owing to the bloodletting proclivities of their hotheaded sons had become intricately involved in one of Iceland's most bitter blood feuds.[11] In the saga the year is 1011 and all involved are Christian, but heathen wrath must be assuaged in the only way known when all compromise has failed: through blood vengeance. Surrounded at home and hemmed in by a confederation of his sons' implacable enemies, the aged Njál faces death by suffocation as the house is put to the torch. Though the servants are allowed exit, Flosi, leader of the besiegers, scornfully refuses Njál's offer of financial compensation for past killings. Njál's sons, the real objects of the attack, are in the house with him. In a sudden burst of Christian conscience or heathen generosity, Flosi offers to allow Njál himself to come out unscathed. The offer is refused:

> I will not go out, for I am an old man and little prepared to avenge my sons, and I will not live in shame.

Flosi then calls out to Bergthora:

> You come out then, *húsfreyja* [a poetic honorific meaning 'goddess of the house'] for on no account do I wish to burn you in.

Bergthora's proud reply rings down through the ages:

> Young was I given to Njál; this have I promised him, that a single fate shall meet us both.[12]

The elderly couple then retire 'to our rest,' and the tragedy continues, with fateful consequences for all concerned.

When the famous Gunnar in the same saga is surprised at home alone by his enemies, one of them, climbing up on the roof to look into a loft window, is caught by Gunnar's spear and slides to the ground. 'Well,' says his impatient leader, 'is Gunnar at home?' 'Find that out for yourself,' is the rejoinder. 'What I do know is that Gunnar's spear is at home.' And the man falls dead. One did not die willingly, but one did not whimper over it, either – best to die with a quip on one's lips, as did that follower of St Olaf at the Battle of Stiklastad (the monarch's last) who, pulling an arrow from his belly, exclaimed 'The king has fed us well; there's fat around my heart roots.'

A man knew his own worth. At the Battle of Svolder, in which the other famous Olaf met his death, his court poet Einar Thambarskelvir, a great archer, stood beside the monarch on the deck of his flagship, loosing his arrows at the foe. Suddenly an enemy arrow smote Einar's powerful, bended bow in the middle so that it broke in two. 'What broke there with such a crash?' 'Norway, King, from your hands,' came the proud, laconic prediction. When Asbjörn Seal's Bane, for good and sufficient cause, slew a slanderer who stood smirking before King (Saint) Olaf, so that the man's head fell on the table before the king and his trunk across the royal ankles, the visibly angry monarch kept his self-control, but when Asbjörn's cousin Skjalg, a member of the royal retinue, stepped forward and offered financial atonement – customary under the code of the times – the king was not disposed to be gracious. 'Do you and your father think it a small matter that he used my feet for a chopping block?' Skjalg answered: 'It's a bad deed, King, if you are displeased; in other respects, Asbjörn did a splendid piece of work.'

Still farther west

The three incidents involving Norway's kings are narrated in the long history of Norway called *Heimskringla*, [13] by the Icelander Snorri Sturluson (1178–1241) who, most ironically, was himself murdered at the behest of a king of Norway. Snorri's distinguished predecessor, Ári Thorgilsson *frodi* (The Learned, 1068–1148), was the author of the oft-mentioned *Landnámabók*, a sort of Icelandic Domesday Book though, unlike William the Conqueror's, it was not compiled for the purposes of tax extraction. Ári was the first Icelandic writer to mention Vínland. In northern Europe the name Vínland had appeared at least once, and possibly twice, before. The first mention was in a tantalizingly doubtful runic inscription from Hønen, Norway. The word UINLAT, acceptable in itself if that is a trustworthy transcription, appears on a stone for which the runologist Magnus Olsen suggested a probable date of 1050. Now most unfortunately lost, the inscription did at any rate refer to a voyage to the UBUKTH (O.N. *úbygd*, 'unpeopled area'), quite possibly the dread east coast of Greenland. A suggested translation is:

> They came out and over wide expanses, and needing cloth to dry themselves in and food, away towards Wineland, up into the ice in the uninhabited country. Evil can take away luck, so that one dies early.[14]

The final sentence would indicate that this was an epitaph over a young explorer. A quarter of a century later Adam of Bremen, principal of the cathedral school at Bremen, claimed to have heard of Vínland from Sveinn Úlfsson (Sven Estridsen), King of the Danes (1068–76). Writing in Latin, Adam says:

> He spoke also of yet another island of the many found in that ocean. It is called Vinland because vines producing excellent wine grow wild there. That unsown crops also abound on that island we have ascertained not from fabulous reports but from the trustworthy relation of the Danes [*certa relatione Danorum*]. Beyond that island, he said, no habitable land is found in that ocean, but every place beyond it is full of impenetrable ice and intense darkness.[15]

The shaky Hønen inscription and Adam's 'trustworthy' reference comport reasonably well with one another, and though neither locates Vínland, the one indicates an unsuccessful voyage thither, and the other, if in any way reliable, can rest only on at least one successful voyage there by *somebody*. By about 1122 Ári the Learned was writing his *Book of the Icelanders* (*Íslendingabók* or *Libellus Islandorum*, preserved in a second edition). Ári's concise history is conscientiously documented, his sources and informants specified. In the work, he casually mentions Vínland in association with the Icelandic colony in Greenland:

> Both east and west in the country they found human habitations, fragments of skin boats and stone implements from which it was evident that the same kind of people had been there as inhabited Vínland and whom the Greenlanders call Skraelings.[16]

Ári's uncle, the distinguished Thord Gellisson, had had the account from a man who had followed Erik the Red to Greenland

and would have been well informed. While Ári was compiling his account, Vínland was the subject of more intensive interest to the missionary Bishop Erik *Upsi* (codfish) Gnúpsson. According to the Icelandic annals *sub anno* 1121 (as preserved in 13th-century documents), Erik set out in that year 'to find Vínland' (*leita Vínlands*). Vínland was consequently known to exist, and it had evidently become lost, as did the good bishop himself, for he was never heard of again. In the following generations Vínland is mentioned in several of the sagas, sometimes with the addition of 'the Good' and save for implacable Skraelings, an early Shangri-La, a new Ultima Thule, and becoming in time a generalized name for the eastern shores of North America below Markland, yet never aught but a vague annex to an industrious Nordic civilization in southwestern Greenland.

Born in Iceland of Norwegian parentage, Erik Thorvaldsson the Red was a great-grandson of Øxna-Thórir, a Norwegian *hersir* or baron who was a brother of the Viking Naddod, early discoverer of Iceland in the 860s. Erik's own date of birth is not known for sure, though a circumstantial guess might make it 945–50, for he was very active throughout the 980s but deceased by shortly after the year 1000, it appears. Erik's wife Thjódhild came of an important family with royal connections. These were no ordinary people. Like his father, Erik was a man of stern disposition, but no common roughneck, and the term 'criminal' breezily applied to him by a recent writer is quite misleading. Erik had bad luck in the beginning, had suffered wrongs, and under a code that required that one seek one's own justice, more or less, there being no police system or public prosecutor, he did something about it. The consequent charge of manslaughter brought by his enemies resulted in conviction by the local assizes (district *Thing*), and the formal sentence amounted to one of 'lesser outlawry,' i.e. he was obliged to remain away from Iceland for three years. Had he remained, like the famous outlawed Gunnar of *Njál's Saga*, or Grettir, or Gisli, each the subject of a saga named after him, he would sooner or later have been killed through private or group assault as soon as that matter could be contrived. For once 'outside the law,' whether justly or not, one's life was forfeit to vengeance-seeking unfriends or even to a 'contract' killer or common bounty hunter.

Now, Erik's father Thorvaldr had not belonged to that early generation of *landnámsmenn* who had acquired all the best land years before. Settled on marginal land in western Iceland, Erik had less to sacrifice than the tragic Gunnar ('Fair is the lea, I shall

57 Ornament on a 10th-century thistle brooch from Orkney.

remain and not go'). And so, quietly disposing of his real property, and keeping a wary eye on his lurking enemies the while, Erik gathered a crew – he was far from friendless – and put to sea. His purpose was precise, and few banishments of a single individual have been so fruitful in their results. His plan was to explore the reputed lands to the west of Iceland which, if in any way suitable, would become his dominions. In his coveted rôle of primary landtaker, Erik planned to make his choice of grazing lands and assign the rest to relatives and friends and decent men generally, for in unity there would be the strength requisite to a colonizing project. In the event, Erik proved that he had leadership, foresight and the ability to command respect. During the three years that he and his crew spent exploring the east and west coasts of Greenland, it would appear that not a single man was lost through misadventure or disease. All things considered, that is remarkable.

How could Erik know for sure that a great, unnamed land mass lay to the west? That can be answered in two ways. The shortest distance to Greenland from the mountain Snæfjöll in northwestern Iceland is 155 nautical miles (287 km). When the wind is from the Arctic, visibility is excellent and Greenland can actually be discerned from the Westfirth mountains. Owing to atmospheric conditions of optical inversion that sometimes prevail over the sea, the high parts of Greenland's east coast can be seen or easily surmised from ships at sea west of Iceland. Secondly, adventurous or wind-driven mariners had already sailed close enough to detect a land region of consequence.

Greenland, like Iceland, was in a sense thrice-discovered. The first discoverer was Gunnbjörn Úlf-Krakason, a Norwegian who, on his way to Iceland some time before 930, was driven off course and saw what subsequently came to be known as Gunnbjörn's Skerries. Gunnbjörn settled in Breidafjörd, western Iceland, where his descendants continued to live in Erik's time. For his skerries, or rocky islets, people searched fruitlessly for decades. The skerries may have been islands off the east coast of Greenland at Angmassalik above the 65th parallel; or else Gunnbjörn, who did not land, may only have seen Greenlandic mountain tops from a distance. The port he sought was after all in Iceland.

The second discovery took place half a century or so later (981–82), when Hrólfr Thorbjarnarson and Snaebjörn Holm-steinsson with two dozen followers, seeking Gunnbjörn's Skerries, landed on the inhospitable eastern coast. During the stay the explorers had a falling out. Snaebjörn and his followers were killed by Hrólfr and his men who, after dreadful hardships, succeeded in making their way back to Iceland by a circuitous route.[17] There is a literary echo of this episode in the later horrid tale of Freydís in *The Saga of the Greenlanders*, the murders there all the more repulsive for being credited to a woman.

But the third time is the charm. Erik the Red sailed west in 982. Three years later, his sentence of outlawry up, he was back in Iceland with a glowing tale of adventure and anticipated prosperity. He gave likewise a promising name to the land he had explored. Cleverly, but not at all dishonestly, Erik named the land, after the best of its qualities, the Green Land (*Grönaland/Grönland*), and by this name the world has known it since.

58 Bronze lion ornament for a harness, Gotland.

The ultimate step

Of Greenland's approximately 850,000 square miles, 84% is covered by inland ice. From Cape Farewell at 59°46′ N. lat. it stretches 1670 miles northward to Cape Morris Jessup at 83°39′. Though precise accounts of ice conditions around the millennium are naturally lacking, it is known that even in that warmer period the eastern coast was stern, more than inhospitable and the seat of many an unrecorded human tragedy and some recorded. Greenland sealers and whalers from the southwestern area (to the bafflement of outsiders referred to as the *Eastern* Settlement[1]) must have rounded the southern tip of the island and fared a way northeast during the short summer seasons, but he who risked a winter on the east coast was almost surely doomed. Their own southwestern shores, on the other hand, afforded stimulating opportunities to men of vision and resolve. Succeeding generations of life in Norway, followed by the meager conditions of existence in Iceland, had schooled them in exploiting northerly environments. It must be remembered, to be sure, that the Norse were very far from ready to live the nomadic life, or beat skin drums and sing the *Pisiit* songs or the *katadjait* ('competitive throat songs') of the Eskimos. Though skilled and adaptive huntsmen, the Norse were a farming and cattle-breeding people, their clothes and implements had European antecedents, their laws and customs, their folk-memories, their language and history, the religion that had come to give shape and meaning to their lives, would all prevent so drastic a transformation. Furthermore, when they arrived and selected their farms in southwestern Greenland, no Eskimos of any kind were settled there, and the implements and boat remains that they are reported as having found indicated some previous habitation, probably from decades or centuries before. An explanation for these came to them retroactively.

Erik the Red had penetrated to the heads of many of Greenland's deep fjords and assessed their capabilities to sustain colonizing Icelanders. After experimentation he had made his

59 Ketilsfjord, Greenland, a graphic representation of the harsh landscapes encountered by the Norse.

choice of farmstead. It was at the head of newly-named Eriksfjord that he set up his establishment, calling it *Brattahlid* ('Steep Slope'). That name is not entirely clear, for the land does not slope precipitously and the hills behind are not especially impressive for Greenland. Nevertheless it was Brattahlid, 'capital' of the main colony of this New Iceland and, at least until the establishment of the bishopric at Gardar, not too far away, 140 years later, the spiritual center of the world's least populous free state; Brattahlid, manor of the chief squire and magistrate upon Greenland and the place to which all distant visitors steered their course; and Brattahlid, anchorage to the Vínland sagas and magnet to the historians and archaeologists of a much later age.

One of the more successful 'estate agents' of all time, Erik the Red had a way with people. Seemingly, he experienced no difficulty whatever in promoting his discovery. His stories of ample pasturage – the *green*, remember – summer flowers in brilliant abundance, sea-birds all about, large sea mammals in the offing, wrack and driftwood on the beaches, fired the imaginations of friends and neighbors, each of whom nourished some private or public reason for making a move. Some were involved in financial difficulties, others felt the pressure of feuds and litigation, most were settled on land that they were not unhappy to sell. A number of them were sufficiently attached to Erik personally that they simply wished to throw in their lot with him. In all, the seldom dormant spark of adventurousness must have quickened at his descriptions. In the end, twenty-five shiploads of them assembled for the voyage. There would have been the usual sad goodbyes, parting admonitions, forecasts of doom and disaster. For some of the emigrants such prophesies must have borne sad fruit. Of those ships that set out in the year 986, fourteen arrived safely at their destination. The episodic nature of early records allows one only to guess at the fate of the hapless eleven. A few may have been beaten back to Iceland and whatever bitterness awaited them there. Some may have been successful on a second try. Others may have joined the throng who slipped tracklessly into the waves or whose lifeless bodies and fragmented ships were so often found on Greenland's eastern shore. These vessels were, after all, heavily freighted with people, domestic animals and goods. The margin of safety was small between the gunwale and the brine.

By agreement, unquestionably, with Erik, chief captain of the little fleet and chief authority ashore on all pertaining to the

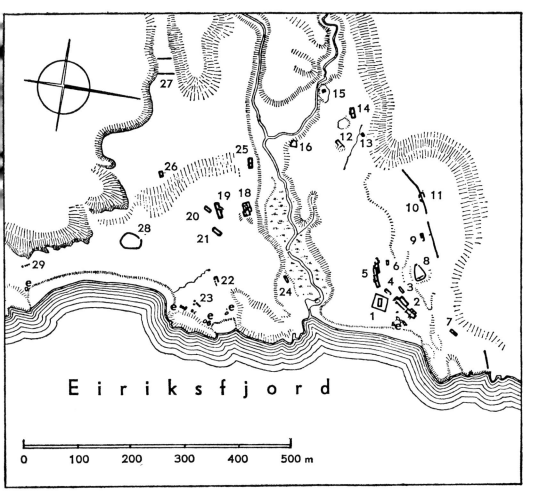

E i r i k s f j o r d

```
0    100    200    300    400    500 m
```

Green Land, the settlers, after rounding Cape Farewell or, perhaps, passing through the channel behind it, moved into the fjords and set to work at their most immediate task: that of erecting shelter against the coming winter. For as to that, the Icelanders would not be fooled by the bobbing daisies and bluebells of 'a summer so short.' After the sea-sickness of the voyage their animals went joyously to meet the luxuriant grass that grew virtually as one watched it under an almost continuous northern sun. But they would not be able to graze during the protracted winter, and so the grass must be mown and stacked, tang and mosses and angelica collected, crowberries and whortleberries and lingon picked, all the natural products located and assessed, the physical features of the environment carefully noted for future reference. Men, women and children all worked. Such slaves as they had were put to their tasks, the more reliable among them sent on exploratory or foraging errands. Only exceptionally would a slave try to escape, for

60 Sketch of the northern area of Brattahlid: 1, church; 2, manor; 3, 4, storehouses; 5, byre and barn; 18, neighbouring farm; 19, byre. Remaining numbers indicate various ruins. The *Thingvöll* or assembly place is off map to left.

where in that place could they go that they would not be hunted down and punished? Furthermore, a slave's interests lay in community, as part of the household. Ultimately, all were manumitted at one time or another, and set up in small holdings of their own around the edges of the greater farms in a relationship of interdependence that was of mutual advantage to cottager and squire.

So: there was game on land, from hares to reindeer, and larger than those of Norway; various kinds of fish in the sea – cod, capelin, herring, halibut – and fish such as salmon trout (*Salmo alpinus*) in lakes and streams fed by snowclad mountains behind; seal, walrus and whales; ptarmigan and other game birds in the air, and birds' eggs in quantity. Just as in Iceland of the early period – the saga of Egil Skallagrímsson tells us so – animal life in these regions, whether on land or at sea or in the air, was unsuspicious of man, for the Eskimos had not in generations penetrated this far south, and the human population even now was small.[2]

Life on Greenland

Houses were built of rock and turf, with thick walls both to bear the roof and to keep out the cold. Trees were available, but few of these were of any size. There was driftwood aplenty in the early days, used, as were peat, manure and fishbones, largely for fuel, but also adaptable for tools, household articles, and the building of the small boats used in local activities, especially on the fjords and the waters of inland lakes. In time the settlers would cross Davis Strait and harvest the giant timbers to be found in the forests of central Labrador. Sadly, their own birches were soon cut down. The houses first erected, as judged by their remains where these can be distinguished from later structures that modified or supplanted them, were of the long-house type (*langhús*), whose principal feature was a single room or hall. This type of hall was particularly known in the Norwegian province of Jadarr (modern Jaeren), from which Erik's family derived. Originally built in that style, Erik's Greenlandic Brattahlid was subsequently enlarged, and became a *ganghús* ('passage house'). Ultimately, the Greenlanders developed the so-called central house, a complex that included stables and storerooms, built together, but the great house at Sandnes in the Western Settlement, owned by Karlsefni of Vínland fame, though it had many rooms, was still essentially a *langhús*.

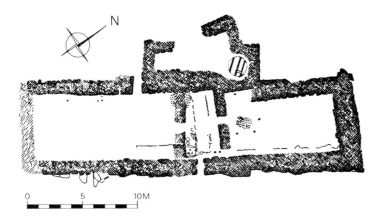

61 The Sandnes Farm in the West Settlement, a typical long-house.

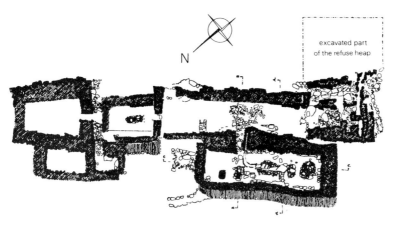

excavated part
of the refuse heap

62 Erik the Red's establishment at Brattahlid. The large room at the bottom is the original long-house, to which the rest was subsequently added. In the middle of the room is the partially covered water course.

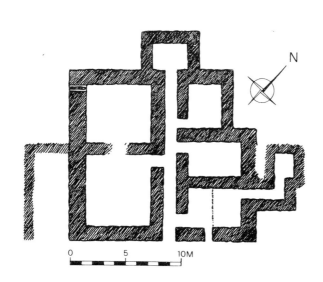

63 A so-called passage house from the Eastern Settlement – the ultimate development.

83

Whichever system was followed, warmth was a basic consideration for man and beast. Horses and sheep could usually make shift outside, but even they required some protection in the worst weather, and some feeding with fish meal, kitchen scraps, seaweed, leaves and whatnot to eke out the precious hay. 'Big cattle' – and curiously small they were by present-day standards, pygmies in comparison with the huge and friendly creatures that nuzzle one in the mountain pastures of Switzerland – *bos domesticus* of both genders, had chiefly to be kept inside during cold weather, in narrow stalls in a stable of stone, with thin rock slabs for partitions between stalls. The importance of the stabling has been illustrated in a shocking manner by events during the Greenland winter of 1948–9, when half the cows in the Julianehåb district (which includes ancient Brattahlid and Gardar) perished for want of planning in the face of an exceptionally cold season.

Dairy products were esteemed by the Greenlanders and even exported in return for needed articles, like malt, grain, iron and salt. Iron for knives, axes and arrowheads could with some difficulty be extracted from bog iron deposits, and no fewer than four forges have been discovered, but the process was exceedingly costly in terms of fuel production. Grain of a sort the colonists could harvest from the vicinity in the form of strand rye (*Elymus arenarius*) that grows even in unlikely sandbanks. It is laborious to pick but one can make porridge or even bread of it, and the stalks were added to the animals' feed. Various seaweeds and mosses served as food for humans as well as livestock. Not merely belly-fillers, such moss types as *Cetraria islandica*, or the tang *Rhodymenia palmata*, or the willow herb *Epilobium angustifolium*, or brackens, contain invaluable nutrients and were highly regarded by the Greenlanders as they had been by their fathers in Iceland and Norway. For wheat, rye and barley there are of course no real substitutes if the choice is at hand, but testing by Norway's State College of Agriculture has indicated that 3 kg of dried reindeer moss (*Cladonia rangiferina*) contains a food value equal to 1 kg of barley.

Beer brewed from imported malt, when available, may have been their only alcoholic beverage, and that blessing in disguise furnishes a background to the excitement over reports of a land of grapes somewhere to the west. Salt was another rarity. Distillation of sea-water is a laborious process, there were no salt licks round about, and in consequence salt was little used in conserving food products. Instead, fish and meats were dried or smoked, or else preserved in sour milk, tubs of which were kept on hand. As for the body's basic need for salt, meat and the ocean fish in their diet would have provided that, not to speak of seaweed. Helge Ingstad describes his visit to Brattahlid several decades ago, where he found, in Eskimo ownership, a potato patch. Old Erik the Red had never seen or heard of a spud. A native of South America, the potato reached southern Europe via Spanish explorers and reached North America via England, where it was known by 1596, but the Scandinavians were not acquainted with the versatile tuber.

Any establishment of size had need of numerous outhouses for storage, stables, dairy work, smithying, cooking etc.[3] A turner's bench has been found. The Eskimos who, in the end, though apparently only after some centuries, succeeded the whites, must very soon have appropriated what objects of iron they could use, but humans are careless and such artifacts have remained scattered around: arrowheads, worn knives, axes, scythes and sickles, scissors and tongs, awls, weapon blades and fire steel, each item precious to the modern investigator. How much iron the Norse settlers had or produced cannot now be determined, but they got along excellently with implements of wood, walrus ivory and bone. Soapstone, used by their ancestors in Norway for centuries, was not available in Iceland, but there were soapstone deposits in Greenland. Exactly how soon the colonists found these is not known, but once the discovery was made, they lost no time in employing the substance for oil lamps, cooking and dining utensils and a variety of other purposes. Easily carved, soapstone brought out the artistic urge in many a Greenlander.

The oil that burned in the lamps was whale oil or the rendered lard of seals, which gave light and warmth and supplemented the cooking fires. Nails were made of wood, and lashings were prepared of walrus hide, reindeer sinews and, it is believed, of whalebone. Though the colonists hunted with bow and arrow, it is not known what they made their bows of. For swords there was little use, but spear, axe and knife were major necessities, fish-hooks and harpoons known and used, and stone weights that turn up in the ruins indicate a use of nets. Almost certainly they employed the leister or fishing spear, which had ancient antecedents in their homeland.

Transport, other than by Shanks's mare and bended back, of all that was gathered from shore or hill, fjord or lake, was by boat wherever necessary or practicable, otherwise by *klyfjahestr*, the faithful and hardy packhorse. Useful in war, agriculture and commerce, the horse had been bred and esteemed in Scandinavia since ancient times and had followed the Vikings abroad. Graves of Vikings who had received a proper burial during the heathen period reveal that a favorite horse, in some cases a pair of horses, had been interred with their master for use in the afterworld. In exploring the wilderness areas of Greenland away from the settlements, the Norsemen could have made small use of *equus caballus*. The species native to the western hemisphere had died out long before. If the Greenlanders' efforts to colonize the American continent had been at all successful, it would have been stocky horses of northern breed in the 11th century, rather than the Spanish horse of Arab antecedents in the 16th, that first proliferated on North American soil. The putative effects of that on the history of Indian warfare and the later colonization by the English and French, are worth contemplating.

The house at Brattahlid and many another Greenland residence had running (cold) water, in the sense that a brook ran straight through it under floor level from the back long wall to the front. Presumably it could be covered over with thin stone slabs or wooden planking. Except during the winter season, when water barrels would have to be maintained inside, this conduit would save the housewifely trouble of going outside for water and would in addition handily carry away offal and sweepings. This type of arrangement had long been known in Iceland and parts of Norway, and was of such obvious usefulness in times of uncertainty and strife that we know of at least one Norwegian case in which, when a besieging enemy took steps to divert the precious stream, the blockaded householder immediately surrendered. He well understood that the damming would be followed by the torching of his house, as had been done in the case of Njál. At some time during their tenure the Greenlanders developed irrigation systems of a sort to irrigate some of the holdings. The practice may have started, or at least reached its highest development, at the bishop's seat Gardar, where still visible pits in the ground are apparent witness to the technique. Though fertile, those areas are surprisingly dry, and artificially introduced moisture made a world of difference. Fertilization with animal dung was another practice that the Greenlanders may have brought with them from Iceland and Norway, where the dung basket was an important farming adjunct. Possibly they followed the practice called by the Norwegians *grindgang*, or fertilization through the use of a moveable corral. Seven months of stabling each year provided amounts of either fuel or fertilizer that would have made a perceptible difference to the domestic economy. Unthinkable that they would have wasted it.

Settling in

The Eastern and Western Settlements were approximately 400 miles apart, reckoned from center to center. In between was what is sometimes referred to as Middle Settlement. In visiting back and forth, poking into every fjord, the Greenlanders soon became familiar with the geographic and economic features of the nearest areas. And early, it appears very early, they pushed northward along the coast and then across Davis Strait to those farther lands they had already had such startling word of. Though such things are manifestly impossible to quantify, it seems almost certain that the expansionist spirit, the colonizing urge, must have been strong in those early years. Augmented by seafaring merchants and adventurous hopefuls from Norway and Iceland, awash in the surging ambitions of young men as yet unburdened with family cares and who sought some exploit that would bring profit and fame, the new colony was still in the initial stages of assaying its possibilities and, in the current idiom, establishing its identity. Not until later, when the notion of migration still farther westward had proved fatuous, did the Greenlanders settle for a sensible approach to the northern and western spheres as hunting grounds and, following upon northerly contacts with the Eskimos, as profitable trading places.

Looking back a thousand years we can imagine them of a winter's evening around the long fire pit in the main room at Brattahlid and in the houses of the neighbors, the women at their work that never ends, the men repairing nets or carving and fashioning implements and spinning tales, youth matched against age in games like *hnefatafl*, a forerunner of chess (*hnefi*, 'knight', + *tafl*, 'board, table'), the whole a buzz of talk and laughter, of reminiscences and ambitions made audible. No television to sedate their minds, no chattering wireless to bring news from abroad, no home movies, no coffee or tea or tobacco or the bottled soft drink around which so much of modern civilization revolves, no magazines or books or mail order catalogs – nothing but what the mind could produce and hold and exchange with family and companions. As with all generations before them, they must have had their ditties and songs, their riddles and jokes and folk tales, their genealogies and heroic verse, their legal formulae and their maxims for conduct. Their viewpoint was not that of modern science but they understood well enough what was reasonable and what was absurd, and in their attitude toward nature they belonged to a tradition of keen observation and sober analysis. Their dialect had developed scores of words to describe the texture of snow and ice, the ever-shifting manifestations of the sea or the sailing qualities of a ship. They did not feel deprived, this self-selected tribe of emigrants, offshoot of the great Viking expansionist urge, the *Drang nach aussen*, but rather, well filled with confident belief in future opportunity. They were chiefly nonliterate save for two poems in the Eddic canon which survived to the age of writing,[4] plus a few terse and moving messages carved in runes, and their deeds and their conditions were only recorded – ever so sparingly – by collaterals in Iceland, generations after the fact. When the art of writing on parchment developed among Iceland's intellectuals early in the 12th century, tales of life in Greenland were common enough in some quarters. A portion of this material ultimately found its way into several major sagas of life in Iceland, to which a character's experiences in the western colony add an occasional bit of spice. Some of that material is fanciful, other episodes have the ring of truth and can be reliably attached to known persons and reasonably corroborated events.[5] Despite incidental references from time to time, after several centuries of continuous if not uninterrupted traffic between Greenland and its mother countries Iceland and Norway, the land would lose precision in the consciousness of annalists and novelist–historians. Ironically, it was the very failure of the Greenlanders to plant a daughter colony in America that brought them the measure of fame that was to be theirs. That failure and that fame are recorded in the two short Vínland sagas, to which we shall turn in a minute. Before that we must say a word about religion among the Greenlanders.

The Greenlandic mini-state – it never had an official name or ruler as such – was founded at a time when the heathen gods were fading. The White Christ loomed on the horizon, for some an ominous sign of the deterioration of all good institutions, for others a glorious symbol of hope for a good life, if not in this existence, then in the next. Among those who sailed off to Greenland some, not yet a majority, must have been strongly influenced by the New Wave, but they were cautious enough not to make an issue of it, for they had not yet learned intolerance in

64 Hvalsey church, Greenland.

matters of belief. Their heathen inheritance of multiple gods, all equally valid if not equally powerful, was enough to ensure that for a while. We are told of one exception, the famous case of Erik's strong-willed wife Thjódhild, who had found in Christianity a welcome excuse not to sleep with a heathen husband. That Erik should take it ill was to be expected, and the incident received enough attention to be recorded in *Erik's Saga*, though the *Greenlanders' Saga* makes no mention of the matter. Thjódhild built herself a chapel 'not too close to the house,' and indeed, a minute church has been found about 200 yards from the main house and obscured from view by a slight elevation. Though often referred to as 'Thódhild's chapel,' the identification is not certain.[6] Erik seems to have died shortly after the year 1000, but we are sure neither of the date nor the manner of it, knowing merely that he died and was succeeded at Brattahlid by his son Leif. Christianity became the accepted frame of reference for the colony's activities, and *Erik's Saga* manages to emphasize this through the recording of a classical exception. This is in its description of a heathen séance conducted by a seeress called upon for prophesy in a time of crop failures and hardship. This fortune-teller of the late 10th century requires the assistance of someone who could sing the incantations essential to the ceremony. As an emergency measure, the young woman Gudrid, who learned the incantations in childhood from her foster-mother, accedes to the general request that she sing them now. The saga is properly apologetic regarding this, for Gudrid later became the wife of Karlsefni, chief hero of *Erik's Saga*, and the great-grandmother of three Icelandic bishops.

More sophisticated in tone, with traces of Christian hagiography around the figure of King Olaf Tryggvason that are quite unknown to the *Greenlanders' Saga*, *Erik's Saga* clearly reveals an intention of magnifying the achievements of Karlsefni. On top of that, it demonstrably utilizes building blocks, i.e., words and turns of phrase, drawn from the earlier *Greenlanders' Saga*, ringing tiny changes on them in the process.[7] It reduces Leif Eriksson's exploration to an accidental discovery, crediting him by way of compensation with palpably fanciful actions in the Hebrides, where he has a love affair and fathers a son, and in Norway, where Olaf Tryggvason charges him with bringing Christianity to Greenland.[8] Bjarni Herjolfsson, represented in the *Greenlanders' Saga* as the true discoverer, though not explorer, of America is not mentioned at all, for if it is Leif who gets the credit for stumbling upon America, what narrative room would there be for Bjarni? But out of a guilty (Christian) conscience the sagawriter creates a new Bjarni, with the patronymic Grimólfsson, and credits him with heroically giving up his life to save another man at sea. This cannot detract from Karlsefni's explorations, which nevertheless are of the greatest interest and set forth in both sagas.

65 Christian grave at Sandnes. Skeletons of a man, woman and child, with a small wooden cross between them.

The voyages: one version

The Bjarni Herjólfsson of the *Saga of the Greenlanders* – I think he was real – was a youngish merchant with his own *knörr* or merchant ship. Accustomed to spending his years alternately abroad and with his father Herjólf in Iceland, he comes home to Iceland with a full load of wares only to find that his father in the interval has moved to Greenland with Erik the Red and taken up land at Herjólfsnes in the extreme south. After a brief consultation with his crew, Bjarni decides to visit his father as usual, but now in the new and to Bjarni quite unfamiliar environment. The voyage starts out auspiciously but, soon deprived of sun and stars, the voyagers become lost in the North Atlantic fog. Drifting for days or weeks before wind and current, they come at length within sight of some point in North America which, from the descriptions given to Icelanders by Erik the Red after his reconnaissance of 982–5, Bjarni knows cannot be Greenland. The sun's position tells them that they are too far south, this unknown coast faces east instead of west, and its forests are visible from the sea, whereas in Greenland trees are visible only at the heads of fjords, far in the interior. Furthermore, here the mountains are low, unlike Greenland's, and no glaciers are visible.

Though the crew, after the foggy frustrations at sea, clamor to go ashore for water and firewood, Bjarni's caution prevails. The season is getting on, known and unknown hazards must be faced, and there is no time for trifles. Despite the grumbling they sail north, coming within several days to another forested land of low elevation. Again the crew mumbles and grumbles, again Bjarni sails sternly on, coming 'in three days' to an island with both mountains and glaciers on it. Before a vigorous southwest wind they now sail for four days (across Davis Strait) and hit Greenland exactly at the projecting Herjólfsnes. Such precision, or such good luck, was not usual in the age of sailing with neither chronometer nor compass. It can of course be that the saga known to us – a copy of a copy of an oral account – however conscientiously the latter was transmitted by generations to whom people were more important than details, has shed one step of the voyage. Bjarni may well have sailed across Davis Strait at a latitude that he considered comfortably *north* of Herjólfsnes, then taken a southeasterly course keeping the Greenland coast in sight. Even from out at sea, Herjólfsnes is visible in clear weather from a distance of up to 90 miles. To miss

66 Procession crucifix from Greenland.

67 The Sandnes Christ, a wooden crucifix found in the Western Settlement.

the great island for a second time would surely have been too much to risk! The *Greenlanders' Saga* relates that Bjarni makes a subsequent voyage to Norway, where he receives much criticism for not having landed or made any exploration of the coasts he has landed upon. From a perfectionist point of view, of course, the criticism was justified. At all events, after returning from Norway, Bjarni gives up sailing and settles down at Herjólfsnes. Whether he knows it or not, he has a ship for sale.

The *Greenlanders' Saga* now goes on to narrate five further voyages, of which the first is made, just possibly by as much as a decade and a half later,[9] by Leif Eriksson. Leif goes down to Herjólfsnes to bargain with Bjarni about purchase of the latter's ship which has, if not a warranty, at least a pedigree (in physics, this would be a chain reaction). Firmly determined to explore, Leif and his crew sail, first of all west to the land that is described as being the one Bjarni saw last. Then they sail southward, making various observations and coming at last to a region which excites them sufficiently to induce them to winter there. Included in Leif's crew of thirty-five men is the famous little 'southerner' Tyrkr, who dazzles them all with his discovery of what he has recognized as grapevines and grapes. Solar observations indicate to the voyagers that they are well south of Greenland, and the winter that year proves to be unusually mild. After living for a while in *búdir* ('booths'), or temporary dwellings consisting of walls of turf or stone – in this case doubtless the former – which can be covered over with canvas or other temporary roofing, they decide to build houses. After that they systematically explore the countryside. In the spring, loading the ship with timber, they depart for Greenland, rescuing fifteen persons from a reef-wrecked ship on the way. His successful exploration and this rescue bring Leif the epithet of 'Lucky.' Leif has given appropriate names to the newly visited lands: *Helluland*, 'Slabrock Land' (perhaps Baffin Island), *Markland*, 'Forest Land' (Labrador/Newfoundland), and finally *Vínland* 'Wineland.'[10] Its location is the subject of a complex dispute, which will be discussed in later chapters.

The third voyage is made, presumably several years later, by Leif's brother Thorvald. Sailing with a crew of thirty, he finds Leif's property (referred to in the saga as *Leifsbúdir*) easily enough and winters there, devoting two summers to exploration north and south. Thorvald becomes the first of the Greenlanders to meet with the indigenes, eight of whom the explorers kill. This precipitates an attack during which Thorvald is wounded by an arrow. With a quip on his lips, he dies, and at his request is buried there, with Christian crosses at his head and feet, for which reason the burial vicinity is named by his companions *Krossanes* ('Headland of Crosses'). A recent commentator sees in Thorvald's death the sagawriter's intimation of Divine retribution for the slaying of the natives. I doubt that a medieval Christian would be offended by the killing of alien heathens, in this case *heathen* heathens.[11]

There follows the account of an unsuccessful voyage by Leif's other brother (half-brother?) Thorstein, who has meanwhile married Gudrid, widow of the Norwegian (Thórir) whom Leif had saved from the reef. Thorstein and his crew of twenty-five are storm-tossed all summer, never see land at all, much less Leif's Vínland, and barely manage to reach shore in the Western Settlement. Thorstein dies that winter in an epidemic, after prophesying that Gudrid will marry an Icelander and produce distinguished descendants. Supernatural incidents now intrude on the narrative. The prophesy is fulfilled when Gudrid marries a newcomer to Iceland, the wealthy merchant Thorfinn Thórdarson, usually known as Karlsefni (Makings of a Man). Karlsefni decides – this will be voyage Number 5 – to do what no one else has done so far. Taking sixty men, five women, livestock and equipment, he sails to find Leif's Vínland with the purpose of colonizing there. Not fully reconciled to abandoning his own plans for Vínland, Leif says he will *lend* them the houses. Karlsefni finds Leifsbúdir and a quiet winter ensues. In the spring, after being visited by curious Skraelings who come to trade their furs, and who are fed milk in return, Karlsefni takes the precaution of building a stockade around their dwellings. Gudrid now bears her son Snorri, stated to have been the first white child born in North America. The Skraelings return in the autumn with more furs. Unfortunately, one of them is caught pilfering a weapon, and is killed by the Greenlanders. This precipitates a third visitation and general combat, in which Karlsefni's bull plays a part by roaring at the savages, who are demoralized and flee. Though unmolested the following winter, the *soi-disant* colonists prefer safety to valor, and retire to Greenland.

The sixth and final voyage included in the *Greenlanders' Saga* is the ghastly and quite suspect account of a voyage made by Leif's illegitimate half-sister Freydís, who along with her wealthy but nonentity of a husband Thorvard undertakes a two-ship commercial venture in partnership with two Icelandic brothers, who bear the clearly formulaic names Helgi and Finnbogi. Each party is to take thirty men, women not counted, but the treacherous Freydís has brought along five extra men. Almost at once there are difficulties, and in the end, on the basis of trumped-up allegations, Freydís and her followers murder the other party, Freydís herself murdering the women when her men refuse. Then swearing her men to secrecy on pain of death, she sails home with them, the whole expedition as pointless as can be. When Leif uncovers the nasty story he is horrified and predicts that she and her descendants will be shunned for evermore. Without further details, the saga asserts that the prophesy became fulfilled (prophesies must be fulfilled). Karlsefni has meanwhile sailed to Norway and disposed of his cargo at a profit, being praised likewise for his voyage to Vínland. He sells his *húsasnotra* to a merchant from Bremen. This is a figurehead carved out of the wood of a tree called *mösurr*; the word has been variously translated as 'Vínland maple' and 'veined birch.' Returning to Iceland, Karlsefni lives there until his death, whereafter the now thrice-widowed Gudrid makes a pilgrimage to Rome, then builds a church at Glaumboer, where she ends her days as a nun. Her Vínland-born son is the grandfather of two bishops and the great-uncle of a third.

The voyages: a parallel version

The sextuple account of Vínland voyaging is compressed into three voyages by *Erik's Saga*, which was set to parchment about sixty years after the writing of the *Greenlanders' Saga*. The first section has Leif, returning from Norway as King Olaf Tryggvason's Christianizing emissary, stumble upon unnamed lands of unspecified location which grow wild grain and grapes, as well as impressive trees including the aforementioned *mösurr*. Leif rescues some mariners at sea and becomes known as 'the Lucky.' Thjódhild builds a chapel and refuses old Erik his conjugal rights. As a result of Leif's accidental discovery his brother Thorstein, using the ship that Gudrid's father, Thorbjörn Vifilsson, has come to Greenland in (not just a generic ship but now pedigreed), sets sail with a crew of twenty to find Vínland. The voyage is grievously unsuccessful.

Thorstein marries Gudrid and later dies of a pestilence. Some time later Gudrid is wed to Karlsefni. The latter organizes a gigantic expedition to Vínland with three ships and 160 men and women. Leif's brother Thorvald is here made a member of this expedition, and another is Thórhall Huntsman, a heathen curmudgeon and retainer of Erik the Red who is widely knowledgeable about wilderness areas. The men find and give names to a variety of topographical features, but Leif's old neighborhood they are unable to find. After a period of scarcity, Thórhall Huntsman's incantations provide them with a whale, the flesh of which, however, makes them ill.[12] Disappointed over their inability to find Vínland, Thórhall composes a satirical poem on the subject and sails off in one of the ships – more probably a ship's boat – whether to find Vínland or return to Greenland is unclear, inasmuch as both of these conclusions are warranted by the text. However, in the end he and the nine men who are accompanying him are wind-driven to the Irish coast and enslaved, that being an obviously suitable end for heathens.

Karlsefni with the remainder of the company now sails south to some area they call *Hóp* ('Landlocked Bay'), a tidal estuary. It is a place rich in halibut and wild game, and both grapes and wild wheat are found. Before long the expedition is visited by Skraelings in nine skin boats, described as small and evil-looking, with coarse hair, large eyes, and broad cheekbones. After staring for a while, the Skraelings withdraw. There is no snow that winter, and the cattle manage well outdoors. In the spring the Skraelings are back in great force, eager to trade furs for strips of red cloth and, if possible, for swords and spears. This last is prohibited by Karlsefni, but the trading goes on until Karlsefni's bull, which has been grazing in the woods, comes out bellowing. The terrified natives run for their boats and are not seen for three whole weeks. Then they return in battle formation and discharge arrows and a ballista at the Norsemen, who flee to where they can have their backs against a cliff. At this point the pregnant Freydís, waddling after them, picks up the sword of a dead Norsemen and pretends to cut off her breast with it. Always frightened by madness, the Skraelings flee in their turn. Freydís has saved the day, but the plan for colonization in this locality is nevertheless scrapped. Various explorations and experiences with the natives follow, and a bit of medieval lore about Unipeds is introduced. In Markland the men capture two Skraeling boys who tell them (in what language?) a great story about men in white clothes who march about with banners. Inserted at the end is a bully tale about Bjarni Grimólfsson on the 'wormy sea,' followed by a few lines concerning Karlsefni and Gudrid and their descendants.

The two sagas, then, are in essential agreement about some things, in great disagreement about others. Each contains a certain amount of inventive nonsense, and these inventions do not match. Some things match, or semi-match, partly because the matching items are based on probable fact, partly because one saga imitates, to a certain extent, the other. Imitation is not always direct: it can proceed by indirection and even by inversion. That is the relation of the *Saga of Erik the Red* (composed *c*. 1260) to the *Saga of the Greenlanders* (composed *c*. 1200). The intricacies upon which that demonstration rests have been discussed by me in more technical publications and cannot occupy us here.[13] The critical waters have often been muddied through the efforts of translator–editors to harmonize apparent discrepancies through the practice of conflation of texts, essentially a patching operation in which the seams are not apparent. Though useful for some purposes, this can be greatly misleading in cases where the end purposes of a given investigation are not merely the pursuit of pleasant reading, but historical and geographical knowledge involving specialists in the sciences. If these latter are to do their best, they require as reliable a definition of the problem as the student of texts can give. In solving a problem in physics, or chemistry, or biology, it would never do to mix, for the sake of harmony, the results of one experiment, or set of experiments, with another. That such procedures may be analogously fatal to reliable conclusions in a matter involving written texts, is not uniformly perceived.

There is much about the geography and history of the Vínland voyages that we may never know. The first step is to consider the two anonymous Vínland sagas as discrete literary entities that deal with a similar historical theme. The cast of characters is partly the same, but their rôles are not identical, and their speeches and actions have been conceived differently. Their final formulation in the manuscripts available to us took place in different sections of Iceland, at different times and among people with differing knowledge and understanding of the original events, as well as differing interests in presenting them. We may use one set of criteria in evaluating the two short masterpieces as literary works, outrunners of a major narrative tradition embodied in the Icelandic Family Sagas. The judging of them as guides to geographical location involves additional criteria, as we bear in mind that these sagas were written rather to record the impressions of the people involved than as general chronicles or sober research aids to a distant future.

In Chapter 1 we noted the archaeological evidence for northerly travels by men of the Viking Age and their medieval descendants along both sides of Davis Strait. We know that the Greenlanders systematically exploited the timber resources that lay across from them, even though not one in a hundred of these voyages had the slightest chance of being recorded. As to that, we know likewise that the greater part of Iceland's precious inscribed vellums were in one way or another lost, not merely to the appetites of worms and mice, nor to the ravages of soot and dampness or the poverty of farmers reduced to using them for shoe-leather, but also to major, recorded disasters. Thus, a load of Icelandic manuscripts collected on the island by the Danish Royal Antiquarian, Hannes Thórleifsson, perished with him at sea in 1682 on its way to Copenhagen, and in the following century, two-thirds of the selectively amassed Icelandic manuscripts acquired by the learned Árni Magnússon for the uses of scholarship went up in the great Copenhagen fire of 1728. 'Here go writings nowhere to be found in the wide world,' was Árni's sad commentary on the disaster. What remains of his assembled manuscripts is now the so-called Arnamagnaean Collection (Arnamagnaeanske Håndskriftsamling) at Copenhagen University.[14] How many materials elucidative of the geography of Vínland may have perished, we shall never know.

What one does know is that in the onomastic competition of later centuries, the name Vínland, frequently as Vínland the Good (this probably derived from medieval references to '*la dulce France*[15]'), gradually became a generalization for America, 'which some people think extends from Africa.'[16] To the north was Markland, remembered for its timber resources. The rest was recalled chiefly for its ice and snow. As to Greenland itself, we must once again remember that the saga accounts were after all Icelandic products and subject to all the vagaries of Icelandic conceptions of a place which the climatic deterioration of the later Middle Ages had made it increasingly perilous to reach. The Western Settlement was the first to be deserted. After 1349, the time of the Black Death, the Eastern Settlement's ties with hard-pressed Norway, whose dependancy Greenland had become, were loosened. Greenland's last resident bishop died in 1377. Communications and external stimulus all but failed. As far as the world was concerned, Greenland as a geographical reality began to take on legendary features.

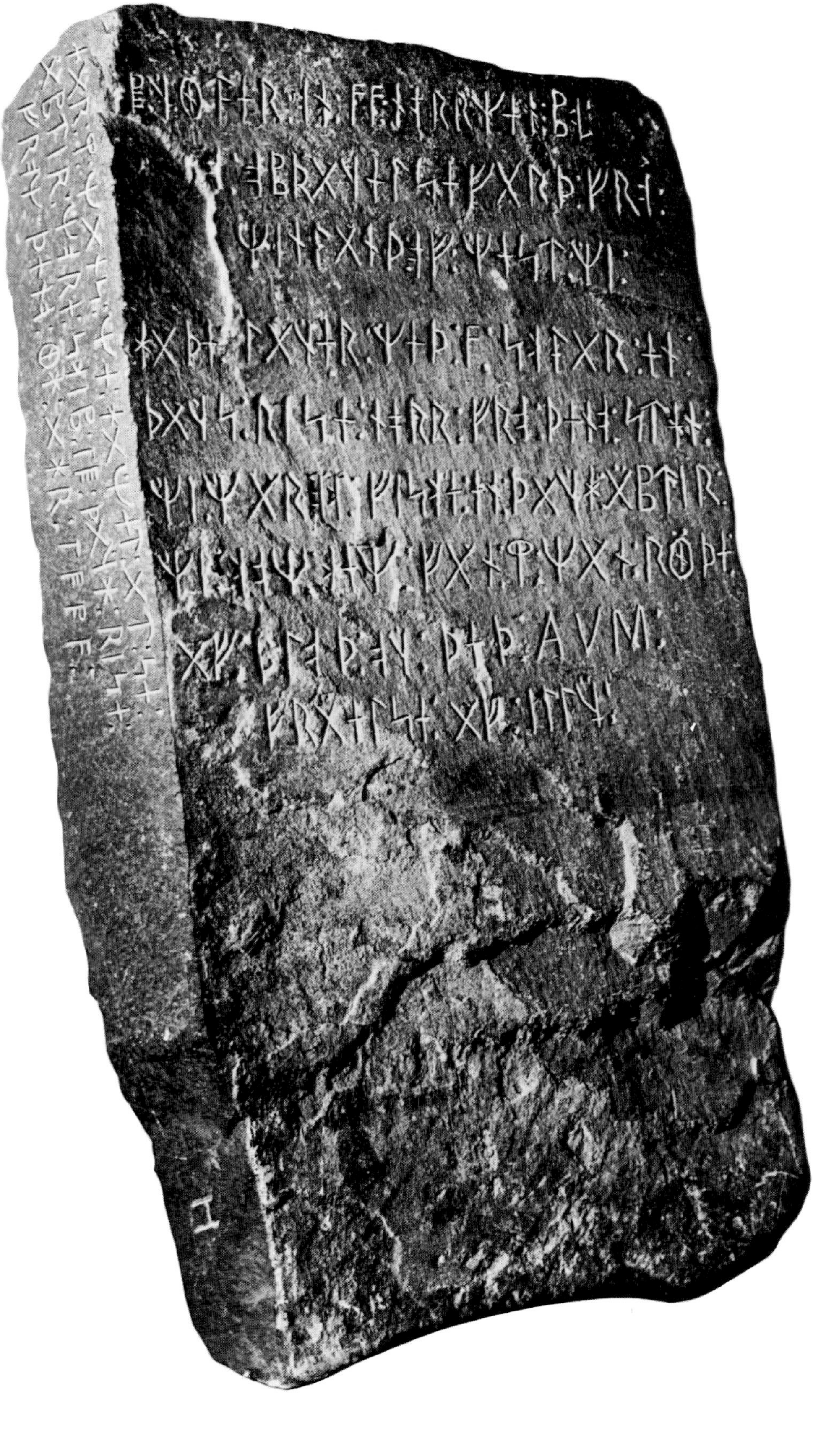

6

Buckram Vikings

My startled eyes moved from the printed letterhead to the typewritten text, then back to the letterhead: 'M. B., Registered Patent Attorney, Electrical and Mechanical Engineer.' Attorney–Engineer B. was outraged:

> Your so-called review . . . has given me a good laugh. Of all the unscientific, ignorant and childish poppycock on this subject you have easily produced the most outstanding example. If you were not such a nincompoop I should have answered you in print and made a real fool out of you by scientific proof which you could never answer, but you have made a fool of yourself already in the eyes of those that know (not those like you who just think they know), that no public punishment is necessary. Has it never occurred to your befuddled brain . . . etc.

It was difficult, back in 1950, to imagine Mr B. as having a 'good laugh' about anything at all. My malfeasance had consisted in a short review, printed in a philological journal that has never been expurgated to fit the tender sensibilities of lawyers and engineers, of a newly published booklet that had retroactively provided North America with twenty-four ancient runic inscriptions, interpreting these in a variety of fanciful ways in order to document Norse explorations in New England, New Jersey, West Virginia, Nova Scotia and Ontario. Though ancient Norsemen may well have visited some of these places, the rock scratchings adduced in evidence of their travels provided, rather, evidence of a different phenomenon: that of self-hallucination. 'Rise ye, men and women, by the Cross,' read one of the alleged inscriptions. 'Dwelling years of Jesus are 3,' read another. 'The Swedes took out charter,' read still another. With sovereign disregard of Old Norse vocabulary, syntax, grammatical form and idiom as well as of proper rune forms, and equally impervious to the dictates of common sense, the rune-happy

68 The Kensington stone, face. Found in western Minnesota in 1898, it is self-dated to 1362, but is indisputably modern.

pamphleteer had compiled his strange readings almost with abandon. His lawyer friend, less critical and certainly less circumspect as a letter-writer than most members of the legal profession, had constituted himself *defensor fidei runicae*. The wrathful vituperation was no isolated sally. Chance crevices in rocks, Indian petroglyphs, schoolboy pranks, outright hoaxes were all being 'interpreted' by enthusiasts with no training in linguistics but who wished to people America's past with Viking hordes. Roaming from Maine and Massachusetts to Minnesota and Oklahoma, from Florida to Mexico and Yucatan, these asserted Vikings once chiseled mooring holes and foolish runic messages as they went.[1]

A truly impressive number of citizens will rally round any asserted exploit, however disprovable, by early Vikings. As press releases proliferate, deviants from the 'Viking faith' are excoriated. It is no defense that one believes in Leif Eriksson and would welcome authentic Viking traces in New England or New Orleans. Let one challenge a favorite inscription or a phony battle-axe, and one has not merely transgressed against local pride or offended an ethnic claque: one has fomented rage even in unexpected quarters. One's name and felonies circulate in a multitude of infra-literate *samizdats*. One's general lack of veracity is featured in widely distributed books. The mailman brings weird missives. Supportive colleagues are vilified in their turn. Gratis entertainment of this nature is of course a legitimate perquisite of academic life. To avoid addiction, one may on occasion seek the company of individuals innocent of any concern for Viking forts, mooring gadgets or runic divulgations. But what is the clue to so much turmoil over chiseled rocks?

The Kensington stone

In the 20th century, the key word is *Kensington*. Once known, if at all, to most Americans as 'something over in England,' Kensington has become a rallying cry for American exponents of Pan-Vikingism. An inscribed stone found in 1898 on a farm near the village of Kensington in Douglas County, Minnesota, and commonly referred to therefore as the Kensington stone, has been the subject of many books, thousands of articles and lectures, numerous radio and television programs and newspaper publicity without end. In 1949 Dr M. W. Stirling, Director of the American Bureau of Ethnology at the Smithsonian Institution, publicly referred to it as 'probably the most important archaeological object yet found in North America.'[2] The Smithsonian had already collaborated with *National Geographic*, whose September 1948 issue contains a photograph of Neil M. Judd, Curator of Archaeology at the Smithsonian, as, magnifying glass in hand, he studies the Kensington stone, along with the statement: 'Later studies indicate that it was carved by white men who had traveled far into North America long before Columbus's first voyage.'[3]

From 17 February 1948 to 25 February 1949 the stone was on exhibit at the Smithsonian. It was then called back to Minnesota in time to be unveiled at St Paul on 15 March 1949 in honor of Minnesota Day on the occasion of the Minnesota State Centennial. In 1951 the Smithsonian directed the attention of the whole world to the by then hotly disputed artifact by publishing in translation a Danish monograph on the Kensington inscription by Denmark's leading authority on Eskimo culture, Professor William Thalbitzer, who had opted for authenticity.[4] On 12 August of that year the 202-pound slab of Minnesota graywacke was granted a signal honor through the establishment at Alexandria, the seat of Douglas County, of a Runestone Memorial Park. Chief feature of the park is a giant reproduction of the Kensington stone in rune-inscribed granite. Sitting on a four-ton base, the mighty stone is 180 times as heavy as the original. By now, millions of tourists have seen the reproduction. Surely, anything so titanically impressive must be genuine?

When the present writer obtained permission (1953) to interview the Kensington stone, it was hiding in the basement of the Alexandria Chamber of Commerce, the subject of an unadjudicated lawsuit. But now it is boldly on exhibit in Alexandria's Rune Stone Museum. In 1964–5 it was exhibited in a tent at the New York World's Fair. In Alexandria one may purchase miniature replicas of the inscription, and the park has been enlivened through the addition of a large, carved Viking, on whose shield is printed 'ALEXANDRIA. BIRTHPLACE OF AMERICA.' This is heady stuff. It would be only fair to say, however, that Alexandria is home to more than a few scoffers as well. There have been local skeptics ever since the discovery of the stone was first announced in 1898 or 1899 – as with everything else connected with the Kensington affair, accounts vary considerably. But decade after decade the skeptics were held at bay through the efforts of one man. We shall return to him in a moment.

This mainstay of Viking lore in the New World measures approximately 30 × 16 × 5½ inches and is inscribed on the smooth face and left edge with 221 (or 222) characters. These are runic symbols derived from the ancient Scandinavian runerows of varying centuries, along with some home-made letters resembling the modern printed symbols known as Bible aids. Circumstances surrounding the discovery and initial presentation of the artifact are curiously contradictory.[5] The date of the find in 1898 was 'August,' or again '8 November.' The location was either at spot A, in a swamp 500 feet from a certain house, or at spot B, on a hillside 700 feet farther west, that time with runes on it. When announced to the press in January 1899 it was either freshly discovered, or had already been on exhibit for months, etc. That the poplar tree from the roots of which it had purportedly been extracted speedily disappeared did not keep the estimates of its size from constantly growing – seldom has a slender tree attained such enormous girth *post mortem*.

The inscription purports to record a disastrous expedition to the future Minnesota in 1362, several hundred years after the close of the Viking Age. There is an attempt to touch up the writing with medieval features derived from the misunderstood reading of implied 'recipes' for 14th-century Scandinavian texts. These were found in the little private library of the Swedish immigrant farmer Olof Ohman (Öhman), who claimed to have made the discovery. Furthermore, the grammar and vocabulary are curiously modern and indeed quite reminiscent of the colloquial Norwegian–Swedish lingo formerly heard among immigrants to Minnesota. In translation it reads as follows:

> 8 Swedes and 22 Norwegians on exploration journey from Vinland westward. We had camp by 2 rocky islets one day's journey north from this stone. We were out and fished one day. After we came home found 10 men red with blood and dead. AVM save from evil. Have 10 men by the sea to look after our ships 14 days' journey from this island. Year 1362.[6]

This expression of a date in terms of calendar years is out of place in runic inscriptions. Where dating occurs it is anchored to important events like the reigns of kings. Numerals, in the rare cases in which they appear at all, are cumbrously written out or, in late times, expressed in Roman style. The astonishing thing here is the use of seven numerals or sets of numerals, including the date, all expressed through symbols purporting to be runes, but with place value based on the Hindu–Arabic system of notation, a system that could not possibly mix with runes. The amusing language of the inscription includes the English word 'dead' (spelled DED), and a slightly disguised modern Dano-Norwegian compound purporting to mean 'voyage of exploration' (OPTHAGELSEFARTH, cf modern D.-N. *opdagelsesrejse*, Sw. *upptäcktsfärd* vs O.N. *landaleitan*). Unlike genuine medieval rune stones, this one presents a smooth and relatively unweathered face. A puzzled and reluctant geologist was induced to conclude in 1909 that the inscription was ancient because he was told that the language on it was medieval, and that it had been dug out of the roots of a very large, hence rather old, tree. But to judge by *geological criteria* alone, he wrote, the inscription was carved no more than thirty, and perhaps no more than fifteen, years anterior to his own inspection of it that year.[7] Most damning of all were several contemporary paper texts purporting to be copies from the stone, but comparative study of which indicates that they are experimental variants, or rough drafts, of a proposed inscription, made by one or more persons involved in promoting the hoax. In brief, they *anteceded* the actual carving. Anything as time-consuming (and expensive) as carving in stone calls for preliminary preparation that includes line arrangement, calculations of space, etc. Lacking paper, the ancient Scandinavians made charcoal tracings or scratched their preliminary copy onto boards or the inner side of bark. At Kensington, either out of pure, naive carelessness, or in a deliberate attempt to impede scrupulous investigation, the conflicting versions were released by persons unaware of the investigative resources of textual research.[8]

From the very beginning the Kensington inscription was recognized by linguistic scholars on both sides of the Atlantic as a simple, though certainly humorous, modern forgery. The stone and the writing on it would have been forgotten long ago save for its resurrection in 1907 by a Norwegian–American resident of Wisconsin, Hjalmar Rued Holand (1872–1963). A gentleman farmer and holder of an MA from the University of Wisconsin, Holand was also a writer on historical topics. Coming across the stone either by accident or through intent – he has told it both ways – Holand sized up its potential at once. For more than half a century he piloted the gray slab and himself to international fame as an ancient monument and its official keeper. Listing himself in *Who's Who in America* as a 'runologist,' Holand understood little and cared nothing for linguistic and historical methodology. Scholarly responsibility he disdained as 'the consistency of petty minds.' But his ability to persuade the untutored, baffle the educated, obfuscate the evidence and create a favorable climate of opinion for his views entitles him to a leading rank among promoters. Shrewdly conceiving the project as primarily a matter of public relations, he planted in his supporters, who were by no means limited to Scandinavian–Americans, the notion that criticism of Holand's theories amounted to persecution of a blameless scholar by the small-minded and jealous. At one point, even the distinguished archaeologist and director of Denmark's Nationalmuseet Professor Johannes Brøndsted was enough impressed by the clatter to consider the Kensington inscription genuine, subject, however, to the verdict of runology, which he soon found it necessary to accept.

American Catholic clerics and historians hastened to welcome the religious fervor and Mariolatry of the 'medieval' runecarver at Kensington.[9] That was not known or properly surmised by the anonymous Protestant who, writing from Fort Worth, Texas, had just read my 'disgusting' article and accused me of being in the pay of the Knights of Columbus. In the same week I was blasted by a priest in Illinois for attempting to suppress evidence of early Catholic exploration. A school superintendant in Iowa lectured me sententiously on my lack of knowledge. A newspaper editor promised to 'hold a court of judgment and tie up the tails of these ignorant and fat-bellied academics' (that exempts me, for I was, and still am, quite scrawny). The '11th Duke of Penelosa' sent me ten pages of typing filled with zodiacal intricacies. A Swiss gentleman living uncomfortably close to my campus wrote me a series of twenty-four letters, complaining in the twenty-fourth that I had answered only the first two and requesting that, in view of all the effort he had gone to in refuting me, I should recommend him to the Academic Senate for an honorary doctorate. The replies he had received from East Coast universities were 'devious and unsatisfactory.' Another local activist solicited a meeting with the Vice Chancellor in order to initiate disciplinary action against 'wayward and irresponsible scholars' (my translation: 'this viper in our midst'). A prominent Minnesotan sent a Midwestern university president an eight-page warning against encouraging 'unpatriotic research,' lest the state legislature cut the university budget.

Professional scholars will gleefully point out one another's errors, the pointing out, if not the glee, being a manifest part of their academic duty; but those outside the portals take great comfort in assuming the contrary. Thus, time after time, it has been proclaimed that the anti-Kensington attitude is a 'conspiracy of scholars to vindicate the prestige of members of their own select coterie who guessed wrong.' Or it is a 'twisting of fact, misrepresentation, sly insinuation and vicious personal attack upon other men, living or dead.' Unused to any objective distinction between *res* and *persona*, such complainants identify their own theories and their heroes with themselves. Resenting academic snobbery, which does indeed exist, lay activists frequently demand exemption from the rule that criteria applicable to a disputed artifact must apply impartially to all works of the same category. Small wonder, then, that the English runologist R. I. Page, in reviewing for *Speculum* one more foolish book on the Kensington inscription, starts out: 'It is with bewilderment that European runic scholars survey America.'[10]

Whereas Europe has had its share of hoaxes and frauds – the Constantine Donation, Piltdown Man, Glozel – the weight of academic authority, however onerous on occasion, does put the brakes on facile promotion of the patently fraudulent. The more ambiguous status of intellectual life in the United States, where egalitarianism is so often confused with democracy, can lead to curious results. It has been seriously suggested that the United States hold a national plebiscite on whether the Kensington inscription is genuine. A recent book suggests that the President and Congress should 'pass a law' to establish its authenticity. Ah, but what if they voted against it? In an imperfect world there are of course worse things. In some countries history is officially rewritten in the name of the Leader, or the Party, or the Revolution. Entire archives are altered or disappear, and persons who 'know too much' disappear as well. Why not the democratic way of 'one person, one vote' to determine the facts of science and history? It is a fetching notion, though scarcely an appropriate alternative to tyranny.

Earlier discussions

Although the Kensington stone has been the centerpiece of modern Viking propaganda in America, it is actually a latecomer. The first object to acquire wide popularity as a 'Scandinavian antiquity' was the so-called Viking tower of Newport, Rhode Island. An English colonial product from, at the earliest, 1640, it was referred to by Governor Benedict Arnold in 1675 as 'my stone-built windmill.'[11] But two discussion-filled centuries later, so distinguished a scholar as Sweden's Oscar Montelius was

69 The 'Viking Tower' of Newport, Rhode Island, cannot be much more than three centuries old. It is first mentioned in 1675 by its owner, Governor Benedict Arnold.

willing to accept it as a Norse structure from the 12th century. The tower helped influence Henry Wadsworth Longfellow, already a Scandinavian enthusiast, to write his famous ballad 'The Skeleton in Armor.'[12] This was the Age of Romanticism. In southern Sweden, on a surface known as the Runamo rock, one may see an 'inscription' which puzzled scholars for centuries. By 1833 a spokesman for the Danish Academy of Sciences had pronounced it an alliterative poem, carved in runes, on the hazily remembered 8th-century Battle of Bråvalla. Three years later the Swedish chemist Jakob Berzelius visited Runamo and found the 'runes' to be natural crevices in the rock. And so they are. At about that time the Dane C. C. Rafn was publishing, in Danish, Latin and Old Norse, his account of the early Norse voyages to America, *Antiqvitates Americanae.* [13] Writing to every historical society in the eastern United States, mustering every possible inscription or other likely Norse object, Rafn was far from the first to discuss the subject, but it was his trilingual publication (1837) that attracted the greatest notice.[14] By 1862 the American James Russell Lowell, in the Second Series of his famous *Biglow Papers,* had published a marvelous satire on Rafn and his work. Pretending through the person of the Rev. Mr Wilbur, AM, that he has acquired a rune stone, Lowell comes out with an essay on 'lithick literature':

> Touching Runick inscriptions, I find that they may be classed under three general heads: 1°. Those which are understood by the Danish Royal Society of Northern Antiquaries, and Professor Rafn, their Secretary; 2°. Those which are comprehensible only by Mr. Rafn; and 3°. Those which neither the Society, Mr. Rafn, nor anybody else can be said in any definite sense to understand, and which accordingly offer peculiar temptations to enucleating sagacity. These last are naturally deemed the most valuable by intelligent antiquaries, and to this class the stone now in my possession fortunately belongs.[15]

To his great joy, Rev. Wilbur finds that the inscription on his stone reads the same straight up, on the diagonal or upside down. It is a memorial stone erected in honor of the first smoking of the herb *Nicotiana tabacum* on the American continent. This pristine smoker was Bjarni (Prof. Lowell had 'Bjarna') Grimólfsson, who consequently had not perished at sea, after all. Another first for the Norsemen. And a double first for Lowell, whose device of the poly-oriented runic inscription anticipated by almost precisely a century the recent presentation by a Scandinavian–American physicist-inventor of an elaborate – and perfectly serious – cryptogram theory which he finds to underlie an assortment of runic inscriptions claimed for America. That will be discussed in a moment.

In 1867, five years after Lowell's little spoof, a runic hoax was reported from the vicinity of Washington, DC. The first part of the hoax consisted of a Latin manuscript of the year 1117, assertedly found at the Icelandic episcopal see of Skálholt and dealing with the Vínland voyages. It records the death at age twenty-five of 'Syasy' or 'Suasu' (the runic symbol for Y/U is ambiguous), granddaughter of Leif Eriksson's contemporary Thorfinn Karlsefni. A learned Dane, we read later, visited America and located the young lady's burial inscription in 'Nevak' runes, whatever those are (*Nevak* does sound a bit like a Greenland Eskimo place name), dated 1051. No less a periodical than the London *Anthropological Review* bit on the hoax, terming the discovery 'a very important contribution to the archaic anthropology of the American continent.'[16]

H. R. Holand has been dead for more than a score of years, but his legacy in the form of newly discovered, or newly interpreted, inscriptions and peripheral theories continues to flourish. In 1971 I received a letter from the mayor of Yarmouth, Nova Scotia, enclosing a neat photograph of an inscribed red sandstone boulder (*c.* 30 × 29 × 29 inches) that had been known from at least 1804 on the shore of Yarmouth Bay. The mayor wondered politely whether the inscription could be validated as runic. It could not. Quite undecipherable by me, and so far not reliably interpreted by anyone, the curious arrangement of dots (drilled holes) and grooves does bear a superficial similarity to shorthand, several systems of which flourished in 18th-century England. Several years previously I had received a similar request regarding putative runes, this time from the wife of a mayor. The town was Heavener, Oklahoma. Careful tracings and a photograph of some kind of runic word were enclosed. The word, without meaning in Scandinavian, was GAOMEDAT. Of eight runes involved, all but the second and eighth belong to the ancient *futhark* or runerow (AD 200–750), whereas the remaining two are later, Viking Age forms. It has subsequently been suggested that these latter two are reverse runes. That would change the inscription to GNOMEDAL, a word offering immediate possibilities.[17] In a modern mix of English and Norwegian, such a word could be construed as meaning 'gnome valley,' 'valley of gnomes.' More likely by far is the interpretation 'G. Nomedal,' Nomedal being a recognized homestead in Norway with a family name deriving from it. Again, the forms indicate modernity. Known since at least the final decade of the 19th century, and officially recognized by the Oklahoma Historical Society in 1959 (though Mr Holand had been displeased at this watering down of his Kensington monopoly), the inscription shows no indication of inspiration from the Kensington carving and probably was never intended as a hoax at all. In any case, disappointed in the obtuse verdict of Scandinavianists that their runes were post-Columbian, the people of Heavener have subsequently found recompense in another theory: along with others that have turned up in Oklahoma, their inscription is now said to be 'Phoenician,' and therefore no longer a Scandinavianist's responsibility.

No American inscription has enjoyed the three centuries of popularity accorded the Dighton Rock of Berkley, Massachusetts. Spectacularly, it has been by turns Welsh, Portuguese, Phoenician, Hebrew, Chinese and, of course, Old Norse. The Algonkian Indians who originally carved it have become lost in the attribution shuffle.

Another ingredient has meanwhile been stirred into the recipe for runic inscriptions, one that H. R. Holand never dreamed of. This is the cryptopuzzle approach, which in fact makes Holand's rendering largely irrelevant. Having arithmetical and even geometric aspects – like the Rev. Wilbur's rune stone – the new doctrine was invented by the retired US Army cryptographer Alf Mongé and promoted by Dr Ole G. Landsverk, founder of the Norsemen Press and the Landsverk Foundation. America's runic inscriptions are all cryptograms, their purpose having been to record secret calendrical data pertaining to the perpetual calendar of the Catholic Church.

The method, and Landsverk's explanation of it, are complex and, according to him, foolproof and exact to the day, though not to the hour. He can date the Kensington stone to 24 April 1362, the Heavener inscription to 11 November 1012. The Newport Tower dates from 10 December 1016, the runic materials at Spirit Lake (see below) are from 27 May and 6 October 1123, the Waukegan Horn (see below) from 15 December 1317. Landsverk has even managed to date the 'medieval' Vinland Map, though his finding differs by many centuries from the 20th-century origin for it recently established through chemical analysis of the ink.

These are only a few of his precision targets, for the method is infinitely distensible. Several mathematicians have laughingly told us that his system is meaningless. Runologists have pointed out the reasons for his errors.[18] Experts in cryptology like the American Kahn and the Swede Karlgren have in published reviews pulled the method to pieces.[19] But they have not shaken Landsverk's credit with true believers.[20] Few of the latter will have read the trenchant review of Sigurd Agrell's book on runic magic by C. N. Gould back in 1930. The brilliant Agrell's mathematical formulae could prove the most improbable things. Employing Agrell's method, Gould demonstrated satirically that the name Chester Nathan Gould was 'the invention of the most skilled gematricians, endowed with ancient secret knowledge.' Among the secret symbols contained in Gould's name were those of the Scandinavian gods Thor, Njord and Frigg. Wrote Gould: 'How can one avoid magic numbers and combinations in such a system? They are everywhere.'[21] To this may be added the major prerequisite to the solving of the new cryptopuzzles: one must decide in advance what one wishes to prove.

One of the mainstays of American Norsemania is the asserted royal Norwegian–Swedish expedition (1355–64) of Sir Paul

Knutsson to the New World and, according to Holand, Kensington, Minnesota. Gloomy factuality indicates that the voyage could never have taken place. Attached to that non-expedition, say the mythmakers, was a Franciscan friar and mathematician of Oxford, Nicholas of Lynn, acclaimed as the author of *Inventio Fortunata*. Nicholas was in fact a Carmelite, not a Franciscan, and there is no reliable evidence for his authorship of that curious and garbled document. Had either Nicholas or Sir Paul ever come to Greenland, as the diligent story-weavers theorize, they would have been mentioned in the *Description of Greenland* written by Ivar Bardarson, administrator of the See of Gardar (*c.* 1340–62), who had combed the Norse settlements and had the official duty of knowing everybody and everything. Ivar is the first person they would have called upon for assistance.[22]

Vikings are proliferating exponentially. Chandler blends African, Scandinavian and Central American tradition by inventing an Icelander named Björn Kukulcan, who anachronistically married the Queen of Sheba and ruled Yucatan. Mahieu posits Swedish Vikings who settled in Mexico, Brazil and Paraguay. Enterline (1972) and Mallery-Harrison (1972) indulge their Viking fancies untrammeled by the rigors of proof.[23] For such widespread interest in these subjects, one may be grateful. For the foolishness to which the public is exposed, one is not.

Halberds, battle-axes and Viking swords have been placed in evidence as Norse antiquities, some of them genuine enough but imported in modern times. The so-called Beardmore finds, ancient Norse implements found in the 1930s on a mining claim near Beardmore, Ontario, are believed to have been brought over from Norway about 1923 by a Lt Jens Bloch. Reportedly deposited in the Royal Ontario Museum at Toronto, the artifacts could not be located by the staff when we visited the museum in 1965. But most of the halberds found here and there are modern, having been manufactured by the Rogers Iron Company of Springfield, Ohio, for the cutting of plug tobacco. The battle-axes were premiums given in exchange for labels from Battle Axe Plug. Lowell would have enjoyed this. Did he know about mooring holes? Minnesota and many other parts of the United States are filled with them, and they have seized the popular imagination in a way that would have astounded Leif Eriksson. Some of the holes, we have learned, are actually surveyors' marks. Others have been drilled into rock as a preliminary to black powder blasting, then abandoned. Still others, including those prepared during this century for Admiral S. E. Morison, were drilled to connect fish nets and traps to pegs.[24] None relates to ancient Norse customs of anchoring boats, in the course of journeys drawn up on shore or tethered to trees, which in New England are frequently found close to the shore. Such mooring holes as were drilled in ancient Scandinavia served only for permanent moorings, where they would obviously be worth the labor involved.

That explanation does not impress Mr Marion Dahm of Chokio, Minnesota. He is indignant over professors who sit in their offices while he 'does the work' of traveling around the country to validate mooring holes. Spending $25,000 of his own money, he has uncovered hundreds of Norse habitation sites, thus 'proving' that thousands of Vikings lived in Minnesota at one time. They came around the year 1000, states Dahm, to avoid Catholic persecution in Ireland for adherence to their pagan gods. The expedition of 1362 was sent to Kensington in search of these pagans (whether that would be to succor them or to exterminate them is unclear). In view of that important disclosure, must we necessarily blame *Indians* for the slaughter of '10 men red with blood and dead'? The inscription, after all, makes no explicit mention of Skraelings.[25]

A map and a runic horn

The year 1965 brought a startling addition to cartography, the history of exploration and the rôle of the Vikings. This was the publication, after five years of joint undercover work by the British Museum and Yale University, of a large volume containing, among other documents, the reproduction of an ostensibly medieval parchment map that included Greenland, Vínland, Markland and Helluland. Greenland is shown with baffling accuracy. Latin captions credit 'the companions Bjarni and Leif' with the discovery of Vínland, and report additionally on Bishop Erik *Upsi*'s (in this case successful) voyage in search of that country. Before long the expensive book had sold 37,000 copies.[26] Late the following year an international conference on the now famous 'Vinland Map' was held by the Smithsonian Institution. The opinions of the participants, though varied, cautiously favored the authenticity of the puzzling parchment, which had been cleverly sandwiched between two indisputably authentic medieval parchment collections, with matching wormholes running through the whole set. Particularly among cartographers, however, skepticism waxed; the map's projections were anomalous in relation to the rest of the world shown on the map. The proceedings of the conference were published by the University of Chicago Press in 1971, shortly preceding a somber discovery.[27] Spectographic analysis of the ink used on the map proved that it could not have antedated World War I; it contained a modern chemical called anatase, a form of titanium dioxide.

The initiation of the Vinland Map forgery has subsequently been traced to Luka Jelič, a professor of history at a Catholic theological seminary in Yugoslavia. Disappointed at having his theories ignored, Father Jelič had, probably around 1922, contrived to make them outlive him. It is not known who his helpers were, and the travels of the map subsequent to his death in 1924 and until it turned up in New Haven, Connecticut, are in many respects obscure. My own observation in 1965 (before the name of Jelič had been introduced into the equation) that the Latinized forms of Scandinavian personal names must have been written on the map by a southern European, presumably Italian, who was unfamiliar with Scandinavian patronymic, or -son names, and their proper Latinization (the Vinland Map has, for example, the droll *Leiphus Erissonius* for *Leiphus Erici*[28]), comported reasonably with the subsequent identification of Jelič, who had an Italian mother, was educated in Italy and lectured and published in Italian, French and Yugoslavian.

It is not to be supposed that any of this has weakened lay support for the Vinland Map, whose hard core adherents now claim that the document in hand, while admittedly modern, is merely the *copy* of an authentic original. Why it should have been so carefully disguised is then a mystery. How the original could have been discovered and copied in this century without becoming the subject of a stir, a book or two, and at least one major conference, is not obvious. By whom was it copied in, say, 1920, and what suddenly happened to the original that had survived ancient neglect? Perhaps the Kensington stone, too, with its freshly cut runes, is merely a copy?

Runes are great fun. Professor Gösta Franzén has written about restaurant menus from turn-of-the-century Chicago, written in runes. A great mural in the hall of Chicago's Norske Klub contained a runic inscription. Over thirty years ago I examined a freshly found inscription comprising three score or so runes that had been discovered on a private estate in a semi-rural part of Sweden. It was in English, no less, and stated in

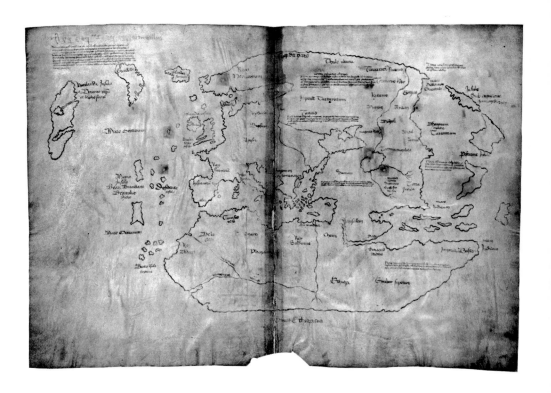

part: 'Joe Doakes went east 1953. He discovered Europe. Holy smoke!' The runologists of Scandinavia tell numerous stories of runic inscriptions carved by chuckling farmers. In Iceland, the pastime of carving runes has sometimes been combined with another Icelandic specialty, that of forming them into verses in bound meter. And that brings us to the Waukegan horn.

In 1952 a young man named Ronald Mason found an object that had been exposed by roadwork near the shores of Lake Michigan in the city of Waukegan, north of Chicago. A drinking horn, it was carved with figures and an inscription. Two decades later the horn was borrowed and studied by O. G. Landsverk of cryptopuzzle fame, who decided that the inscription was in calendrical code, interpreted as 'Audin carved the runes on 15 December 1317'.[29] Dr Landsverk found further that this 'acrostic–telestic' cipher was directly connected with the Vinland Map and the Kensington inscription, being consequently as authentic as those two artifacts. That part of the conclusion is impeccable.

On the basis of photographs, Professor Einar Haugen was struck by the seeming modernity of the pictures on the horn.

70 Map of the world known as the Vinland Map. Allegedly from the 15th century, it has proven to be a forgery from perhaps 1920. The tripartite Vínland is at the upper far left.

After transcribing the runes, he consulted the Icelander, Professor Haraldur Bessason of the University of Manitoba. Bessason reported that the inscription was composed of Icelandic verses of the difficult and complex type called *slettubönd*, a fashion of verse originally invented by Thórdur Magnússon about 1590 and increasingly popular during the 18th and 19th centuries. In this meter, every word in the first half of a quatrain rhymes with a corresponding word in the second half, and the quatrain (*ferskeytt*) reads the same, or the reverse, backwards and forwards.[30] Thór Magnússon, head of the Historical Museum at Reykjavík, recognized the horn as a modern type available for purchase by tourists or emigrants and similar to several in the museum. He suggested – in a population of a quarter million, everyone knows everyone – that the poet–carver had probably been a certain Hjálmar Láruson, whose daughter Margret Hjálmarsdottir was still living. When the beginning of the quatrain was read to the lady, she immediately repeated the rest. 'My father wrote it,' she said. And sure enough, a search among his papers turned up both the poem and model sketches of the pictures on the Waukegan horn. So much for acrostic–telestic cryptography.

That revelation has made no dent in the armor of the cryptomaniacs. This leads to an interesting question. *Is there any limit whatever to human gullibility?* At what point would skepticism set in? Let us suppose that in the late summer of 1997 a runic inscription is found along the Gulf of Mexico, say in coastal Mississippi. Skilfully carved on a large and succulent watermelon, the message runs:

KAL TRAK UIN UK RIST RUNAR A UATSMIL HNA KUTHU TOLU UETR IFT TRAB UL TRUKUS (O.N.: *Karlsefni drakk vín ok reist rúnar á vatnsmelónu hina gódu tolv vetra eptir dráp Óláfs Tryggvasonar*). 'Karlsefni drank wine and carved runes on this good watermelon twelve winters after the slaying of Olaf Tryggvason' (= AD 1012).

Radically contradicting previously held theories as to the location of Vínland, the startling inscription will encounter initial criticism. But negativism will be routed through a dazzling insight: the carved watermelon is merely a copy of a medieval watermelon.

One of the favorite theories of ethnic patriots is that the culture of the now extinct Mandan Indians of North Dakota, painted by Catlin and referred to by Holand and many others, can only have evolved on the basis of contact with the (superior) whites. Concerning this particular delusion, Michlovic and Hughey say that 'even a modest appreciation of Mandan culture and the Mandan people themselves allows an understanding of their uniqueness without reference to European ennoblement.'[31] The Mandans were, at least in the end, a western tribe. The more easterly Algonkians have similarly had to pay retroactive cultural tribute to the theoreticians of white superiority, and this in rather surprising form. According to a monument of misapplied ingenuity by the Norwegian–American writer Reidar Sherwin, a multi-volume work titled *The Old Norse Origin of the Algonkian Indian Language*, Karlsefni's three years in America were linguistically productive, if nothing else.[32] In realistic terms, however, chance similarities, such as Sherwin has mustered, between paired Norse and Indian words, tell us nothing about corporate relations between the languages. The two follow utterly different systems of grammar, morphology, phonological material, lexical relationships, idiom and points of view. American Indian languages, like any other language group, are inter-related and patterned, and the Algonkian shows no trace whatever of Scandinavian influence. Nor was such linguistic pressure to be expected from occasional and unwelcome visits by a few score of troublesome strangers. For a real challenge to ingenuity, one might try to demonstrate that the Scandinavian languages, all of them, have evolved out of the Algonkian.

A multiple hoax

The high point of the Kensington movement was reached on 27 May 1971, when three small stones, to which a fourth was later added, were discovered by a beach-combing carpenter, W. J. Elliott, at Spirit Pond, Popham Beach, in coastal Maine. Inasmuch as Popham Beach had previously distinguished itself as the site of a rune stone assertedly bearing the sad message 'Year 1018 is a famine year,'[33] public attention was not slow to focus on these stones, for they were indeed rune-inscribed. Two of the stones, respectively measuring 5×6 inches and 6×7 inches, are of hard diorite. The third, 8×10 inches in size, is composed of hard, clay-like slate. There is a series of inscriptions in a runic alphabet borrowed in its entirety from the runes of Kensington, to form a quadruple satire on the Vínland voyages, the Vinland Map, the Kensington stone and the theory of runic cryptograms. The language, partly in plaintext but chiefly in

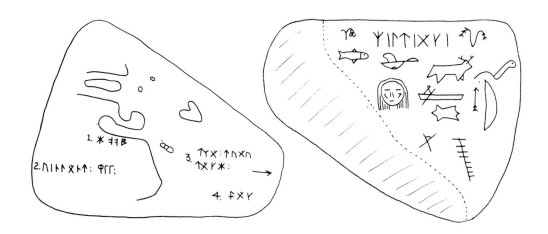

71 The new 'Vinland Map' from Spirit Pond, Popham Beach, Maine. The map is of the immediate area, and this part of the inscription seems to read: 'Hóp. Vínland 1011. To Canada two days. Jack.' (the numerals 1–4 have been supplied).

72 Reverse side of the Spirit Pond stone: the inscribed word 'Miltiaki' (Mild-Acre) may be metonymy for 'Vínland the Good.'

some sort of disguise or code, is, despite the borrowed rune forms, not Kensingtonian Swedish/Norwegian, but rather, a distorted version of Old Icelandic. There are fake runic numerals, anachronistically provided with place value: 10 (twice), 12, 17 (twice), once the word 'two,' together with four dates, or rather, the date 1010 once and the date 1011, written twice as ⏀ΙΙ and the final time as a humorously syncretic ΜΓΓ. Accompanying the text is a labeled map to indicate that the Popham Beach area is (Karlsefni's) Hóp in Vínland, two days' journey south of Canada. The map shows likewise the offshore island that stands off the Maine coast at this point. Popham Beach State Park is approximately 23 air miles northish and east of Portland, and by water approximately 150 miles southwest of the border with Canada's New Brunswick: a pleasant two days of sailing, as prescribed.[34]

The stones exhibit additional features. The carved representations of a sheaf of grain and a cluster of grapes (but no watermelon) confirm saga tradition. A flying duck, an animal pelt, an Indian paddling a canoe, a winking female face, a bow and arrow, a slingshot or ballista and a rattle or flail, a very penile fish and a horned deer or elk almost complete the roster. The final item would appear to be, not Thórhall Huntsman's diseased whale but, more creatively, a sort of Loch Ness monster. And in fact, a word for sea-serpent actually appears in the text. Perhaps the satire should be classified as quintuple.

The fourth stone has a hole bored in one end for the fitting of a thong and appears to be an amulet. On one side is inscribed a cross of the kind known as *baton* or *potent*, on the reverse a sort of comb or simple tree rune of traditional type, almost certainly a well-known type of cryptogram, along with the syllable VIN and the date 1010. I suggest that the five upright arms or teeth of the comb may represent the third letter of the second futhark group (–HNIAS–). Yielding an *I* or *J*, that could stand for either Jesus, or Jack, or both. The name Jack has already appeared twice in the collection of inscriptions.

E. Haugen made a detailed study and transliteration of the inscription in 1972. Without attempting a translation, Haugen demonstrated that the carvings were modern, post 1932, the date of Holand's first full book on the Kensington stone. Another study was published a decade later by the present author who, suggesting a date closer to 1970, had decided that the seemingly chaotic inscription, spread over five separate surfaces on the three stones first found (or at least first reported), could be made to yield sense if one ignored false clues. These were the meretricious word dividers that segment the text into largely incomprehensible syllable clusters. The problem was in esssence optical. To illustrate: so puzzling a message as *W : ecangr : aspsom : eofit* can be intelligibly respaced to yield 'We can grasp some of it.' Such a reformatory procedure applied to the Spirit Pond material produces a text that is definitely the work of neither a disciplined ancient *rúnameistari* nor an imaginative modern raconteur. It is spasmodic, poorly integrated and poorly aimed – quite possibly a literary camel designed by a committee! But modern it certainly is.

The map carved in stone shows the coastline as one sees it today, rather than as it might have been in 1011. Though nothing is known of Viking maps, it would not be surprising if they drew diagrams in the sand as conversational aids in describing distant places. Charts of a sort can be carved with a nail on a piece of inner bark or on a board with a knife. A diagram of any area within immediate vision would of course be pointless. And the Vikings who have left us not a single lithic map among the thousands of rune stones preserved to us in Sweden, Norway or Denmark did not suddenly acquire the art of cartographical epigraphy while foraging in New England. They did not employ numerals for dates. They wasted little energy on trivial information. They did not know what information would be recorded in the Vínland sagas, nor even that there would be such sagas. They did not foresee a Canadian border centuries after their time. Their word for sea-serpent or sea-monster would probably have been *hafskrimsl* or *saeskrimsl* rather than the clever novation *mar(r)orm* of the Spirit Pond inscription (cf modern

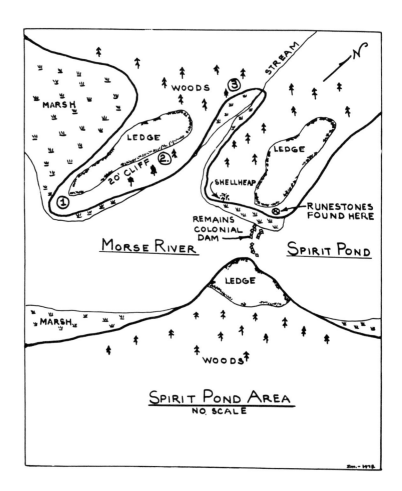

73 Outline map of the Spirit Pond area.

Norwegian *sjøorm*, Swedish *sjöorm*, 'sea-serpent'). *Haf, saer* and *marr* are all words for 'sea' in Old Norse/Icelandic.

It is suggested that the inscription has risqué tones that lend it a modern and juvenile flavor. As an extra joke the runemaster, who refers to himself as 'Jack of the Norse folk,' has inserted the phrase *uiulisa suitlk* (or *suitnk*) into the message. Whether that is a bit of Indian or Eskimo, a phrase from some private language or pure gibberish is not manifest. The Spirit Pond text mentions ice floes, and we do know that the greatest number of Greenland icebergs emerge from a fjord just south of Ilulissat (= Jakobshavn). The ending *-lik* is also found in Greenland Eskimo place names (as in Ameralik).

It must be stressed that, for want of comparison texts, we can not be sure of a translation. The language, non-formulaic and isolated, is fake Old Scandinavian overlying a basically English thought pattern. It would not be inappropriate to call it Pig-Icelandic. A proposed rendering is the following:

Hóp. Vínland 1011. To Canada two days. Jack. Bountiful land [= Vínland the Good]. I declare that this unweary leader saw 17 dead men with scalplocks in dugouts, year 1010. *Uiulisa suitlk* 12 [or 22] days' journey, west 12, north 10. Sagaman young S. K. Eichelman. Haakon found the hart-nixie [walrus?] towards west on ice-floe. Kirsch-drinking men in dugouts years 1011. Skraelings let loose sea-serpent against that sailing-ship. Female friend in kayak take hold of m...p..., wind ship towards land. 17 red, chopped [or: redmen chop] I can choose slain men with scalplocks in dugouts. Year MII. Norse folk's Jack.

Aside from the suggested domestication of sea-serpents, which will be of interest to ethnologists and zoo-keepers, the foregoing document is no world-shaking narrative. No Scandinavian scholar, but obviously proud of his Scandinavian ancestry, its author may feel like correcting any errors. If that prove not worth his while, we shall know only that he has consulted Zoëga's Old Icelandic dictionary[35] in a public or college library, has read Holand, Landsverk, probably Pohl and certainly the Vínland sagas, and enjoyed every minute of them. Possibly he accepted a dare from his college fraternity brothers to have fun with the public and test the ingenuity of scholars. That his runes from 1011 were borrowed from their ancestor, that strange assortment on the Kensington stone from three and a half – or nearly six and a half – centuries later, is anachronism at its delicious best. Readers of the gentle sex will forgive the adherence to the masculine gender in assigning authorship of the hoax, for the manufacture of hoaxes is a male-dominated activity. It can be observed that women rarely involve themselves in such nonsense.

All of these discoveries pale beside a recent announcement by the Harvard biologist, Professor Barry Fell. In West Virginia he has found an inscription written in Tifinag, which we are surprised to learn is 'a Scandinavian script from the Bronze Age' (far antedating runes) that 'linguists' have found in Great Britain, Canada, Libya and North Africa. The inscription in question, a scientific document of note, contains 'information for regulating the calendar by observing the reversal of the sun's course.'[36]

Unlike the generality of animals, which with short memories and limited aspirations, live cheerily in the present, Man has the indomitable urge to mythicize his past while romanticizing his future. Man's constructs, science and the formal study of history, are fluid and adaptive activities rather than fixed assemblages of data. In an age of single-issue thinking at all levels, we have more need than ever of an emotional balance between the hoped-for and the given. Let oddball deviancy be taken for what it is. Seen with the humor it deserves, the occasional hoax, the inevitable daffy theory, help to give us perspective on the equivocal human condition.

7

Archaeology ascendant

The modern search for ancient Norse landing spots west of Greenland has been a long one. When the Norwegian historian Gustav Storm published a monograph nearly a century ago that purported to demonstrate the impossibility of Norse voyagers' having come south of what is now the Canadian border, he stirred up a hornet's nest below that very border.[1] Several years previously the digging up of the Gokstad ship had occasioned worldwide discussions of what the sailing capabilities of such a ship might have been, and by the time Storm had followed up his original study with an additional one published in Chicago and Christiania, the famous voyage of Magnus Andersen's 'Viking' had somewhat deflated his assertions.[2] Whether or not Leif Eriksson had found the United States, the Gokstad replica had done so with style. But we have seen that long before the 1890s, the Vínland sagas and the Newport Tower had centered antiquarian attention on New England as a probative location for Wineland, and numerous treatises appeared in support of the claim. American patriotism apart, a main reason for this was of course the mention in the sagas of *grapes* and *grapevines*, without which detail searches for Vikings below the Canadian border would have lacked persistence, while without the sagas themselves no one would have looked anywhere at all. A favorite New England locality has been Cape Cod. The famous astronomical observation referred to in the sagas has elicited a variety of even more southerly suggested locations for Leif's houses, from the Carolinas to Manhattan, where the traces may be buried under the Empire State Building and unlikely to occupy the archaeologist. Some people, to be sure, place great reliance on a runic inscription found in nearby Brooklyn in 1924. Carved in idiomatic modern Swedish, it states succinctly that 'Leif Eriksson was here.' More conservative thinking has suggested Nova Scotia, Newfoundland or the St Lawrence Valley. Väinö Tanner has suggested that the coast of Newfoundland be combed, particularly the region around White

Bay.[3] Edward Reman expounded the theory that Karlsefni had settled on the western shore of Hudson Bay.[4] Einar Haugen and Halldor Hermannsson inclined to favor Massachusetts, on general grounds and without indicating special locations.[5] The late Professor Assar Janzén once remarked that: 'We are never going to find out.' For a while it looked as though he were right. But though none of us could know it, a startling revelation was on the way.

For some years the author of *Land under the Pole Star*[6] had been searching for Norse habitations along the eastern coastline, following up every possible clue provided by saga texts, topographical features and the suggestions of local fishermen and others familiar with those reaches. It was June 1961 when the Norwegian-born lawyer, navigator, explorer and skilled writer Helge Ingstad and his archaeologist wife Anne Stine sailed their boat *Halten* from Montreal to Épaves Bay in northern Newfoundland. Anchoring far out, for the water here is shallow, they took to their small boat and then finally, hauling the boat, waded to shore where 'a wide, open plain curved around the bay. The small river Black Duck Brook had its outlet here. The land rose in terraces, gradually sloping up from the river. On the largest of these terraces lay some house-sites which Helge Ingstad had found the previous year, and which we were now going to investigate.'[7]

They were near the little fishing village of L'Anse aux Meadows (locally pronounced 'Lancy Meadows') with a population of seventy. Immediately discernible were the deteriorated remains of five ancient sod structures; four more were subsequently discovered. Local villagers were recruited to dig test trenches. Were the houses *really* ancient? Did they derive from Indians or Eskimos, or from white fishermen or whalers of later centuries? An answer gradually became apparent. The first house uncovered not only had many parallels in Norse material, but contained hearths of a type known from Iceland and Greenland along with highly corroded iron rivets. Comparison rivets from later colonial settlements are far less corroded. The search for 10th- and 11th-century Norsemen had now begun in earnest. The Ingstads concluded that after so many years of searching, they must at last have found Leif Eriksson's Vínland.

With financial and professional help from many sources, the Ingstads spent another seven summers at the L'Anse aux Meadows site. The first task was to uncover and measure the

74 Aerial photograph of the marine terrace at Épaves Bay, showing partially excavated house-sites at L'Anse aux Meadows. Black Duck Brook in foreground, Great and Little Sacred Isles in the background.

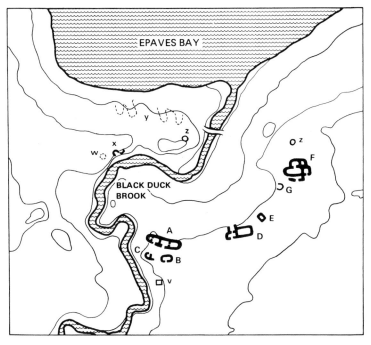

75 Sketch map of the excavation site at L'Anse aux Meadows: A–D, houses; E, work shed; F, large house; v, natural deposit of bog iron ore; w, charcoal kiln; x, forge; y, boat sheds; z, cooking pits.

house plots, which were labeled A, B, C etc. The houses had been built, not of rock, but of turf collected from the neighborhood, and in some cases the discrete layers could still be made out. The roofs had of course fallen in, and the sod walls, laid without the stone footings that would have been expected in Greenland, were hard to discern. Expert opinion is that in the damp climate of northern Newfoundland, the life of such a sod house is limited to twenty, and certainly not over thirty years. Showing no indication of rebuilding, the houses had not been inhabited, even intermittently, during very many years. Following detailed study of the houses and their few remaining contents, the structures have now been taken over and restored by Parks Canada. With their sod roofs and wickerwork fence around the outside, the reconstructions give an authentic, if almost excessively neat, impression and are a fitting Canadian counterpart to England's reconstructed Jórvík.

What special features had brought Helge Ingstad to this particular windswept spot at 51°36′ N., 55°32′ W. in the first place? The prime prerequisite for a Viking location, he had reasoned, would be pasturage. Though the Norsemen would have explored many localities, they would not have tried to settle – the sagas indicate several such attempts – without grazing opportunities. Incontestably, the area around the house sites, along which Black Duck Brook meanders to the sea, exhibits a multitude of grasses and comparable vegetation suitable for cows, sheep, pigs and, if any were to be brought along, horses. Ingstad had searched the barren coast of Labrador in vain for sufficiently promising vegetation. He found that the inhabitants of the village of L'Anse aux Meadows, settled since 1870, had long been curious about the soddy bumps in their community, and this visit from a scholarly explorer sufficed to enlist their knowledge and enthusiastic suggestions.

L'Anse aux Meadows first appeared on a map in 1862, under the name Anse à la Medée, perhaps in connection with a ship named Medée. It has also been known as L'Anse aux Méduses, 'Jellyfish Bay', of which the present English name is clearly a popular etymology, reinforced by the abundance of meadow grass in the vicinity. It is worth mentioning that the French word *anse* means both 'bay' and 'pot handle.' The first settler of the handle or hook-shaped tongue of land at L'Anse aux Meadows was William Decker, whose descendants, living there today, report that French fishermen used to have houses at the end of the hook. Clay pipe fragments and fishing hooks found there

76 Reconstruction of Viking site at L'Anse aux Meadows.

have nothing to do with the Norse remains, and their location so far from Black Duck Brook can be explained only by the latter's extreme shallowness, so that even small fishing boats can not put in there.

The Ingstads and their collaborators found, in addition to the house ruins, the remains of four *naust* or boatsheds, analyzed by Christensen as being of typical Norse type. These consisted of roughly oval depressions in the ground which had in part been dug into the marine terrace and in part built up. Situated on the west bank of Black Duck Brook, these structures lay at an oblique angle to the shore. The walls had been built up of turf, just as the houses had, and it is uncertain whether the structures contained post holes for the now collapsed roofs. Apart from fragments of highly decayed wood and two pieces of whalebone, there were no small finds. Humus layers under the sand should probably be attributed to the storms that had several times covered the area, allowing the vegetation to decompose underneath. The four sheds varied slightly in construction. Christensen thinks that the roofs may have consisted of closely spaced tree trunks or branches, resting on rafters, these then covered by turf, with the gable ends facing the sea either open, or closed by means of a light wooden wall. Their use presupposes a sea-level very little above the present level, considering the danger to the boats from northerly storms. Christensen would allow 1 m at most, while Henningsmoen's estimate is 0.50–0.75

m. In other words, the shoreline has probably risen no more than 2 or 3 feet during the past thousand years.[8] Since the boats were customarily run ashore between trips, both the slope and the distance from the waterline should not be too great. A ship of any size would not have been able to come in close to shore, and the apparent dimensions of the four *naust* at L'Anse aux Meadows would in any case indicate that the vessels they housed were small. Christensen points out that the three boats found with the Gokstad ship ranged from 20 to 32 feet in length, quite normal for small boats of the Viking Age and normal for the coasting fishing boats of Norway well into the 19th century. Curiously, there is no indication for the housing of a *knörr*, or of anything even faintly resembling the size of the Gokstad vessel (length, if the reconstruction was accurate, 76 ft 5 in.). How that should be interpreted is uncertain for the time being. But the problem should be looked at without too many preconceptions. The establishment of a colony at L'Anse aux Meadows can by no means have been the sole ambition of the Greenlanders. The nearby northernmost tip of Newfoundland, surrounded by water on three sides, is obviously an area of strategic importance to explorers for whom travel and transport by water were paramount. The location is perfectly situated as a launching spot for the exploration, at the very least, of the St Lawrence Valley. For travelers from Greenland it must have presented itself as an excellent intermediate landing. For a few years the L'Anse aux Meadows site and neighboring localities may have continued to be utilized by the Greenlanders as summer stations. Further archaeological reconnaissance is certainly indicated. And future discoveries of authentic Norse remains along, say, the southern shore of the St Lawrence Valley, however unlikely at so late a date, are not ruled out.

Characterization

'It cannot have been easy to find straight trees in these parts.'[9] The nearest real forests of such kind as might have aroused the excitement of the Greenlanders are at a distance of 6 to 8 miles, though shrubs and stunted trees averaging a couple of feet in height grow, and grew formerly, in the vicinity of the house sites. Pollen analysis by Henningsmoen indicates that vegetation on the area *c*. AD 1000 differed little from what is growing there today. From all that one can gather of climatological opinion, now that the climate has warmed appreciably since the

intervening cold epoch, the situation at the time of the Norse settlement approached that of the present day. The L'Anse aux Meadows region can experience mild winters with no snow until February, or very cold, blizzardy winters with a great deal of snow throughout, and we recall from the Vínland sagas that would-be colonists could be badly deceived by expectations based on a single mild winter.

One of the house sites, a sunken structure labeled house G, must have been a bath-house, since the fill contains an unusual quantity of brittle-burned stones, much larger than cooking stones tend to be. In addition, a large slate slab was found in the excavation, probably used for covering the smoke opening to prevent loss of steam. As in the Finnish *sauna* today, it was customary in Iceland (cf O.N. *badstofa*) and elsewhere in the north to heat large stones and pour water over them, and it is significant that, inasmuch as house G was situated at some distance from the brook, excavations by Bareis and Winston indicate that a man-made water trench ran down the slope of the terrace immediately southeast of the house.

The excavations revealed a kiln for the production of charcoal. There would certainly have been a sufficiency of fuel, for L'Anse aux Meadows is so situated as to 'hook' driftwood carried by wind and currents from either the south or the north. Such driftwood accumulates there today and has given Épaves Bay its very name, cf Fr. *épave* ('nautical debris'). In connection with

78 Spindle whorl of soapstone from L'Anse aux Meadows, house F.

the kiln there is structure J, clearly a smithy for the extraction of iron from bog-ore, a technique well-known to the Norsemen and practised in Greenland. No smelting pit has been identified, but the telltale slag is evidence enough. A Norse farm characteristically had its own smithy, located away from the dwellings because of the fire hazard and often on the bank of a river, as at L'Anse aux Meadows. Structures similar to the smithy at L'Anse aux Meadows are that on the Norse farm at Jarlshof in Shetland, the building at Sandnes in Greenland's Western Settlement (known as ruin group No. 51)[10] and the smithy on the episcopal farm at Gardar in the Eastern Settlement. Keldur, the oldest farm in Iceland, had an ancient smithy which is still in use today, and though more advanced with its stone walls and roof, it looks very much as J must once have looked: like a grassy mound with a hole, the smoke hole, in the middle.

There is a notable line of development from house A to house F. House D differs from house A in that a small room had been built on to the back, a natural development of the Norse long house, with the nearest parallels to be found in Iceland, such as the well-known farm ruin of Stöng in Thjórsárdalur. Connnected with it in some way is house E, a sunken-floored building or *Grubenhaus*. It may have been a fire house, at all events an early type of building of which many are known from the north, apparently in connection with larger structures. House F, too large to have been spanned by a single roof, doubtless comprises several houses built together. It shares many features with house D. Neither house has parallels in Eskimo or Indian cultures of the region, but parallels are found in Iceland and Greenland, in which main rooms take the form of a so-called sleeping hall with a long hearth of simple type in the middle of the floor and benches along the side walls. Room VI in house F was to all appearances a women's room, facing the sun and sheltered from the coldest winds. It may at one time have been paneled. In this room was found a soapstone spindle whorl of known Nordic type, made from a fragment of a discarded soapstone pot. Soapstone was used a great deal in western Norway, and it is not clear whether the Greenland deposits were being utilized by the time of the L'Anse aux Meadows settlement. Also found in room VI was a needle hone of quartzite, and bits of jasper and iron pyrites for striking fire. In and around the house were bits of iron, a fire flint, lumps of slag, a sandstone fragment and some bone fragments of uncertain origin, together with fragments identified as whalebone. Rivets and nails, or their fragments, were discovered in and around the various houses. In house A was found a ring-headed bronze pin of 9th- or 10th-century Norse type.

C-14 analyses of charcoal, iron, slag, bone, wood and turf were made at several different laboratories, and despite expected variations, seemed to comport with an assumed settlement date of *c.* 1000 or, surprisingly, in the opinion of one scientist, even earlier.[11] Driftwood will of course introduce imponderables into the equation, since it will naturally yield earlier dates than freshly cut wood. Typological criteria for the evaluation of identifiably Norse artifacts easily confirm the C-14 data. Much of the local wood is birch (*Betula*), which seldom survives more than sixty years and decomposes quickly after cutting. In the local climate, such materials as bone, antlers and wood will disintegrate in much less than a millennium. Unquestionably, great use was made of wooden implements including bowls and spoons, just as was the case in Greenland, Iceland and Norway, where wooden utensils were common in all classes of society. The Norse would not willingly have abandoned any useable items made of their toilfully acquired iron, and the aborigines would certainly have cleaned up the leavings.

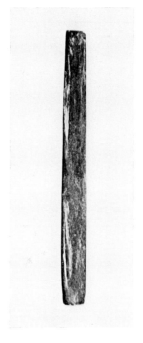

79 Needle-hone of quartzite from house F.

Reporting on the pollen samples preserved at L'Anse aux Meadows, Henningsmoen states that the area lies 'within the transitional zone between the sub-arctic forest and tundra. . . . Small forested parts occur only in those places where hills and ridges provide shelter . . . occasionally the trees may reach a height of a few metres. More common is a low, shrubby vegetation.'[12] The list of trees includes *Picea mariana, Abies balsamea, Picea glauca* on fairly well-drained ground and *Larix laricina* in moist localities, *Alnus crispa* and several types of *Betula,* also *Sorbus decora* and *Juniperus communis.* Spruce, pine, maple, hazel, ash and elm do not grow this far north. Beech, oak, linden, walnut, hickory, chestnut, hornbeam, hackberry, arbor vitae and hemlock are out of the question.

Pondering the relative skimpiness of forest trees, in contrast to the satisfaction attributed to Leif Eriksson as he ordered utilization of the splendid supply of timber, a shadow of skepticism creeps into one's mind. L'Anse aux Meadows is certainly the site of an ancient Norse establishment, however temporary. But which one? And what about the 'wine-withies' and grapes? Were the explorers, who had lots of berries in their background as part of the struggle for living in northerly climes, taken in by the crowberries, red and black currants, raspberries, blueberries, bilberries, cloudberries, cranberries and cloud-berries of Newfoundland? Some of them had certainly seen and drunk imported wine, but they did not know how to make it. Are the grapes, and the grape*vines* emphasized in the *Greenlanders' Saga* – these so utterly unlike the clumpy bushes from which most other berries grow – purely a fiction? It is neither necessary nor natural to think so. Henningsmoen is properly cautious regarding this. She does not attempt to evaluate the sagas. Speaking as a botanist, she finds the name 'Grapevine Land' not unreasonable, 'provided that one accepts the possibility of berries other than genuine grapes being designated "wine-berries".'[13] Currants and squashberry (*Viburnum edule*) are likely candidates for the substitution, she suggests. The matter of grapes will be treated in the following chapter.

Pollen series were collected, for evaluative contrast, from eight different pond and bog localities, including three from the site itself or its immediate vicinity. Three collecting spots were within 3 km (1.9 miles) of the house sites and showed similar characteristics. One was from the border of the forested area, 10 km (6.2 miles) distant, another from within the forest and 14 km (8.7 miles) distant. This was expected to reflect any significant vegetational development from Viking times on down. For comparison during the analysis, pollen was collected from living vegetation during the summer of 1962 and the summer of 1968 to form a kind of 'pollen herbarium.' Samples were taken at altitudes ranging from 1.4 m to 50 m above sea-level in order to gain perspective on possible effects of sea-level change during the past millennium. The list of pollen samples recovered from the soil at various depths and from the house sods represents approximately two hundred taxa, of which many, including the pollen of grapes, were not indigenous but airborn from distant regions. The aggregate indication is that despite seasonal or temporary variations, little vegetational change has occurred during the past 7500 years. No heavy forestation is shown for Viking times, as we have seen: pollen can give no indication of the size of a given tree, which may equally be that of a large specimen or a mere shrub. Shrubs in that vicinity average from 2 to 4 feet in height. Both climatic criteria and the multiple evidence provided by comparison plant types suggest that the trees were not large one thousand years ago. With all due respect to the jellyfish (*méduse*), the area around L'Anse aux Meadows doubtless deserved at that time, as it does now, to be considered a land of meadows.

Altogether, the microscope, spectographic analysis and various chemical procedures have provided a fascinating series of answers to questions that could be put concerning the materials associated with the L'Anse aux Meadows site. It is disappointing, though, that not a single charred bone or bone sliver can be traced to *Bos domesticus*, the common cow or bull. One bone sample is tentatively identified as coming from a pig, *Sus scrofus*, a reminder of the fact that the favorite meat of the ancient Scandinavians in legend and in fact had been pork, though the porkers were far from being the overfed creatures of today. Some whalebone and bone of seal were found, but most of the bone material has been so affected by the cooking fires that it is simply unidentifiable.

From a botanical point of view, there is no trace of ecological influence deriving from Norse activity at or around L'Anse aux Meadows. The human tenure was too short for that. The visitors did not plant anything, and whatever trees and shrubs they chopped up, as well as the meadow plants their beasts may have consumed, soon regenerated themselves, and all went on as before. The structures they built collapsed after a score or so of years and were not repaired or replaced. There is evidence of use of the dwellings by natives, particularly those of the Dorset culture, a puzzling fact that would seem to refute the opinion[14] that the Dorset had already abandoned the region. But there is some possibility of error here: a layer of dug-up turf containing earlier artifacts can in some cases be found superimposed on later items. The Dorset-type objects include a core or core-scraper, and possibly some chert flakes and chips of uncertain origin, found in a layer somewhat above the Norse material. In other words, Dorset people appear to have inhabited the site both before and after the Norsemen. There is also a projectile point of Dorset type found below the Norsemen. From radio-carbon dating there is evidence also that Beothuk Indians inhabited the site, at least sporadically, for long afterwards, probably as late as 1500,[15] while a single group of Indian objects can be identified as contemporary with the Norse finds. These represent two periods of habitation, separated by a layer of sand, offering interpretative complications.[16] It is indicated in any case that the terrace at Épaves Bay was a site favored by various ethnic groups, so that some sort of contact was virtually inevitable.

This was before the age of gunpowder. With the sole exception of their relative size, the Norsemen would have had small advantage over the natives in point of weaponry, and they

80 Ruins of a cairn on the hill-top west of terrace at Épaves Bay.

would in the end have suffered under the disadvantage of inferior numbers. An additional disadvantage would have been their inability, generally speaking, to choose the time and place of an attack. A. S. Ingstad suggests that since the whites and the indigenes were dependent on the same resources, the basis for conflict was obvious. If the Norsemen, as might be expected, brought domestic animals with them in the interests of a permanent settlement, it is not unlikely that the natives would have hunted these. As such a resource was not easily replaced, the settlers would have responded with appropriate fierceness. From saga accounts it is evident that the Norsemen looked on the Skraelings as supernatural beings, to be feared and if possible eliminated. The handwriting was already on the wall.

The remains of four rock cairns of Norse type are found in the vicinity of the house sites. Two of them located on a low ridge west of the houses, they are covered with old lichen and largely collapsed. All are identical in construction type: they are built of long, flat stones set in a circle around an open core. Not visible from the sea, they can not have been beacons, nor would they in that location have been of use in marking paths. Neither were they owl cairns, which are constructed differently. The function here was probably that of the clock. The cairns do not stand on the highest point of the ridge but rather in a slight depression. A.S. Ingstad states that, as viewed from the houses, the sun stood above one pair at 3 pm. Most unfortunately, she does not indicate the *date* of her observation.[17] Though the other pair may have served an analogous purpose, it is too disintegrated for a decision.

Ungava Bay

Right across Davis Strait from Brattahlid, above the northern tip of Labrador (Cape Chidley), lies the entrance to Ungava Bay. The Norsemen could not conceivably have missed it, lying as it does between Baffin Island and Labrador, and sooner or later they would have explored it, probably sailing along its southern shore and around to Payne Bay and up into the entrance to Hudson Bay. Did they establish any hunting stations there, erect any structures, leave any artifacts? The late Dr Thomas E. Lee thought that they did. Birgitta L. Wallace thinks it doubtful on present showing. Professor Schledermann is skeptical but openminded, and stresses the need for careful evaluation of comparison material. A.S. Ingstad considers a possibility of Norse origin for an occasional item. While some investigators think Lee's claims preposterous, Marshall McKusick argues very sensibly for our keeping an open mind on the entire question of Norse remains in Ungava Bay. The Norsemen indubitably visited the area, but that does not of itself make any particular structure or implement Norse.[18]

What story do Lee's excavations, sketches and descriptions actually tell? Lee found a couple of long-houses that he considered to be of Norse type along with implements allegedly traceable to Norse sources. To take the Pamiok Longhouse No. 1, as he has called it: it is a long, rectangular structure rounded externally at the corners, partitioned into three rooms and with an entrance passageway from one side wall. The house contains two parallel rows of postholes lined with slate. Lee calls these ember pits for the preservation of hot coals at night. But Icelandic/Greenlandic ember pits (*feluholur*) – found also at L'Anse aux Meadows – customarily adjoin, or at least are close to, the hearth and, though Norse rooms with more than one hearth have been found, there is never more than one ember pit per room. Nor would there be need for such. Furthermore, the stone boxes at Pamiok did not contain an appreciable amount of charcoal, of which an ember pit would be full. The hearths at Pamiok do not give a Norse impression. The lowest stratum of materials found comprises stone implements of cherty quartz. Lee attributes these to Norsemen who built and lived in the establishment before it was taken over by the Dorset Eskimos whose artifacts lie above them. Before his death Lee may have abandoned his quite untenable belief (1966) that the Norse had mixed with Eskimos and reverted to Stone Age culture. In this idea he was clearly influenced by the historian Tryggvi J. Oleson who, following the Icelandic writer Jón Dúason, was persuaded that the Eskimos of today are essentially a mixture of tall Greenlandic Norse and dwarfish Dorset Eskimos. The famous explorers Vilhjálmur Stefánsson and Knud Rasmussen, the latter himself part Eskimo, had expressed vaguely similar views. In reviewing a book by Oleson in 1965 I expressed a strongly negative opinion regarding the theory.[19] Beards, brown hair and occasional blue eyes among Eskimos have long required no special explanation.

Pamiok Island is on the west shore of Ungava Bay, just off the mouth of Payne River which leads to the 55-mile-long Payne Lake in the middle of the Ungava Peninsula. On the south shore of the lake Lee found a series of structures that seem extraordinary for such a location. He has described them as built of very heavy stone blocks with square corners laid end to end. Examined by him in the summers of 1964 and 1965, one of these turned out to be 16 × 12 feet, the other 16 × 46 with 'a European style wall fireplace' and possessing an astonishing similarity to a Christian church, or at least to a structure erected by people with a knowledge of such churches. Lee found further a stone dam, 37 feet long and, 5 feet from this, towards the lake, a stone causeway 27 feet long and 8 feet wide. 'With such width and care in building, could it have been anything other than a road for a wheeled vehicle, heavily loaded with stones needed for building?' Even an affirmative answer to the question would not be proof of Norse involvement. The Eskimos claim, to be sure (writes Lee), that the structures were built by white men, before the Eskimo. On the river bank, in a low place, stands an incredible monument which Lee asserts is a Thor's hammer, 10 feet high and composed of three stones, of which the main one, a vertical pillar, is estimated to weigh 4000 pounds. There is no earth or stone rubble from which a ramp might have been constructed, and the land is treeless, being even without bushes. The answer to the problem of construction, says Lee, is a ship's hoist. And even at high tide, nothing but a low-keeled Viking ship could navigate so shallow a stream, whose bottom is a mass of great boulders. Ancient eider-duck shelters on the coastal islands furnish, according to Lee, additional evidence of Norse

81 Supposed Hammer of Thor weighing several tons, from Payne Estuary, Ungava.

82 Pamiok long-house ruin no. 1.

residence in the region, and though opinion regarding these is divided, such is possible, for unlike the Norse the Eskimos had little use for eiderdown. That, if so, is evidence for their *not* having gone over to an Eskimo way of life. There is a question, too, of chronology. Were the Norsemen who erected a Thor's hammer the same ones who built the Christian church? If not, which came first?

Ungava Peninsula is a barren land of rocks and lakes, without pasturage, without roads and without inhabitants save for coastal Eskimos. In summer, frost forms on the ponds two nights out of every three. It is rainy, foggy and blown by Polar winds from across interminable fields of Polar ice, − 50°F. in winter with an average of 80 inches of snow. One can believe that frontiersmen would look at the place, might conceivably trap here, living on fish and caribou meat. What the men would be inclined, or able, to build is another problem. Why, if oppressed by Eskimos in Greenland, men, women and children should have moved to the land mass known to be inhabited by Eskimos and Indians, is puzzling indeed. Agriculture and stock-raising, which had been in their blood since the Bronze Age, were out of the question in this desolate waste. Would so fundamental a transformation have been psychologically possible for them? It is doubtful.

However, this area, or something akin to it, did persist in Icelandic fiction during the Middle Ages, as a pendant to the Greenland/Vínland tradition. There are at least two sagas of the non-historical genre that have utilized the ambience of Greenlandic and Canadian waters as part of the setting for ingenious tales about fictional heroes. One is the humorous *Saga of Clever-Fox* (*Króka-Refs saga*), the story of a valiant and resourceful man and skilled woodcarver who escapes his malicious enemies in the Western Settlement by moving with his wife and three sons to a more northerly fjord. Here he builds himself a seamless fort constructed of hollow logs into which he pipes spring water. When his enemies, after half a dozen years of searching, find his stronghold and set fire to it, tiny shutters open on the outer surface of the logs and water spurts out, extinguishing the flames! After further exciting adventures, inventor Ref and family show up in Denmark, where he gives the king some of his treasures: five polar bears and no fewer than fifty Greenland falcons of which fifteen are of the highly prized white variety. Such hyperbole does not spring from mere naiveté, for in these 'lying sagas' (*lygisögur*) hyperbole is the rule. An earlier short story concerning the young Icelander Authun, which is fascinating enough despite its relative sobriety, had made do with the gift of a single polar bear to the monarch, and that had been deemed worthy of great counter-gifts including an entire ship with cargo.[20]

Possibly closer to Dr Lee's Pamiok environment is the wild *Saga of Arrow-Odd*. Odd, claimed in the saga to be a distant relative of Egil Skallagrímsson, has a great enemy in the outlaw Ögmund. Ögmund has sailed off to Baffinland and perhaps beyond and built an impregnable fort, where he reigns as chieftain of Skuggifjördur, which means Shadow Fjord or Spectre Fjord. This is a fitting realm for Ögmund since he is a

Lapp magician – virtually a spectre or troll – from Permia (northern Russia) and hence in Norse eyes easily kindred to the New World Skraelings. Lee translates Skuggifjördur as 'Place of Fogs,' and adds, 'Pamiok is indeed a Place of Fogs. And the adjacent Payne Estuary is well described as a fjord – the only one on the west coast of Ungava Bay.'

The present discussion must rest there, with the sincere hope that some scholar or institution interested in the Province of Quebec's early history will undertake further investigation of the Ungava Bay material.

The undertaking at L'Anse aux Meadows is legitimately the center of gravity for all future considerations of Old Norse voyages to North America. The excavations by field archaeologists have led to fruitful study by chemists, botanists, oceanographers and others concerned with physical environments, as well as by ethnologists interested in the culture of the natives who preceded, coexisted with or succeeded the Norsemen. The stake in this matter of the historian and the scrutinizer of ancient Scandinavian texts is equally patent. The Ingstad achievement, along with a certain warming of the Arctic and sub-Arctic climate during this century, has very properly encouraged further field research in the west and north, and future discovery of Norse artifacts in Greenland and Canada waits only on opportunity. The subject is no longer a vague one, sustained by faith and surmise. The Vikings *were* there.

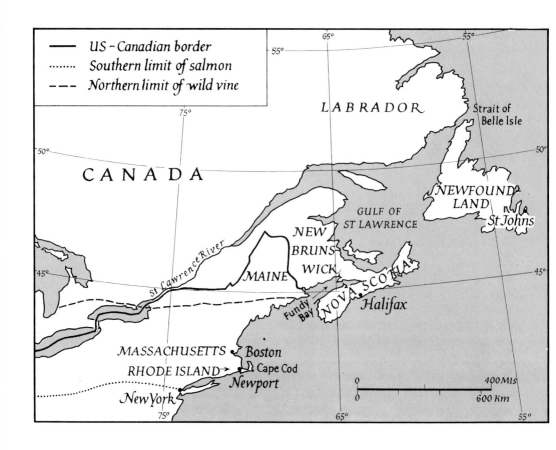

- —— US–Canadian border
- .... Southern limit of salmon
- – – – Northern limit of wild vine

CANADA

LABRADOR

Strait of
Belle Isle

NEWFOUND
LAND

St Lawrence River

GULF OF
ST LAWRENCE

St Johns

NEW
BRUNS-
WICK

MAINE

NOVA SCOTIA

Fundy
Bay

Halifax

MASSACHUSETTS · Boston
RHODE ISLAND
Newport
Cape Cod

New York

| 0 | | | 400 Mls |
| 0 | | | 600 Km |

8
Grapes, gold, and whales

There is now solidly confirmed archaeological proof that the Norse-descended Greenlanders made at least one well-organized attempt at pushing their dominions farther to the west. There is excellent evidence that the explorers, huntsmen, sealers and whalers among the Greenlanders traveled far north on both sides of Davis Strait, ultimately encountering natives and possibly engaging in trade with them. Reason exists likewise for an assumption that they followed the waterways, both salt and fresh, farther into the Canadian interior than indications once would support.

None of those exertions makes it seem unlikely that such capable pioneers would make southerly probes as well. Rather the contrary. The Vínland sagas which first led romantics and sober scholars to comb the American coastline for their traces, speak with an insistent voice: a land of ample pasturage is indicated, by all means; but a land bearing grapevines it must be as well. To a large extent, the recent more northerly triumphs have shaken scholarly attempts to localize Vínland in New England, and observers are beginning to take for granted that L'Anse aux Meadows is literally the tiny 'capital' of the Vínland that Leif Eriksson named and that Thorfinn Karlsefni vainly searched for. That is the easy way out, but a problem remains, for the successful identifications in Newfoundland have obscured several issues. Local patriotism and ethnic or national prestige are not genuine lodestones and will be discounted as an argument in any particular direction. Wishful thinking in the past, misidentifications and the occasional hoax have given the New England theory a worse press than it probably deserves.

The sum total of evidence from various scientific disciplines, while confirming the Norse character of the settlement at L'Anse aux Meadows, will not support its being Leif Eriksson's land of grapes. That means either that 1) L'Anse aux Meadows is not Leif's settlement, or 2) it may well be that, in which case the grapevines and grapes mentioned in the Vínland sagas must be

83 Map showing approximately the limits of wild vine country (northward) and of salmon (southerly). Such features assist in the location of Vínland.

explained away. That is, they may be pure invention, they may result from a misunderstanding of some sort (such as a mistaking of, say, blueberry shrubs for tree-choking grapevines) or, as sometimes suggested, the grapevines which Leif had to chop away from the growing timber were seen on some southerly push but had nothing to do with the place where he passed the winter and built first booths, then real houses. Having personally for some years observed the simultaneous growth of raspberries, blueberries and grapes on my own property in the American Northwest, I incline to be skeptical of any such confusion in the minds of curious and observant Scandinavians a thousand years ago. Secondly, if Leif and his companions had found grapes, along with pasturage and other favorable features in some such place as New England, why would they then deliberately settle for the more meager conditions of northern Newfoundland? Nor are we content with seeing the grapes as somebody's invention. The incident of the Uniped in *Erik's Saga* is a clear case of invention. New England grapes are no invention. Should the timber-suitable trees be regarded as an invention?

Helge Ingstad was aware of the problem when he published the original Norwegian edition of his *Land Under the Pole Star* in 1960, in which the text and map refer to a Vinland I and a Vinland II. Vinland I he locates in northern Newfoundland; Vinland II is in New England, because the label in the map is placed beside Boston. In the English version of 1966, this is repeated. Both times the Newport Tower (Rhode Island) is marked on the map, and though Ingstad is uncertain regarding its age, his text refers to Rhode Island as being part of Vinland II. But this arrangement is ignored, and presumably recanted, by Ingstad in the introduction to his wife's book in 1977, where in corroboration of his theory that Vínland lay in Newfoundland he cites the views of A. W. Munn (1929), V. Tanner (1941), A. H. Mallery (1951) and Jørgen Meldgaard (1961). Gwyn Jones accepts this view (1964). T. J. Oleson and many others suggest Cape Cod; Steensby proposes the St Lawrence Valley. Ingstad's dilemma springs from his natural preference for a thoroughly identified Old Norse habitation site over a theoretical one that has not been physically confirmed. And his preference is strengthened, he thinks, by a philological consideration. Following the lead of the philologist Professor Sven Söderberg of Sweden, he has decided that the first syllable of the critical word is 'Vin-' rather than 'Vín-'. Both the pronunciation and the meaning of these two deceptively similar Old Icelandic words are involved, and the difference is in both cases absolutely crucial.

Digging up the theory of a deceased Norwegian predecessor, Söderberg decided that the place name referred to a land of meadows rather than to a land of grapes.[1] This conclusion would proceed from the ancient word *vin* ('grassy place, meadow'). Inasmuch as the early Icelandic scribes had not yet hit on a way of indicating vowel length in their manuscripts, the latter show *Uinland/Vinland* without the acute accent over the first syllable. *Vin* is pronounced approximately as *vinn* would be in English. *Vín* ('wine') is pronounced like *veen*. The scribes, according to this theory, had intended to describe pasturage, and later readers had mistaken this for a land producing, by indirection at least, wine. Ingstad has with understandable willingness accepted the hypothesis, of which the L'Anse aux Meadows findings seem to be a corroboration. But this is to put the cart before the horse. Supposing that the Söderberg theory can be proven false? Does Ingstad's L'Anse aux Meadows site fall with it? By no means. There is no necessary relationship between the meaning of the critical seven-letter word and the authenticity of a Norse housing site in northern Newfoundland. The existence of pasturage at L'Anse aux Meadows in no way correlates with the specific name that Leif chose to give his land claim. One is not compelled to go on thinking that the explorers had been taken in by fool's grapes, so that, while the indubitable pasturage remains, it is not relevant to the name, and while the name remains, it has a mistaken referent. The simple fact is that Söderberg's thesis is quite untenable. The Ingstad find stands on its own merits and needs no such crutch. By the same token, it is not *Vínland*. Let us consider the matter linguistically.

Ancient Icelanders, and modern Icelanders, have always made careful distinction between long vowels and short vowels, so that the pairs *a/á*, *e/é*, *i/í*, *o/ó*, *u/ú* are sounded differently. Such phonetic differentiation is an important carrier of meaning (cf Eng. hill/heel, sin/seen). Before the adoption of superscript length marks ('accents,' as we sometimes call them), the Scandinavian scribes often doubled a vowel to indicate length, as *aa* for *á*, *ii* (sometimes written *ij*) for *í*, etc. But there is great inconsistency in this. Modern editors of the old texts rectify matters for their readers by supplying the proper vowel indications in their printed texts. This is part of a process called 'normalizing.' We may think of this standardizing process as a form of interpretation. How then can one be certain that the scribes meant *Vínland* ('Wineland'), and not *Vinland* ('Meadow-land')?

To that question there are two basic answers. The first involves *context*. The context of a disputed word can usually elucidate the meaning. A special aspect of context, and one that fully applies here, relates to compound words formed of the disputed syllable *vín/vin*. In the *Greenlanders' Saga* the word *vínber* ('grapes') is used six times (once in the dative plural form *vínberjum*). The word *vínvid(r)* ('grapevines') appears four times in the accusative form (without the nominative *-r*). In each case the usage clearly refers to grapes and could not signify anything resembling pasturage. The word *Vínland*, including the genitive form *Vínlands* and the dative *Vínlandi* occurs seven times. There is one occurrence of *Vínlandsferd* and two of *Vínlandsför*, both meaning 'journey to Vínland' or 'Vínland expedition.' All of these words are found in chapters 4–9 of the saga. *Erik's Saga*, chapters 5–12, uses *vín* once, the dative form *Vínlandi* once, and the genitive *Vínlands* twice. All of these words are of a piece in that none conveys the slightest hint of incongruency with the others. The central core of this collection can be nothing but grapes.

The second answer to any inquiry into scribal intent derives from what is known of how Icelandic sagas were transmitted orally before the age of manuscripts on the island. In such a matter as vowel length, there was no possibility of a 'misreading.' The words were pronounced aloud, and understood perfectly. Several educated Icelanders have assured me of the impossibility of confusing *í* with *i*, and that was true in ancient times. Thus, there has been a continuous, and at all points consistent, use of the long vowel *í* in the word we are discussing. In one place *Erik's Saga* uses a circumlocution, *drykk inn bazta* ('the finest drink'). The speaker was not referring to grass. One manuscript employs the word *vínberjaköngull* ('cluster of grapes'). Once again, the reference is not to grass.

That is by far not all. A syllable *vin-* with short vowel, in the sense of grassy locality, had, with one ancient exception, passed out of usage several centuries before Leif Eriksson's time. In fact, it did not exist as a solitary word, or simplex. It had been used in compounds, usually as *-vin*, i.e., the second element. An example of this is *Björgvin*, the original form of Bergen, Norway. Einar Haugen points out that the syllable *-vin* had passed out of use by 600 and would in any case have designated an entire farm rather than a pasture.[2] Professor Gösta Holm, philologist of

Lund University, calls the Söderberg theory 'untenable' and adds 'That such a word should have been attached to the word for America is utterly incredible.'[3] A suffixed or prefixed -*vin*- denoting pasturage is nowhere found in the extensive corpus of Old Icelandic literature, nor does it anywhere appear in Iceland's place names. It is a will-o'-the-wisp.[4]

How, then, did the Icelanders refer to grass? They called it *gras*, pl. *grös*. What was their word for 'meadow'? The word was *engi*. The word for 'pasture' was *hagi*, for 'pasturage' *beiti*, for 'grazing' the compound *hagabeit*. None of these offers the slightest possibility of confusion with grapevines or grapes. The western discoveries, with all the vocabulary pertaining to them, were endlessly discussed in Greenland – the sagas specifically state so – and since the sagas, as writing came into style, were recorded in Iceland, they had been discussed there as well, both on isolated farms and at such gatherings as the annual meetings of the Althing or Parliament. Chapter 4 discusses Vínland as being mentioned in Arí's *Book of the Icelanders*, some time around 1122, as well as the still earlier (1069–1075) mention by Adam of Bremen who, writing in Latin, spoke of the fine wine produced by Vínland grapes. Though Adam's characterization doubtless represents a German's over-optimistic estimate of what Greenlanders might have been able to do with grapes, he had his information from the Danish court which, speaking the same language as the Icelanders, must have had the information fairly promptly after the fact. And it was to a Bremen merchant that Karlsefni sold his carved figurehead of *mösurr*. Adam himself, after all, was *Bremensis*.

But we are not finished with the linguistic aspects of the case. There has been considerable confusion by the commentators regarding the meaning of the Icelandic word for 'grapes,' which is *vínber*. Some writers triumphantly point out that Scandinavian *vínber*, etymologically 'wine-berries,' can mean 'currants.' This is not true of Icelandic, ancient or modern, in which the currant is termed *kurenna* or *smávínber* ('small wine-berries'), just as shrubbery was called *smávidi* ('small wood'). The modern Swedish word for currant, *vinbär*, preserved its ancient meaning of 'grape' past 1600. Similarly, the word for 'currant,' *vinbaer*, in New Norwegian (*nynorsk*) is modern. In Danish and Dano-Norwegian the word for 'currant' is the quite different word *ribs*, derived from Latin *Ribes rubrum*, *Ribes nigrum*. The various Germanic words for wine are apparently related to Latin *vitis* ('grapevine'), cf O.N. *vínvidr* ('wine withy, grapevine'). In

84 Decoration from the inside of the Oseberg stem.

modern Swedish, the word for grape proper is *druva, vindruva*. The Danish and Norwegian word is *drue*, cf German *Weintraube*.[5] Appropriate comment on wild grapes is found in Babcock (1913), Andrews (1910), Thórdarson (1930) and Tornöe (1964).[6]

M. Thórdarson refers to four varieties of wild grapes that grow in New England. They are: *Vitis labrusca, Vitis aestivalis, Vitis cordifolia*, and *Vitis vulpina*. Tornöe is impressed by the huge grapevines wound around the real trees, maple, birch, elm, oak. Who has not been struck by the almost fantastic grapevines that hang from trees in once cleared areas of New England that now once again are forested? Distinctive, they can by no stretch of the imagination be confused with berry bushes. Growing when undisturbed to great height and girth, they are parasitical, and the basic reference to them in the *Greenlanders' Saga* has repeatedly been misinterpreted.

The grapevines coiling around their host trees were not the stubby plants growing in an environment of lichens, heather and 'poor soil' plants around L'Anse aux Meadows, Newfoundland. Neither were they considered timber by the Norsemen, who coveted the real logs they came upon in the forest. In the saga, Leif very realistically orders his crew to spend alternate days on two separate tasks. One day they will gather grapes and cut vines, the next day they will fell trees to make a load for this ship. A distinction in phraseology is made between the chopping off of the troublesome vines (*höggva vínvid*) and the felling of the forest giants (*fella mörkina*). And a second distinction: their small boat or ship's boat (*eptirbátr*) was filled with grapes; the timber was loaded onto the ship. 'And when spring came, they sailed away.' The small boat would be used to the maximum for local transport, just as in Greenland, for no draft or pack-horses were carried on this exploratory voyage. The Norsemen knew how to esteem real timber. It is doubtful that they wasted much cargo-space on the tree-choking vines that impeded the logging, although slender vines suitable, when kept moist, for use as withies would have had some value. In one spot, where the subsequent voyage of Leif's brother Thorvald is being discussed (*Greenlanders' Saga* chap. 6) the sagawriter nods for a moment and has Thorvald loading grapes and grapevines on his ship. But presently (chap. 7) he comes to his senses – the sagaman, that is – and describes exactly how Karlsefni has logs felled, cut into lengths and dried. The grapes and other products of the land are mentioned afterwards, and separately.

The satire that some commentators have expended on the grapes is misdirected. The saga does not state that grapes were collected in the spring, when they could not have formed. They were of course collected in the fall when available and ready. The grapes must for the greater part have been consumed *au naturel*. If the voyagers were accustomed to drying berries, they may have experimented with these and inexpertly produced raisins. As to wine-making, the sagas soberly report nothing at all. But a maneuvering, or even beached, boat full of grapes will leave many a crushed exemplar, and after a period of sunshine, perhaps a few cupfulls of crude Château Vinlandia were generated, after all. The exciting potential was there.

Some skeptics think that Leif's nomenclature exaggerated the potential of his discovery. Let us therefore suppose that – contrary to custom – on leaving the place Leif had not bothered to give it a name. It is not improbable, then, that as the news spread among the colonists in *Greenland*, precisely the name *Vínland* would have been attached to Leif's new land. In their culture it was practice for every area, every topographical feature to bear a name. We are in fact told that *Vínland* was the goal of a number of later expeditions until, too far away and too dangerous because of the aborigines, it slipped from their expectations.

One does not wish to malign the currant, which certainly can be turned into wine. We know exactly when the Icelanders first learned to do so. It was announced as an important discovery, made in 1203, two centuries after Leif Eriksson's famous voyage.[7] Bishop Jón Smyrill taught the art to the Greenlanders before his death in 1209.

The question of how far south the Greenlanders may have attempted to establish a colony, or even conduct explorations, will never be 'solved' without physical evidence. Nevertheless, the problem has certain parameters. The wear and tear on sails, tackle and ships' bottoms, the ever growing distance from a home base, the concern for winter should supplies run out in a strange land, would set certain constraints on travel. Add to that a suspicion of the natives and the realization that every league covered must be doubled in the end, and one will find it most improbable that they ever deliberately continued as far south as Virginia, let alone the Carolinas or Florida as some have theorized (accidental voyaging can of course never be discounted). In the *Greenlanders' Saga*, chap. 3, Leif makes a famous astronomical observation, the proper translation of which is in doubt. It reads: 'Here day and night were of more equal length than on Greenland or Iceland; the sun had the *mid-morning* and *mid-afternoon* positions on the year's shortest day' (italics by us). The two troublesome words here are *eyktarstad* and *dagmálastad*. Much has been written about this, but we cannot be sure that the well-known terms were always understood by the Icelanders in the same sense.[8] A reciprocal relationship does seem to be indicated between time of day, time of year and latitude. The 'first day of winter' in the Old Icelandic calendar was 21 October, but the shortest day of the year usually falls on 21 December. The two-month differential would suggest some location very far south of Snorri Sturluson's estate in Iceland, which served as a standard for calendrical calculations. This ought to indicate a spot well south of 50° N. lat. Reliability in textual transmission of such precise details can of course not be guaranteed. Neither is it certain whether the phrase 'equal length' was literal or merely an intimation, nor, finally, do we know how accurately the explorers were able or concerned to measure such things. In this case, the 'potential exactness of a quantitative science is almost totally at the mercy of rhetorical vagaries and their mediaeval practitioners'.[9]

The northernmost parameter for an area of grapevines should be in northern Maine or southern New Brunswick. The southern limit, if we continue to pay heed to the natural products mentioned in the sagas, would by the same token be the Hudson River, which is the southernmost boundary of the salmon, also referred to. On this large stretch of coastline no authenticated ancient Norse artifacts have been found except a late 11th-century Norwegian coin found in Maine in an Indian context. Its date precludes any immediate connection with Leif Eriksson, Thorvald or Karlsefni, though it certainly indicates some form of contact, possibly much farther north, during a later generation.[10] By the 1060s, at least, the existence of a Vínland was firmly established in Nordic tradition. If we assume that it was not Leif who built somewhere in New England, we are merely displacing the honor by some years or decades and attributing the deed to a quite anonymous hero. Methodologically, that has little to recommend it.

Gold

A remarkable medieval Latin manuscript turned up a few years ago in the library of Trinity College, Dublin. Written about 1255 by an unknown European missionary, it is a short treatise on world geography penned by way of introduction to a history of the Mongols which he may or may not have been able thereafter to write. In the middle of the document, section 19 is composed of the following sentences, translated:

> Furthermore, there is an island discovered in our own times at the northern part of Norway. To this island persons go in a double-sized ship and return from there within a five-year period. The island is spacious, very abundant in people, but they are pagans. Excellent gold is found in great abundance on the shores of rivers and of the sea. In the summer the people of the island do not know the darkness of night, and in the winter they are completely deprived of light. But about Christmastime, as I have learned from a man who stayed two years on the island and is now still living in Denmark, the people receive light from Aurora Borealis.[11]

The Scandinavian connection is manifest, the high latitude, New World intimation not less so, for such new lands were commonly deemed to lie north of Scandinavia. Whether the 'island' meant is Greenland, Newfoundland, Nova Scotia or some part of the mainland, can only be guessed. This must be the earliest reference to gold in any of those areas, and for the mid-13th century the notice is astonishing. It is not mentioned in the famous Norwegian *Konungs skuggsjá* or *Speculum Regale* (*King's Mirror*) of *c.* 1250.[12] The Danish mention makes it almost certain that Greenlanders were somehow involved in the transmission of this bit of lore, irrespective of whether it is based on actual contemporary knowledge of gold deposits anywhere in the New World. In modern times, of course, gold has been mined in Nova Scotia, Newfoundland and Labrador. The mention of a five-year period is realistic enough in an historical sense, though not

85 Gardar cathedral after excavation. Located across the fjord arm a dozen air miles south of Brattahlid, the cathedral was the episcopal seat of Greenland's bishops beginning with Arnald in 1126.

147

86 Crosier head, Gardar.

87 Wooden crosses, the largest with runic inscription.

because the round trip *per se* required, if all went well, more than some weeks of sailing in two successive summers. But regular sailings were an unknown concept, a round trip during a single sailing season a rare exploit. Though non-stop voyages between Norway and Greenland could be made, a stop-off in Iceland was usual, and considering the casual nature of ocean transport, might well involve a winter's stay. Many a person arriving in Greenland by accident or design had to wait several years for a return voyage. The unknown geographer doubtless had his information from a fellow cleric, via the international fellowship of the Church, whose well-informed bishops and administrators were constantly on the move. Greenland must have had priests since shortly after 1000. Beginning in 1126 it was constituted a diocese with a resident bishop, Arnald. The Church was constantly concerned for its own material support, and we saw in Chapter 1 how important the matter of tithing had become to the Church by the 13th century. The Greenlanders paid their tithes in what treasures they had: walrus and narwhal tusks, pelts and hunting falcons, an occasional polar bear cub (adult polar bears could be killed but scarcely transported alive). Inasmuch as the utilization of gold would have influenced the Greenland economy and the relations with Rome – to say nothing of bringing in a plague of foreign adventurers – one is forced to conclude that gold did not play any rôle in the domestic life or foreign relations of medieval Greenland.

Navigation

There are great differences of opinion regarding the sailing capacities of ocean-going Norse ships. It is often assumed that the merchant ship or *knörr*, heavily laden as a rule and not easily rowed – oars were used in emergencies and when maneuvering in harbor – could for the greater part only sail on latitude because, square-rigged, it could only sail before the wind.[13] Such authorities as Brøgger and Shetelig are vague on this point. But recent nautical authorities in Denmark, Norway and Sweden are doubtful of such limitation. The Swedish museum man and practical sailor Harald Åkerlund, with a specialty in the reconstruction of ancient Scandinavian vessels, has suggested that the Gokstad replica *Viking* that so successfully sailed to America in 1893 was actually built half a meter too long owing to inadequate keel curvature, and that along with other old Scandinavian ships the original had had much more clever

88 The bishop's tomb in the chapel at Gardar, crosier *in situ*.

reefing devices than has usually been recognized. The sail was broader and lower, thinks Åkerlund, than assumed, nearly as wide as the mast, or 12 m.[14]

Much of this is confirmed by Tornöe, who stresses that Viking ships were constructed so that the bow would rise out of the water when the ship attained speed, greatly reducing water drag, as is true of the modern hydrofoil. Writing of his own experience with west Norwegian reefing devices, Tornöe stresses in particular the use of a device for handily decreasing sail through *svipting*. The Old Norse verb *svipta* (pron. svifta), modern Norwegian *svifte* and *svifta*, means to gather a sail, which is divided into vertical strips by ropes sewn into the fabric, by means of another rope running at right angles to the others and through wooden thimbles. One can very handily adjust to changing wind pressure by hauling or slackening the horizontal rope, and in case of storm one can reef as required. Brøgger and Shetelig had found a pile of ropes in the Gokstad ship and could make nothing of them. Tornöe suspects that the Gokstad vessel as well as the ships that sought Vínland were equipped with the west Norwegian type of sail, specially adapted to *svipting* and resembling a lateen, or triangular sail with the top cut off. The otherwise puzzling location of the Gokstad mast, which is quite far aft, is an accommodation to this type of sail. Whether that disposes of Åkerlund's idea on keel curvature is unclear. For that matter, declares Tornöe, a square-rigged vessel equipped with a *beitiáss* or tacking boom to hold the leading edge of the sail taut can certainly tack well enough to sail to windward. An expert

89 Rune-inscribed tombstone from Gardar. It reads: 'Vigdís daughter of Magnus rests here. God gladden her soul.'

crew can tack quickly by lowering the sail, bringing it round the mast and hoisting it on the other side of the ship, and this can be done in 'half a minute.'[15] Skill was everything. Not all navigators were equally skilled, of course, and we know that the Norsemen met many a defeat at the hands of wind and wave.

The distances and speeds logged by early Scandinavian mariners deserve our study. Sailing times were normally measured in terms of *doegr* or twenty-four-hour days. While at sea it was normal to sail round the clock. Near shore, for obvious reasons, the more prudent practice of daylight sailing prevailed. In northern waters, of course, the summer nights are short. From Stad in Norway it was theoretically seven *doegr*'s sail to Horn on the southeast coast of Iceland, rather slow time because of the often contrary winds and currents. Magnus Andersen's *Viking* (the Gokstad replica) required seven days from Bergen to the longitude of Horn, but other routes could be covered at much greater speed. The sail from Snaefellsnes in western Iceland to Hvarf, the southernmost tip of Greenland, was stated to be 4 *doegr*, the voyage from Reykjanes at the southwest tip of Iceland to Joeldhlaup (Oldefee) in northern Ireland was estimated at 3 *doegr*. From Langanes in northeastern Iceland to Svalbard (Spitzbergen) was 4 *doegr*, from the island Kolbeinsey off Iceland's north coast to the desolate region now called Scoresby Sound was accounted one *doegr*. That such schedules were not consistently attained is obvious. It must be remembered that a voyage was expressed in terms of ostensible time consumed as a surrogate for *distance*, for which concept no all-purpose expression had developed.

In Old Norse skaldic poetry[16] 'the whale's path' was a picturesque kenning, or metonymy, for the sea in general. To those who sailed from Norway to Iceland and beyond, the path of the whale was literal reality, regularly incorporated into sailing directions. In voyaging non-stop from Bergen to Greenland in medieval times, after the route became established, one was to sail twelve miles south of Iceland, but more helpfully, to follow the birds and the whales that congregated on the banks off the coast to feed on the masses of plankton found there above the undersea mountain chain running from the Faeroes to Iceland. Today this is called the Iceland Ridge. The location of these and other fishing banks could be determined also by means of a long line. Captain Tornöe has measured and summarized the various distances involved in such voyages as we have mentioned above, and worked out the respective speeds involved. Varying from 8.2

to 11.8 knots, they yield an average speed of 8.5 knots, which is considerably greater than the averages indicated by some modern writers but possibly confirmed by Magnus Andersen's *Viking* which, at one point in its voyage, easily outdistanced an American clipper ship without even the use of its auxiliary sail or jib. 'With the right kind of sail,' opines Tornöe, 'it is very likely that the Viking would have made even greater speed than the 11 knots measured by Magnus Andersen.' When storm-tossed or hopelessly lost in fogs (like Bjarni Herjólfsson) one could not make good overall time, but very fast voyages are recorded. Despite contrary currents a Viking named Thórarin sailed from Norway and around to Reykjavík, a distance of 900 miles, in 4 *doegr*. Líka-Lodin, reporting to King Harald Hard-Ruler in 1066 near Sogn, where the king was preparing his invasion of England, said that he had been on the way for 'seven nights.' That would have been 1600 miles at an average speed of over 9 knots. The well-informed king was not astonished. Without a compass, Líka-Lodin would frequently have deviated from course, so that at times he must have made well over that speed. Graham-Campbell asserts that the Viking ship could be made to sail across the wind and even into it! A speedy Viking ship might have been capable of 14 or 15 knots under the best conditions, easily yielding an average of 10–12 knots.[17]

But speed is certainly not the primary consideration. In 1967 J. R. L. Anderson sailed from Scarborough via the Faeroes, Reykjavík, Frederikshåb and Halifax to Edgartown on Martha's Vineyard. During the actual hours of sailing, 1095 in all, he covered the 4941.6 miles at an overall speed of 4.51 knots. His diet, less monotonous than that of Leif Eriksson, included 150 varieties of food, from marmalade to ginger pudding, oranges to tomato ketchup, herring roe to sliced peaches, ravioli to milk chocolate. More important than the banqueting on board was what Anderson calls his 'navigational detective work,' reconstructing ancient voyages by his experience of current and wind. Anderson points to the importance of water temperature as a navigational guide, having observed a spread of as much as $9°$ F. $(41°/32°)$ between adjacent warm and cool ocean currents. He would place Vínland between $40°$ and $50°$ N. lat., i.e. from central Newfoundland to southern New England (Newfoundland lies between $46° 30'$ and $51° 40'$). Remembering Bjarni, Anderson stresses the prevalence of fogs produced under such circumstances.[18] How early the Norsemen discovered the use of the *sólarsteinn*, or sun-seeking piece of feldspar or cordierite (now employed in air navigation), is not known.[19] They would have noticed that damp winds come as a rule from the northeast, dry winds from the southwest. Constant vigilance was in order. The rest was up to the gods, or God.

Modern Scandinavian experiments with wind tunnels, water tanks, and the sailing of reconstructed models are providing us with new insights into early navigation. The ships dug up from Roskilde Fjord, now rebuilt and displayed, have yielded a treasure of information.[20] The most recent find, a ship at Hedeby, was made in 1979. Within a decade, a great deal more will be known about the subject, as ships built on the Viking pattern sail back and forth between the Old World and the New.

The most recent example of such voyaging was announced by Associated Press on 4 September 1984, based on the previous day's interview in Boston with Ragnar Thorseth, the Norwegian writer and expedition leader who had just arrived from Norway with five companions on the good ship Saga Siglar. A 57-foot replica of a 10th- or 11th-century *knörr*, or sea-going cargo vessel, it had made the trip to Boston by way of Greenland, Labrador and Nova Scotia. With stops along the way, the trip had taken forty-five days. Between Greenland and Labrador the open–decked vessel had run into a storm with 70-knot winds and 45-foot waves, handling them competently but forcing the crew to bail, exactly as the Vikings had done. Praising the seaworthiness of his vessel, built of Danish oak and Norwegian pine, with an overall weight of 27 tons, Thorseth declared:

> We have conclusively proved that Viking ships can sail up to 45 degrees into the wind using a square sail. That disproves the theory that they had to use oars to turn their ships when there was no tail wind. We also found that the rudder on Viking ships was not nearly as important in steering as the sail.

Two years earlier a slightly larger Viking ship, the 76-foot Hjemkomst *Homecoming*, modeled on the Gokstad ship and built by the Minnesota schoolteacher Robert Asp, had sailed in similar triumph in the opposite direction, from Rhode Island to Bergen, Norway. Though Asp did not live to make the voyage, his three sons and a daughter were included in the crew.

It seems almost ludicrous now that so many scholars of distinction could have doubted the reality of the Vínland voyages. With this background, let us now look into the ancient voyages of those sturdy heroes Bjarni Herjólfsson, Leif Eriksson, Thorvald Eriksson and Thórfinn Karlsefni.

9

Where was Vínland?

Unrecorded are the names of the Norse-Greenlandic huntsmen who met speedy death under the crushing paws of *amarok*, the intractable white bear (*nanook* in the dialect of the more westerly tribes), or of those whose chilled, final hours were spent on an ice-floe which, with sudden treachery, had parted from its shore-fast anchorage. Not one wide-ranging early Norse colonial has left us his impressions of the gregarious reindeer and caribou, of the solitary moose, or of *ooningmakk*, 'the bearded one', whose *quiviut* or downy, inner layer of fine wool keeps the musk-ox warmer than the hardiest sheep. Of such things could novels and poetry be spun. Our more prosaic task in this chapter is to strip the Vínland sagas of all save what may elucidate the explorations and, in particular, the discovery – and loss – of Vínland.

In so doing, we see that the inheritance of energies that had sustained the Scandinavian migrants was not immediately dissipated on the ordinary details of housekeeping and survival. An eager curiosity, an alertness to opportunity, a willingness to face danger still motivated the new Greenlanders and their trickle of Icelandic recruits. However, the adventurous among them now faced challenges of a different order of magnitude. The confusing immensity of geographical possibilities posed by a vaguely discerned American continent contrasted starkly with the minuscule number of humans available for its exploitation. Selective manpower, economic capital in the form of ships, equipment and supplies, together with exceptional leadership, all had to be drawn from an astonishingly small population already concerned with 'settling in' after the move from Iceland. No one has to my best knowledge tried in print to estimate the population during the first quarter of a century, and inasmuch as the population maximum during the colony's prime can never – to judge by the excavated house sites – have exceeded three or four thousand individuals, it is safest to assume fewer than half that number in the time of Leif Eriksson. Though we shall never know for sure how far south these early explorers were able or willing to travel, there is good reason for the surmise that the farthest pushes to the south were made during the very first years, when the flush of expansionism was upon them. Having sensed the endlessness of the new shores along with their dangers and their remoteness from a safe base, the Norsemen, following this assumption, would concentrate on what they could do with the greatest prospect of a reasonable return on the investment.

It will be recalled that there are two Vínland sagas proper. They have acquired rather arbitrary names. One, now generally referred to as the *Saga of the Greenlanders*, might be thought of as Leif's saga, for it was he who found and named Vínland. It is believed to have assumed written form by 1200. The other work, now usually called the *Saga of Erik the Red*, ought to be thought of as primarily the story of Karlsefni. It was written in the early 1260s by a scribe who had his own story to tell, but seems to have had a copy of the earlier saga before him, the details and phraseology of which he has modified to suit a purpose. That purpose, apart from a clear emphasis on Christianity, is to emphasize the exploits of Karlsefni, who spent his later life in Iceland and had influential descendants including three bishops.

The *Saga of the Greenlanders* narrates six separate, early voyages to the mainland of America. The first, that of Bjarni Herjólfsson, took place by chance as his ship emerged from one of those North Atlantic fogs of which S. Morison can say 'the sails slatted monotonously and the yards and rigging dropped rime.'[1] The second was a deliberate voyage of exploration by Leif Eriksson, scion of Greenland's founder Erik the Red. It was Leif who found and named Vínland, returning to Greenland a year after his departure. A third voyage was undertaken by Leif's brother Thorvald, whose expedition lasted two years, although Thorvald himself was killed in combat with the natives after perhaps one year. Leif's landmark descriptions were adequate to enable Thorvald to find Leif's houses in Vínland, but Thorvald sought a land claim of his own, found it, and left his bones there. A fourth voyage, this one by their brother Thorstein, was totally abortive, and no lands were found.

The explorer's mantle is now taken up by the visiting Icelandic merchant Thorfinn Karlsefni, who mounts an expedition with sixty persons including some women, and bringing cattle and possessions. They find Leif's houses in Vínland and, after a trading visit from the natives, Karlsefni builds a stockade around them. Unfortunately they clash with the natives and deaths ensue on both sides. After two winters the party decides to return to Greenland. Karlsefni, following upon a voyage to Europe, settles down in Iceland. The sixth and final voyage in this series is undertaken by Leif's half-sister Freydís. It is a murderous disaster, and in every respect so pointless that I think it to have been made up out of whole cloth on the model of an actually recorded episode on the east coast of Greenland shortly before the settlement.

The parallel *Erik's Saga* chooses to know of only three voyages. Bjarni's accidental discovery, and his existence as well, are dispensed with, and Leif is made the accidental discoverer of unknown lands bearing grapevines and self-sown grain.[2] A voyage made by Leif's brother Thorstein is a fiasco. The third, major and final, expedition is made by the visiting Icelander Thórfinn Karlsefni. The number of participants has swelled to 160, and Thorvald and Freydís are subordinated as members of Karlsefni's party. They spend three years in the New World, spend winters in different localities, despite their wanderings never find Vínland at all and, in the end, shaken by a bloodshedding encounter with the natives, give up the project entirely and return to Greenland. As in the previous saga, Karlsefni and his wife Gudrid go back to Iceland after a visit to Europe. No further expeditions are mentioned. The time span of the entire Vínland story in the two sagas probably centers on the year 1000, the possibility being that Leif found Vínland in the 990s, and that Karlsefni may have given up on the new lands by 1012 at the latest. No greater degree of chronological precision is currently possible.

Routes and Sites

The foregoing synopses are of course no substitute for a reading of the translated sagas themselves which, properly examined, give good guidance. A proper examination takes into consideration the practicalities of textual transmission. The *Greenlanders' Saga*, for example, states that from the time when Bjarni emerged from the fog and caught his first sight of land, until he reached his father's place Herjólfsnes in Greenland, a total of nine days elapsed. Some leg of the journey may well have been lost through generations of oral narration preceding the tale's commitment to parchment. If we take the statement literally, his coast-hugging course from, say, northern Nova Scotia, arching northward (rather than a straight diagonal sail northeast with its attendant risk of a second failure to make

Greenland), would have amounted to some 1900 miles, plus allowance for course deviations. Capt. Tornöe plots Bjarni's course as from Nova Scotia to southeastern Labrador (*c.* 600 miles), from Labrador to Loksland (Baffin Island) (*c.* 700 miles), from Loksland to Greenland (*c.* 600 miles). The 1900 miles would make for an average speed of 8.8 knots.[2] That seems excessive. A Viking ship, as we have learned earlier, could exceed that speed under ideal conditions in open sea, and Bjarni, in a hurry now, pressed his ship as hard as he dared. But, heavily laden, it must have been low in the water, and Bjarni was a cautious rather than reckless navigator. It would be safer to accept an overall speed of perhaps 6 knots. What conclusions should be drawn from this? Accepting the reality of the voyage – it makes no sense not to – we either accept the higher speed of 8.8 knots, or posit a greater number of days, and of the two alternatives, the second is the likelier.[3]

We are not tied to a magic number of voyaging days as though they were Holy Writ, and if the commentators who have so valiantly tried to account for virtually every league and every hour of these voyages had relaxed under the rule of common sense, the entire problem might have seemed less formidable. Bjarni was in a hurry, he seems to have had consistently favourable winds with no stops or setbacks, and he obviously employed excellent judgment in evaluating his situation. Should one then retroactively extend his sailing distances in accommodation to the views of those who think that his first landfall was Cape Cod, for example? I think not. Observers who make that assumption are under the spell of Leif Eriksson's later voyage.[4] If Leif reversed Bjarni's course and found an area of fruit-bearing grapevines, they reason that Bjarni must momentarily have stood off that same bit of coast before sailing northward. But nothing in the saga indicates this. To the frustration of his later auditors, Bjarni had ascertained nothing about the products of the lands he viewed from a prudent distance. He could not have seen or mentioned grapevines. Leif's subsequent voyage was therefore not made in expectation of finding grapes, and his surprise at the discovery was surely unfeigned. That surprise and his delight are reflected in the name he gave the land. The saga states that 'Leif saw first that land [Baffin Island] that Bjarni saw last.' Knowing now that lands lay to the south, Leif was on his own. With no obligation to duplicate Bjarni's course he was out to discover what lands there were and how they might be turned to advantage.

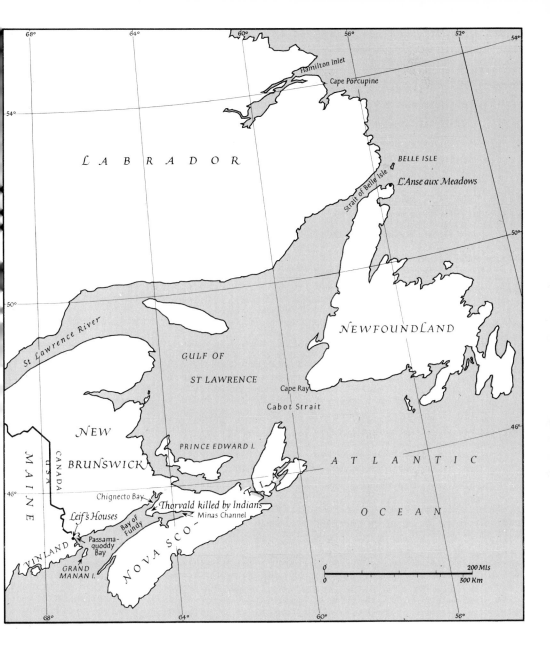

The saga does not even intimate that Leif saw last the land that Bjarni had seen first, and Bjarni's chance discovery relates to Vínland only insofar as it accelerated the interest in western lands. The landing spots of Leif and his brother Thorvald can be guessed at with some show of reason, as can the voyaging of Karlsefni, provided we accept the account of this last as set forth in the same saga (*Greenlanders' Saga*), which puts him in Leif's houses in Vínland, which he reinforces by building a stockade around them. But the account of Karlsefni's travels presented in

90 Did Leif and Thorvald come here?

Erik's Saga leaves the reader quite as baffled as that hero himself seems to have been. The saga plants him squarely in the center of a major ambiguity. He and his followers are made to wander all over the map, liberally bestowing names as they go but never finding Leif's Vínland. What is several times reported concerning grapes and wild wheat is vague and unconvincing: the author of *Erik's Saga* knows that something about grapes is supposed to be included but, mystified, cannot quite come to terms with them. When that old heathen pessimist Thórhall Huntsman, a frontiersman who has been of precious little help on the expedition, decides after a harsh winter to leave the company, his disgust over the failure to find grapes is nothing if not vocal:

> These oakhearted warriors
> Lured me to this land
> With promise of choice drinks;
> Now I curse this country!
> For I, the helmet-wearer,
> Must now grovel at a spring
> And wield a water-pail;
> No wine has touched my lips.

In a second stanza he declares his intention of returning home to Greenland, although the prose text, rather than cope with so bald a defection, sends him off, with nine companions, to find Vínland in the north. But Karlsefni knows that it has to lie somewhere to the south. The stanzas have been much discussed by literary historians. If Thórhall, as is quite possible, did in fact exist,[5] and if the verses do stem from him, they tell a clear story. If, on the other hand, they are the invention of the sagawriter, the suggestion of explorational failure is equally strong. Karlsefni's ultimate discovery of the landlocked bay he calls Hóp, in an area of grapes, sounds like a not too convincing afterthought, though the wild grain and halibut described in the saga are acceptable enough *per se*. The puzzling statement in *Erik's Saga* that Karlsefni's party thereafter returned to Straumfjord, the scene of their disastrous first winter, competes with the selfsame saga's suggestion that, following Thórhall's departure, Karlsefni's force splits up, with the main force remaining at Straumfjord while Karlsefni and some followers spend two months in the south in an attempt to vindicate his search for Vínland. All things considered, something like that version seems realistic enough. Chastened by their experiences, the colonists are prevented through unknown circumstances, through hope or simply through pride, from returning home at this point. What we glean from the *potpourri* is that the return to Greenland takes place after three years in all.

The reconstructed Norse houses at L'Anse aux Meadows represent a first-class achievement in modern archaeology, and a major enrichment of our geographical and historical knowledge. A sizeable group of Scandinavians must have spent, not just a single winter, but several years at the site close to a millennium ago. I think that the founder of the tiny community could not have been Leif Eriksson, whose location is described in terms utterly dissimilar to conditions that prevailed at L'Anse aux Meadows. The expedition leader could of course have been someone unknown to the sagawriters of Iceland who alone codified the Vínland reports, for it is estimated that eighty per cent of all Icelandic saga material has been lost in one way or another. However, though there are collateral reports concerning both Leif and Karlsefni, there is none concerning other explorers from which we could deduce any appropriately dated anonymous settlement of the size and relative persistence adequate to account for the finds at L'Anse aux Meadows. The indicated answer is, of course: Erik the Red's distinguished guest Thorfinn Thórdarson Karlsefni from Reynines in Skagafjord, accompanied by Snorri Thorbrandsson of Alptafjord and Thórhall Gamlason (not the Huntsman) from Austfjord, all mentioned elsewhere in Icelandic sources.

If this could be assumed, a great deal would fall into place. With Captain Munn, Professor Jones and others we could conclude that Karlsefni's Marvelstrands are the forty or so miles of sandy beach just south of Hamilton Inlet on the southeastern coast of Labrador, a stretch now called the Strand. Extending two miles out to sea from the Strand is the important landmark Cape Porcupine, a perfect turned-up keel and many times more likely to have given rise to the name Keelsness than the finding of a ship's keel, through which narrative invention the writer of *Erik's Saga* seeks to authenticate his story by tying it in with the *Greenlanders' Saga*, in which Thorvald Eriksson has lost a ship's keel. That would ostensibly compensate Thorvald, in narrative terms, for being absorbed into Karlsefni's expedition in lieu of his own. The Strand and Cape Porcupine are within an easy two days' sail of L'Anse aux Meadows, leading to the strong possibility that Karlsefni's Straumfjord is Belle Isle Strait. Well used to immense fjords, the Karlsefni expedition, or any other such group, could easily have taken the strait for one more fjord. J. R. L. Anderson is one of many writers who stresses how easy it would be to do that.[6] Straumey or Stream Island, called thus because of the strong (or perhaps simply broad) currents around it, may have been the modern Great Sacred Island or the more distant Belle Isle, but there are other islands in the vicinity as well. The names given by the Norse explorers served convenience and afforded comfort. Once established, such designations as Straumey and Straumfjord were unlikely to be changed in saga tradition despite the inevitable discovery that the strait was not a fjord after all, and that Newfoundland was not attached to the mainland as originally assumed by some.

That Karlsefni's southern trip would have taken him along the western coast of Newfoundland seems certain enough. Whether he thereafter rounded Nova Scotia and touched on any part of New England, or merely sailed west along the northern shores of New Brunswick, i.e., into the southern part of the St Lawrence, is unclear. It seems likely that such a voyage, or voyages would not have been long delayed. One may surmise that Newfoundland was circumnavigated, but the voyaging described in *Erik's Saga* is too unclear for us to plot his course. The sagawriter was laboring under great difficulty in attempting to clarify a confused tradition. One source of that confusion, as previously stated, was the medieval writer's own obsession with redoing the *Greenlanders' Saga*. Despite his rationalizing efforts, one senses Karlsefni's frustrations. Conditions in the New World had not lived up to expectations, whether in terms of climate, natural products or freedom from rival populations. There had been disappointment and vociferous dissension within the colony's ranks. Leif's happy voyage had set too high a standard. In the end, prudence triumphed over ambition, and the settlement at Straumfjord/L'Anse aux Meadows was abandoned to Indians, Eskimos and the scholarly diggers of another age. And partly for want of a clear distinction in their minds between the two Vínland sagas, some of the diggers are convinced that this was the site of Leif's houses and should therefore be called Vínland or Vinland. Incidentally, no traces of a stockade have been found at L'Anse aux Meadows.

Let us now turn to the expedition captained by Leif Eriksson, which must be evaluated in its own terms. It is possible, though not really material, that Leif's *first* landfall was on latitude with Bjarni's *last*: perhaps some part of the coast between Hall Peninsula (on Baffin Island) and Resolution Island. The land

there the voyagers deemed 'worthless.' How long and how far Leif sailed thereafter before conferring the name Markland upon a great area of forests, is nowhere stated. He was investigating everything, he obviously sailed for a long time, and we may not hold him to a time/distance schedule.

Sailing southeast along the coast of Labrador, and probably considering it the more southerly reach of his 'first' land, Leif would inevitably discover the 'fjord' Belle Isle Strait and observe a distinct change in topography. From an east-facing coast he had now come to a west-facing coast. We assume that, continuing south, he entered Belle Isle Strait, then went down the west coast of Newfoundland with land on his port side. Bjarni, knowing that he must be west of his goal, would have instinctively come north along the east coast, fearing to put land between himself and his goal, Greenland. It may well have been somewhere in western Newfoundland – the saga does not say that land lay to starboard – that Leif went ashore for the second time and gave the region a name, Markland. The country was wooded and low-lying with white sandy beaches that 'sloped gently down to the sea.' If he sailed along Newfoundland on the east, his descriptions would have been different: the frontages would have been steep, rocky and often barren. He doubtless knew that already, from Bjarni's descriptions, surely given in detail at the time that Leif purchased Bjarni's ship.

While they were ashore, then, on the west coast of Newfoundland, the saga states that they hurried back to their ship *sem fljótast* ('as quickly as possible'), and sailed off. The sagawriter forgets to tell us why, or thinks it unnecessary. This was clearly a common type of navigational emergency, and the saga can guide us after all. A northeast (off-land) wind had come up. Their ship, straining at the hawser, might easily have blown southwestward out to sea and left them stranded. Thereafter, states the saga, they sailed 'into the sea' for two days before sighting their third land, Vínland.

The phraseology at this point has led to a modern misunderstanding. Leif would have sailed very cautiously in coastal waters, and he was, after all, exploring the coast. To 'sail into the sea' in Old Norse parlance was to head into open water when the coasting segment of a voyage was over. In reality, as various sagas make clear, this often meant many days of sailing along the coast of Norway, or Iceland, or wherever, before heading into the open sea for a distance jump. Was it owing to a change of wind, or to pure chance, that Leif, after reaching land's end and rounding Cape Ray, sailed southeast through Cabot Strait and then down along Nova Scotia instead of into the Gulf of St Lawrence? The factors involved must, once again, include information received from Bjarni, who had pursued the outer path on his way north. St Lawrence would have been described differently than it is in the saga.

The elliptic saga phraseology allows us to believe that their 'two days' of sailing (it may well have been more) brought them far enough south of Newfoundland to clear Nova Scotia, the northern part of which had probably been Bjarni's first land. Bjarni had allegedly sailed north 'for two days' before sighting his next land, and that fetching phrase 'two days' sail' may be contamination here, for such precise quantifications are easily the first victims of errors in transmission. This would be particularly true if the sagawriter, like so many of his modern readers, persuaded himself that Leif's three lands were the reverse of Bjarni's three.

At all events, Leif did not land on Nova Scotia but sailed on until, clearing it, he sighted a land mass. This must have been the continent. Holding in towards it, i.e., sailing west, he came upon an island lying 'north of the land.' Inasmuch as the continental shore is continuous, north of the land is most logically seen as north of the nearest land, which would not be the continent but the southern tip of Nova Scotia. There are islands, and in particular one largish island, that fit the description of lying north of that land, that is, the land that is nearest, as one sails in towards it from the east. That is Grand Manan Island, 5 miles by 13, grassy and timbered, with heights up to 400 feet, a landmark of distinction. The men went ashore on the island, and after their days of facing salt spray they were greatly impressed by the sweet-tasting dew they found on the grass. Reboarding the ship, they 'sailed into the sound that lay between the island and the headland that went north from the land; they went westward around the headland.' The tide was at low ebb. Impatient to get ashore, they left the ship in the shallows rather far from the sea, and ran inland to where a river was flowing out of a lake. When the incoming tide refloated the ship, they towed it via the river to a safe anchorage in the lake. The 'lake' may have been no more than a tidal lagoon. These come and go during the centuries and this one may long ago have ceased to exist. Building temporary booths for shelter, the party became so pleased with the territory that they soon decided to build houses suitable for a winter's stay. The river and lake were full of salmon, and bigger than those they had previously known. This is realistic: the 12- or 14-pound fish of Greenland are eclipsed by New England specimens weighing 30 to 40 pounds. The pasturage was so rich that they thought it would be unnecessary to winter-feed livestock (they had none with them on this surveying voyage), and in fact the winter was very mild by their lights. We can see how such a report, honestly made, would mislead poor Karlsefni later on. The solar observation, the discovery of grapes, the loading of timber all follow.

Everything indicates that the voyagers had reached New England. A host of writers have wished to locate *Leifsbúdir* in Massachusetts, perhaps around Falmouth or Follins Pond, at all events in the vicinity of Cape Cod. Some have claimed to pinpoint the spot almost exactly. If there were the slightest bit of physical proof, there would be no need to debate the matter. There is a strong chance that we shall never know. Considerations of travel time and distance probably speak for a more northerly location, yet one well within the northern boundary for grapes which, now that L'Anse aux Meadows has received its due, simply cannot be wished out of the equation.

Of all the locations suggested during this century, that for *Leifsbúdir* proposed by Edward Reman impresses me as having come the closest, just as his suggestions for Karlsefni's route may have gone the farthest astray.[7] The main requirements for Leif's temporary settlement, later visited by his brother Thorvald, are: a notable island lying 'north of the land' as one approaches the mainland; the strong and sudden (Bay of Fundy) tide; the probable existence of a tidal lagoon; a location between the northern limit of the grape (northern Maine to southern New Brunswick) and the southern limit of the salmon (the Hudson River); the immediate availability of impressive timber; a location so far south of their customary haunts that the voyagers would attempt to quantify it through such procedures as were available to them. A place somewhere between 40° and 50° N. lat. is strongly indicated. A location in Passamaquoddy Bay comports very well with both Leif's experience and what is narrated concerning Thorvald's voyage several years later. And Grand Manan Island, lying before the entrance to the bay as well as north of intervening land as one approaches from the sea, seems to fit perfectly.

The headland that they steered round was no great thing like Cape Cod, which I think would have called for more comment in the saga. Five hundred or so years afterwards Giovanni da Verrazzano (later killed and eaten by cannibals at Guadaloupe) described Cape Cod as *promontorio prominente*,[8] and so it is indeed. The Norse explorers would have made something of it. The headland that Leif and Thorvald steered round would have been of more modest size, such as West Quoddy Head or East Quoddy Head. The exact state of the channel in their time is of course unknown, and it is likely that changes have taken place. The tides in the Bay of Fundy exceed 20 feet, and the fall may reach a speed of 5 knots, a circumstance that seems to be reflected in the saga account of Leif's striking experience with the ship. It is not stated that Leif crossed the bay to erect his structures on the opposite side. Thus, I incline to place his houses on the south side of Passamaquoddy Bay, barely within the present border of the United States with Canadian New Brunswick and probably not more than a few hundred paces from where the motor highway Maine 1 now runs. In canvassing the neighborhood Leif and his companions would, for what it is worth, become the first whites to set foot on any continental portion of either country.

The explorers had luck with the weather as they had had with their sailing. Another winter, another voyage might have been different. Their rudimentary astronomical observation fits well the latitude of 45° N. on which the presumed settlement, under my theory, would have lain. Unlike their successors in exploration, they were not to experience the uncertainties of co-existence with indigenous claimants to the territory. The information that they gave on their return to Greenland enabled Thorvald to duplicate the voyage, proved a will-o'-the-wisp to Thorstein, a tough row to hoe for Karlsefni and a perennial challenge to navigators and bookworms. If the explorers left any artifacts, these have long since returned to the elements. Supposing, in a moment of harsh skepticism, that no grandson of Norway, no son of Iceland, no unmarried and adventurous resident of Greenland would have been likely to stumble on a land of grapes in North America, we should then have to inquire into the rationale for Karlsefni's subsequent and complicated expedition in search of Vínland. It, or its facsimile, did after all take place.

Thorvald finds Vínland

The voyage undertaken in the *Greenlanders' Saga* by Thorvald Eriksson sounds historical, and it is quite possible that, as the saga assures us, Thorvald actually found his brother's houses, guided by such an unmistakable landmark as Grand Manan Island. Leif was willing to lend his houses, but not to convey title to his legal property under their concept of law. Through the centuries one can sense Leif's reluctance to abandon a dream of one day returning to the scene of his early exploit. But according to the saga, his father Erik had died the winter following Leif's voyage, and Leif was now entered upon the responsibilities of a chieftain. He was fated never to return to his claim. Thorvald, once arrived in Vínland, devoted two summers to sailing north and south of Leif's houses, perhaps assuming that Vínland was one more island that could be sailed around. Sailing east, then northward in the Bay of Fundy, the party landed on the west coast of Nova Scotia, and soon they had an encounter with the natives. Their only intimation of inhabitants previous to that had been somewhere to the south of Leif's houses, where they were disturbed to find a grain-stack or protective covering for grain. In the physical encounter Thorvald was mortally wounded by an Indian arrow. At his request his men buried him on the headland with Christian crosses at his head and feet, naming this spot Krossanes ('Headland of Crosses'). Reman suggests that Krossanes lies towards the northern end of the Bay of Fundy. The site that Leif had chosen was not exactly ideal, lacking as it did secure harborage, and with no possibility of the dredging that is possible today. Thorvald had kept looking east, and on the western shore of Nova Scotia, facing New Brunswick, Reman finds the heavily wooded headland jutting out between the two fjord mouths – mentioned in the saga – Minas Channel and Chignecto Bay. At this spot Thorvald must have made his famous remark, 'Here I should like to make my home.' In the event, he was not called upon to leave it.

Ethnologists have held various opinions regarding the identity of the natives encountered by the Greenlanders on the North American mainland and its islands. Both Eskimos and Indians have during various periods inhabited northern Newfoundland. Indians of the Algonkian group apparently were making seasonal visits to the area around L'Anse aux Meadows at the time we must assume for early Norse habitation there. One has the impression that the attack on Karlsefni's company, whether it took place at Leifsbúdir (*Greenlanders' Saga*) or at L'Anse aux Meadows/Straumfjord (*Erik's Saga*), was by Indians rather than Eskimos. The ballista referred to in *Erik's Saga* is evidently based on tradition of which the *Greenlander's Saga* had also retained a trace in the form of the great crash that so frightened the explorers. This was some such object as a boulder or large leather ball filled with things that would produce noise, likewise projected by means of a catapult. The corn stack was certainly Indian. The natives who attacked Karlsefni are portrayed in the *Greenlanders' Saga* as coming out of the woods and fleeing back to the woods, and no boats are mentioned, whereas that same incident in *Erik's Saga* depicts them as coming in hide boats. The natives who in the *Greenlanders' Saga* attack Thorvald's company and fatally wound him with an arrow have also come in hide boats and are evidently accustomed, when on expeditions, to sleeping under them 'three men to a boat.' These do not sound like kayaks. But why are they described in both sagas as *hide* boats if, as one is usually told, American Indians usually paddled dugouts or birchbark canoes? The Greenlanders probably had lost their ancestral memory of the cowhide boats that, back in Scandinavia centuries before, had foreshadowed the thin-planked Viking ship. But their observation in this case was doubtless correct. And the answer is not too far to seek.

The ancient Indians of northern and central Maine and Nova Scotia, precisely the areas that we are concerned with, employed *moose-hide* boats, a practice that persisted into the 20th century.[9] That fact should have confirmatory relevance to the story related in the *Greenlanders' Saga*. As to the hide boats mentioned in *Erik's Saga*, they are either a genuine reminiscence of some actual experience in Maine or Nova Scotia, or, once again, a detail borrowed from the *Greenlanders' Saga* by the author of *Erik's Saga*.

It is an irony of literary history that in those points at which the Vínland tradition is comparatively logical and clear, it cannot be confirmed through concrete physical evidence, and that where it is at its vaguest and most confused (the account in *Erik's Saga* of Karlsefni's wanderings), there are physical remains to prop it up (as at L'Anse aux Meadows). Without the evidence provided by archaeology the very existence of the Greenland colonies might still be doubted, and their offshoot, the Vínland voyages, often have been. In numerous quarters, a New England location for Leif's settlement is doubted still. We shall have to leave it at that.

The end and the beginning

In Chapter 1 we gave details concerning Norse artifacts retrieved from Arctic Canada, some of these matching similar finds from northeastern Greenland. The items include pot fragments, bits of a shirt of mail, various pieces of smelted iron and copper – the Eskimos used meteoric iron but lacked the art of smelting – ships' rivets, chisels, knife-blades, a carpenter's plane of wood with the blade removed, a piece of oak reworked by Eskimos, bottom sections of wooden casks, part of a chair, and bits of woollen cloth. Also found were a couple of figurines, one carved in wood, the other in walrus ivory, both seeming to represent the Eskimo impression of a Norseman. Norse cairns have been found, along with cairns, or ruins of cairns, that cannot with certainty be culturally identified. Then, too, there is the Kingiqtorsoaq runic inscription, now preserved in Copenhagen, the world's most northerly record in a Scandinavian language.

If financial and human resources are available, there is small doubt that discoveries will continue to be made. The Arctic Institute of North America at the University of Calgary in Alberta is currently preparing a two-volume report on finds which span over four thousand years of prehistoric activities in the Ellesmere Island area. It is in the nature of things that the great bulk of material derives from native inhabitants, the Dorset and Thule Eskimos and their ancestors, but there are dozens of scattered finds that indicate Norse influence from as early as the 12th century in northwestern Greenland and the regions to the west of it.[1] Though some items claimed as Norse have unfortunately disappeared, like the two stone cairns reported from Washington Irving Island ($79°$ N. lat.) over a century ago by Captain, Sir George Nares[2] enough has turned up to warrant a surmise that some structures, such as bear and fox traps and eider-duck shelters, reflect cultural influence from the Norse, despite some small suspicion that the last-named, at least those around Ungava Bay, may have been introduced to the Eskimos by later Moravian missionaries. It has been argued that the

92 Prow of the Oseberg burial ship.

Eskimos, though having no use themselves for eider-down, could nevertheless learn to use it in trade. An alternate proposal is that such structures are slab-box hearths of a type known for between two and four thousand years.

We saw in Chapter 1 that many of the Norse or Norse-influenced items have been picked up very far north, particularly from the east coast of Ellesmere Island facing across Kane Basin towards northern Greenland, with the majority from the areas of Bache Peninsula. Knud Peninsula and tiny Skraeling Island are the site of Thule culture winter houses in which a great deal of such material has turned up. Skraeling Island lies just north of Alexandra Fjord (79° N. lat.), at the south side of Buchanan Bay. A natural question is whether these articles, or some of them, were dropped by, or taken from, Norsemen near the locations in which they are found; or were some acquired as gifts or in trade directly with Norsemen at those locations or at a greater distance; or are the finds the result of inter-tribal trading? In that last case, articles can have traveled a considerable distance. What we are asking is, in effect, how reliably can the Norsemen be placed in these high latitudes?

Concerning the carpenter's plane, Schledermann points out that it could not have traveled very far as an item of trade. The useful iron blade removed, it had been thrown out of an Eskimo winter house ruin as an article of no value. The bits of wool cloth, found together with discarded scraps of leather cut off from items of clothing, support the idea of direct contact in the Smith Sound/Baffin Bay area.[3] The fact that only one of a dozen ships' nails found had been reworked indicates that they had not been long in the Eskimo owner's possession. The chain mail rings are quite similar to items found by Holtved forty years earlier in the vicinity of Thule, Greenland. These would have struck the natives as mere curiosities without real value. The Eskimos have left a surprising amount of iron objects in their dwellings, but iron was not unique among them. The Canadian snows are strewn with meteoric iron, and the Eskimos had been working it for centuries, the art of iron-working having come with their ancestors from Siberia. They extracted the iron by hammering it and were unacquainted with the smelting process. McCartney has reported pieces of iron of probably Norse origin on the west coast of Hudson Bay (Silimiut).[4] In view of Reman's extraordinary theory (which I do not accept) concerning such a general location for Karlsefni's Straumfjord and Hóp,[5] the McCartney find is startling but not proof of Norse visits, much less residence. Concerning it, Schledermann states: 'The iron from the west coast of Hudson Bay is not too unusual, iron was a good commodity for trade and could have found its way southward from the Smith Sound area.'[6] It is amusing to think of Norse objects that had gone so far north, now coming south! But that is the unpredictable nature of trade. For that matter, Schledermann would not be at all astonished if the Norsemen had made landfall on the shores of Ungava Bay, and agrees that the Payne Lake structures present unsolved puzzles. If T. Lee's stone 'causeway' and 'Thor's hammer' actually are Eskimo after all, there is certainly a great deal about their culture that has eluded outsiders to date. A suggestion has been made that the houses at Payne Lake were merely unroofed structures for Eskimo ceremonial purposes, or as side-wall protection within which individual family tents were erected. On the face of it, either of those suggestions sounds reasonable enough. The fragment of an axe found by Lee at Ungava is consistent with origin either as an ancient Norse tool or as a European trading axe of the eighteenth or nineteenth century, and one suspects that there would have been rather more of the latter than of the former.

Fragments of Norse iron and a cast bronze bowl have been found at Port Refuge on Devon Island. In an Eskimo house on the south side of Baffin Island, D. and G. Sabo found the very European figurine in wood that has already been mentioned. It must have been carved locally, inasmuch as the manner of carving is not that of the Greenland Eskimos.[7] According to McGhee, this indicates immediate contact between Norse and Eskimos, doubtless impelled by the Norse need for ivory. Though more occasional than systematic, this trade must have been much more frequent and wide-ranging than ever recorded. Most interesting of all the Norse items found was a portion of a folding balance, of the type used by traders to weigh merchandise. This find was reported by P. Sutherland from an Eskimo tenting spot on the west coast of Ellesmere Island. The east coast of Cumberland Peninsula has never been investigated by professional archaeologists. Being the first landing spot encountered as one crosses Davis Strait from Greenland, it would be likely to contain evidence of Norse activity.

To the Arctic ethnologist, the fleeting Norse influence is just a minute part of a fascinating perspective on forty-three centuries of brilliant human adaptation to the challenge of ice and snow. But far from inconsequential to the student of history who has followed the trail of Viking warrior-merchants and explorers from western Europe to Turkey, from the Caspian Sea to the White Sea and from Iceland to an uncertain fate in the Newest World of All, is the notion of finding their traces in a land of the musk-ox at 79° N. lat., far west and 500 miles north of the Kingiqtorsoaq rune stone that once served as their northernmost monument. Roving members of a stationary population must have roamed the fringes of a vast continent along 35° or more of latitude, covering several times the mileage that a straight air flight would entail. They failed to colonize it. As Einar Haugen phrases it, 'in the year 1000 Europe was not ready to discover America.' Hundreds of years later, large and powerful nations with ambitious centralized governments, confident church establishments, the great wealth which breeds a demand for ever greater wealth, found that task laborious enough, attempt after attempt ending in starvation and disaster. Unlike the French and English – Ribaut, Cartier, Roberval, White – Karlsefni and his associates soon learned to cope with hunger. What alone their slender numbers could not cope with was the challenge of a much greater native population. And so, not driven onward by tyranny, religious persecution, political ambition or the greed for wealth, they licked their wounds and quietly withdrew. To the geographers and mapmakers of a later world they bequeathed the Skraelings and the legacy of a pair of place names which were eagerly utilized by 16th-century European cartographers. These are Markland, the region of great forests, and Promontorium Winlandiae, this last an inexpert but recognizable depiction of northern Newfoundland.[8]

Norse Greenland falters

And of the Eastern and Western Norse Settlements in Greenland, what? That so small a population could endure in one form or another for half a millennium without appreciable renewal and despite the weakness, ineptitude and neglect of its nominal superiors in Europe, is almost a miracle. These superiors were both civil and clerical. Despite occasional bursts of ambition or stirrings of conscience in Copenhagen and Rome, Norse life in Greenland was ultimately victimized by the economic and political problems of the Dano-Norwegian monarchy, and not until the time of Hans Egede beginning in 1721 was Greenland re-colonialized and made a practical subject of administrative solicitude. As to the Church in Rome, it

93–101 Northern garments typical of what has so far been recovered from Greenland soil (these are all from Herjólfsnes).

93 (*far left*) Woman's dress.

94 (*top left*) Burgundian cap.

95 (*top right*) Hood.

96 (*left*) Girl's costume.

97, 98 (*below left*) Two men's coats.

99–101 Stockings.

winked at the ambitions of prelates who, one after another, accepted the pleasant-sounding but empty title of 'Bishop of Gardar' with no intention whatever of visiting their nominal diocese. With never a bishop to ordain their priests and consecrate their churches, the chain of religious legitimacy was broken, and no ceremony, whether of baptism, marriage or burial was strictly valid. Indeed, it was sacrilegious and one of the Seven Deadly Sins. Of all the trouble that might and did oppress a medieval people living under the Arctic circle, that all-pervading insecurity must have been the most grievous of all.

The more northerly of the two settlements, Vestribygd, was considered 'deserted' by 1364 at the latest, and in 1379 eighteen men were reported slain by the Eskimos. Bishop Alf, the last resident bishop, died in 1377. The royal trading vessel, periodically – though not the once promised 'every second year' – sent out from Bergen had foundered in 1369. Though the crew was saved, the ship was not replaced. The southerly colony, Eystribygd, continued, and a wedding is reported by a visitor for the year 1409, conducted for want of a priest by a lay *officialis*. The northern hunting grounds were now blocked off by the Eskimos, moving south for the ice hunting as the Arctic chill crept down the coast. Stock-breeding was more and more difficult as the animals, less hardy than humans, became emaciated and weak, so that the colonists grew more and more dependent upon the seal for sustenance. No fewer than half the bone remnants preserved at Brattahlid (Quagssiarssuk) are seal bones.

What became of the Norse Greenlanders in the end?[9] Many theories have been launched to account, in whole or in part, for their disappearance. Half a century ago it was believed that they had probably died of disease or malnutrition. Medical examination of human skeletons seemed to indicate severe malnutrition, shortened stature and reduced brain capacity.[10] Those findings are now discounted by the archaeopathologists. The fertility of the Greenlanders must have declined markedly, but there was neither starvation nor mass illness in the picture. Nor was their economy crushed by a temporary plague of the moth *Agrotis occulta*, as sometimes posited. There is evidence that life may have continued at Herjólfsnes (Ikigait) until 1480, and an Icelandic visitor to Greenland reports – one does not know whether to believe it – that as late as 1540 he had seen a dead Norseman on the beach, final survivor of a farmstead inside an unidentified fjord.[11]

102 Battle between Eskimos and Norsemen, as narrated in Eskimo legend.

Some writers believe that the Norse were driven out to an uncertain fate on the sea, where they likely perished, for they were no longer expert navigators, these farmer-hunters, and their available shipping was poor. Some think they managed to emigrate to Canada, or Minnesota, where they turned into natives or died out, as you prefer. Nothing in Greenland, by the way, indicates amalgamation of the races. Preserved skulls in the Norse graveyards are clearly differentiated as Norse. Steinert motivates a shocking conclusion: the whites were relentlessly massacred by the Eskimos, fjord district by fjord district from north to south.[12] That was certainly part of it, but only part. Eskimo legends preserved until recent times tend to confirm what reason tells us must have been the case, namely, that relations between the two cultures were alternately good and bad. Trade between the the two races was clearly of great mutual benefit. Occasionally whipped up by their local *angakoq* or shaman, the Eskimos would recall the wrongs suffered at Norse hands and conduct a bloody raid. There were times when the Norse treated Eskimos with hair-raising callousness. On other occasions, the two could indulge in reciprocal altruism, illustrating the virtues of symbiosis at its best. The Eskimos were on the whole somewhat fearful of the Norse, and with exceptions, preferred to keep a safe distance between their respective dwelling areas, the Eskimos living by choice on the coastal rim and at the mouths of fjords, the Norse at the heads of fjords. There were dark times, never fully clarified, during which one race sheltered individuals or whole groups attacked by 'foreigners' never satisfactorily identified but apparently European pirates of one or several nationalities.

We know that there were kidnappings, in an age when piracy was commonplace. Some Greenlanders were kidnapped by the English, and released only after a sharp protest from Copenhagen. But there was, I believe, a greater danger from another source: the Basques. According to their own subsequent claims, the latter had been sailing in these waters since at least 1372. Basque whaling gradually reached large proportions, and as late as the 16th century they maintained a considerable factory for the processing of whale blubber on the shores of Red Bay, Labrador, at the entrance to the St Lawrence.[13] Raiding the Greenland colonies for pillage, the Basques could easily have disposed of dead bodies by tossing them into the nearest fjord. No telltale indications of general slaughter have been found on land, and apart from certain orally preserved legends among the Eskimos, the interpretation of which is far from clear, there is naturally enough no record of the matter. Always secretive about their routes and their fishing grounds, the marauders would certainly have kept quiet about such deeds.

Despite conflicting theories and assertions, there is inadequate documentation of any single factor behind the disappearance of the white Greenlanders. Pending future discoveries, it seems most rational to assume that the underlying causes were multiple and reciprocally reinforcing. I propose, therefore, that there was a conjunction of debilitating forces, environmental (the waxing cold), economic (increasing denudation of the soil, the wasting away of their cattle and their few crops, the dwindling supply of fuel, the pressing competition with the Eskimos for marine game), physiological (a gradual reduction in the birth rate) and spiritual (religious deprivation and the lack of cultural stimulus). Assimilation, cultural and biological, by the Eskimos would certainly have preserved the Norsemen as members of a mixed race. Inasmuch as neither artifacts nor preserved skeletal remains give the slightest indication of such an amalgamation, one must conclude that it did not take place to any appreciable extent. Psychological barriers between the two races must have been too strong.

It seems likely that enterprising individuals on occasion found a way to emigrate, since, piracy apart, there is some spotty evidence for commercial visits by foreign ships. These would usually be of an illegal nature because of the theoretical monopoly whose privileges continued to be asserted from

Bergen and Copenhagen. It is believed that some colonists were actually able to purchase passage to Iceland, to Norway or even to England.

That the surprisingly long-lived and tenacious little Norse civilization west of Iceland came to its unheralded end around the year 1500, give or take a few years, should not be allowed to obscure the obvious fact that, enfeebled and outnumbered, Norse institutions would have been absorbed quite rapidly into any major attempt at colonization by England or a Continental power. None such was attempted. The Great Age of Exploration was about to begin, but there is no European nation whose people would have been competent to replace the Norsemen as colonial Greenlanders. In terms of western civilization there was a hiatus that lasted several hundred years, but that hiatus was by no means a vacuum. The Inuit or Eskimos resumed their heritage and remain in Greenland today. The mixture with Scandinavians that evidently did not take place in the Middle Ages is now a fact of life in Greenland, whose inhabitants, Danish, Inuit, or mixed, are happy to consider themselves Greenlanders.

103 The dead Norseman. Eskimo legend.

Notes

Chapter 1

1 See in Select Bibliography under 'Works on Greenland.' Photographs in Thorén, *Picture Atlas.*
2 Cf Oleson, *Early Voyages,* pp. 75–6. Various writers express varying opinions on this expedition. For discussions of the Greenland colonists during this period, see esp. Gad, *Greenland,* Chap. 4. On the Church see H. Ingstad, *Land,* Chap. XXI.
3 Cf Gad, pp. 146ff., 138ff.
4 Cf Select Bibliography under 'Translations.' For a variety of reasons, the most satisfactory presentation of the Vínland sagas in English dress is that published in 1960 by M. Magnusson and H. Pálsson.
5 Gad, pp. 137–8, Jones, *Norse Atlantic Saga,* p. 49, Thalbitzer, *Two Runic Stones,* Wahlgren, *Kensington,* p. 200.
6 Danish sovereignty was reasserted in 1721; see under Bobé.
7 The Kingiqtorsoaq stone is on exhibit at Copenhagen's Nationalmuseet.
8 He and his father thought they resembled seals. Bobé, p. 48.
9 McGhee, 'Contact.'
10 The term 'Dorset' refers to an early Eskimo culture named after Cape Dorset, the southern tip of Foxe Island, which dips into the Hudson Strait; cf Gad, *Greenland,* p. 15. Extensive discussions of the Eskimos, with distribution charts, will be found in Gad, *passim,* as well as in Oleson, *Northern Voyages.* The latter's views are unfortunately affected by his feeling that the Norsemen blended with the Eskimos.
11 Holtved, 'Archaeological Investigations'; comment in Schledermann, 'Notes.'
12 Schledermann, 'Notes,' and 'Nordbogenstande.' The oak was found by Eigil Knuth.
13 Ibid., together with 'Eskimo and Viking' in *Nat. Geographic.*
14 Ibid.
15 Schledermann, 'Nordbogenstande,' pp. 222–3.
16 Ad. Jensen, 'Concerning a change of climate.'
17 See in Steinert, *Tausend Jahre,* his index under *Kleine Eiszeit,* and *Klima.* Differing opinion in H. Ingstad, *Land,* pp. 299ff. See in A. S. Ingstad, index under 'Climate.' From the discussion there it would appear that the climate worsened during the later Middle Ages but is now warming to what it probably was when Greenland was settled.
18 Compare the long house of the Sandnes Farm with the passage house and the intermediate structure, after rebuilding, at Brattahlid (sketches in Gad, p. 36, p. 72, p. 43).
19 Steinert, p. 234.
20 Steinert, pp. 235–6.
21 Ibid. Few scholars would estimate the population at higher than 5000. I think that is somewhat on the high side.

22 The reader is referred to the Select Bibliography, under 'Saga Translations' and 'Representative Literary Works.' It would be advantageous to read the translation of the two short Vínland sagas by Magnusson and Pálsson, together with their excellent Introduction.
23 Nansen, *In Northern Mists.*
24 See under Jaubert, p. 346.
25 At Barrow and several other locations in Alaska.
26 Linklater, *Ultimate Viking,* p. 10.

Chapter 2

1 Cf Select Bibliography, under 'Vikings.'
2 Alcuin, 735–804, English humanist, educated in the cathedral school at York. Invited by Charlemagne *c.* 781 he became the leading figure of the Carolingian renaissance.
3 See in Select Bibliography.
4 See in particular W. Douglas Simpson, 'The Broch of Clickhimin,' in *The Viking Congress* (of 1950), Edinburgh, 1954, pp. 19–35; and B. H. St. J. O'Neil, 'The Date and Purpose of the Brochs,' pp. 46–52 of the same volume.
5 Nestor was a monk of Kiev *c.* 1070–1115. The chronicle attributed to him is an account of Russia's history from ancient times. N. gives many descriptions of the *Rus,* whom he regarded largely as intruders. Written in the French cloister of St Bertin, the *Annales Bertiniani* are the first written source to use the word *Rus.*
6 Best known of these is Ibn Fadlàn, who in 922 described the *Rus* (Swedes) on the Volga. Cf extract translated in Leach, *Pageant,* pp. 299–301. Other early Arabs who described the *Rus* are Ibn Khordadbeh or Horradadbeh (9th century), Ibn Rustah (early 10th century) and Ibn Miskawayh (died in 1030).
7 Fritz Askeberg, *Norden och kontinenten i gammal tid,* Uppsala, 1944. On the word for 'Viking' see pp. 115ff. See also the etymological dictionaries in Select Bibliography.
8 Ibid.

Chapter 3

1 The quotation is from Brøndsted, *The Vikings,* p. 139.
2 See Brøgger/Shetelig, *The Viking Ships.*
3 Ibid., pp. 130ff. Still extant in Chicago's Lincoln Park, the ship is now being repaired.
4 See in Select Bibliography under Olsen/Crumlin-Pedersen, *Five Viking Ships.*
5 Hedeby (*Haithabu*) was an important, fortified Viking center.
6 The Bayeux tapestry is an approximately 230-foot strip of embroidered linen that depicts the famous struggle over the English crown between William the Conqueror and Harald of England, concluding with Harald's death at Hasting in 1066. The tapestry, believed to have been commissioned by William's half-brother, Bishop Odo of Bayeux, is an important source of our knowledge concerning Norman military equipment and technique.
7 See Graham-Campbell, *Viking World,* p. 42. A

splendid account of the ships and the Viking art of shipbuilding, including a visual glossary, is found in Graham-Campbell, pp. 38–63. On the ship of Sutton Hoo see also Brøndsted, *Vikings*, pp. 18–19.

8 Photographs in Graham-Campbell, pp. 19, 172–3.

9 On weapons, see especially Brøndsted, *Vikings*, Chap. 6; Graham-Campbell, pp. 24–5. On clothing, Brøndsted, Chap. 7; Graham-Campbell, pp. 114ff.

10 Depicted in numerous works on runes, these are most clearly represented in the *Atlas* (= Vol. 1) of Jacobsen/Moltke, *Danmarks Runeindskrifter*, pp. 12–16.

11 Defined by S. Einarsson as 'compound circumlocutions,' kennings, or substitute ways of referring to things (metonymy) are discussed by Einarsson, *Icelandic Literature*, under the reference word *kenning(ar)*. See also Hollander, *Skalds*.

12 Ibid.

13 Brøndsted, pp. 132–3.

14 See in Select Bibliography under 'Runic collections.'

15 A notable exception to test the rule is the rune-written *codex runicus* known as the *Law of Skåne*, a Danish exertion from about 1300 and an early example of court-sponsored antiquarianism. Cf Haugen, *Scandinavian Languages*, p. 194. Runic antiquarianism was cultivated in the monasteries of England, and a number of manuscripts are preserved; see under Elliott, *Runes* and Page, *Introduction*.

16 Some so-called rune-staves (*runstavar*) seem to have been in use as calendrical aids in parts of rural Sweden down to this century. An excellent depiction of an example from Dalarna is found in S. F. B. Jansson, *Runes of Sweden*, p. 166; see also Brate's handbook, *Sveriges runinskrifter*, p. 102.

17 All things considered, the number is surprising. See Haugen, *Scand. langs.*, p. 194. Greenlandic runes are discussed in *Greenland Runic Inscriptions* I–IV as follows: I: Finnur Jónsson, 'Grønlandske runestene,' *Det Grønlandske Selskabs Aarsskrift*, 1916, pp. 63–6; II: Jónsson, 'Interpretations of the Runic Inscriptions from Herjolfsnes,' *Meddelelser om Grønland*, LXVII (1924), 273–90; III: Jónsson, 'Rune Inscriptions from Gardar,' *MoG*, LXVII, 1929 (1930), 171–9; IV: Erik Moltke, 'Greenland Runic Inscriptions,' *MoG*, 88 (1936), pp. 222–32, with plates following.

18 That is discussed in Chap. 6 of the present work. See also in Select Bibliography under 'Kensington.'

19 See R. A. Hall, *Jorvik*; see text and pictures from York and Dublin, Graham-Campbell, pp. 99–100.

20 *Saga of Eigil Skallagrimsson*, chaps. 55–61.

21 Icelandic text from Gordon, *Introduction*, p. 114, lines 183–6. Variant translations in the edition by Gwyn Jones (Select Bibliography under 'Saga Translations') and by Pálsson/Edwards, *Egil's Saga*, New York, 1976.

22 Hall, *Jorvik*, p. 21.

23 Hall, *Jorvik*, p. 17.

24 See in particular the beautifully illustrated work *Scandinavian Mythology* by H. R. Ellis Davidson; Turville-Petre, *Myth and Religion*.

25 Stanza 77 of Eddic poem *Hávamál*; see in Select Bibliography under *Edda*.

26 The Roman historian Tacitus (AD 55–117) was the first to record the antics of Germanic berserks in battle, in his *De origine et situ Germanorum*, commonly referred to as *Germania*. The phenomenon of the gun-happy returned war veteran is known in our day.

27 Linklater, *Ultimate Viking*, p. 109.

28 *Not* the spouse of Erik Blood-Axe.

29 Quoted from Graham-Campbell, p. 26.

30 Quoted from Graham-Campbell, p. 31.

31 Quoted from Marvin L. Colker, 'America Rediscovered in the Thirteenth Century?' *Speculum. A Journal of Medieval Studies*, LIV, no. 4 (Oct. 1979), 712–26, p. 712.

Chapter 4

1 Dicuil, *Liber*, cf Select Bibliography under 'Various Topics.' *Landnámabók* ('Book of the Settlers') and *Íslendingabók* ('Book of the Icelanders') are both well discussed by Einarsson, *Icelandic Literature*. On the latter work see also in Select Bibliography under Ári and under Hermannsson in section 'Basic Texts'.

2 Excellent account of this in Jones, *Norse Atlantic*, pp. 16 ff.

3 Ibid.

4 See the story of Gardar's son Uni, Jones, pp. 129–30.

5 Iceland was brought under Norway in 1262. Suggested reading is Knut Gjerset, *History of Iceland*, New York, 1924.

6 Jones, p. 17.

7 It would be more accurate to say that Norwegian traveled the farthest from the once common language.

8 Jones, p. 19.

9 Narrated in *Kristnisaga* (cf Einarsson), XII, 14, *Íslendingabók*, VII, see Hermannsson's edition in *Islandica*, XX.

10 There was a branch of saga literature called the *lygisaga* (pl. *lygisögur*). On this see Einarsson; Gordon, p. 150; Margaret Schlauch, *Romance in Iceland*, New York, 1934.

11 This is the *Saga of Burnt Njál*, particularly Chaps. 128–30.

12 Bergthora was fifteen at the time of her marriage to Njál.

13 These three scenes are translated in Leach, *Pageant*, on, respectively, pp. 251, 235, 241–2. Cf Hollander, *Heimskringla*.

14 Cf Olesen, *Early Voyages*, p. 29.

15 Translated from Book IV, Chap 38 of *Adami Gesta*. . . . Cf text in Hermannsson, *Islandica*, XXV; Wahlgren, 'Fact and Fancy,' p. 47.

16 From Ári's *Íslendingabók*, Chap. VI, see in Hermannsson, *Islandica*, XX, text p. 52.

17 Narrated in *Landnámabók*, cf Jones, *Norse Atlantic*, pp. 128–9.

Chapter 5

1 Though it was known since 1794 that the Eastern Settlement was not located on the east coast of Greenland, the distinguished explorer Adolf Erik Nordensköld (1832–1901) of Finland and Sweden tried as late as 1883 to find it there.

2 Excellent accounts of early Greenlandic conditions are found in H. Ingstad (*Land*), whose descriptions are almost lyrical, and Gad, *History of Greenland*.

3 Select Bibliography, 'Works on Greenland.'

4 These are *Atlakvida in groenlenzka* and *Atlamál in groenlenzko* (Neckel, *Edda*, 234–41 and 242–57; Bellows, *Edda*, 'The Greenland Lay of Atli,' pp. 480–98, and 'The Greenland Ballad of Atli,' pp. 499–540. They appear to be of late (11th-century) composition, and to reveal an attempt to adapt the heroic-legendary material to the tastes of a Greenland audience.

5 *Einars Tháttr Sokkasonar* and *Flóamanna saga* are among the sagas in this category. A character in *Grettir's Saga* is Thórhall Gamlason, called *vínlendingr* ('the Winelander'), who is mentioned as a companion of Karlsefni in *Erik's Saga*. *The Tale of Tósti*, the *Saga of Gisli*, and *Eyredwellers' Saga* are likewise tangential to Greenland.

6 Note the necessary inconsistency between the spellings of the woman's name. I use 'Thjódhild', but Father Wolfe's article in *ASR* uses an *eth* for the 'd' and no acute accent on the 'o'! On Thjódhild's little church, see 'Thjódhild's Church,' *American–Scandinavian Review*, LI, No. 1 (March, 1963), 55–66, by Michael Wolfe, OMI, the only Catholic missionary priest in Greenland. It is not certain now that the little church actually was Thjódhild's chapel as mentioned in *Greenlanders' Saga*.

7 Corroborative details in Wahlgren, 'Fact and Fancy,' pp. 61ff. The Icelandic scholar Björn Thorsteinsson doubts the existence of a Vínland, cf Select Bibliography under 'Largely Relating to Vínland'.

8 Wahlgren, 'Fact and Fancy,' pp. 40ff.

9 Ibid., pp. 42ff.

10 On the spelling of Vínland, see the comment in the Preface to this volume.

11 H. Bessason in *Mosaic*, 1967.

12 The incident of the whale need not be total fiction, for we know from the sagas that Icelanders were occasionally poisoned by the flesh of a stranded whale. Though cetacean pathology is still not fully understood, it is likely that the disorientation of beaching whales is sometimes the result of disease.

13 Cf Wahlgren, 'Fact and Fancy,' pp. 68–9, 74.

14 On the printed catalog, see Select Bibliography. The catalog lists the manuscripts under *Eiríks saga rauda* and *Groenlendinga Tháttr*.

15 On this cf Wahlgren, 'Fact and Fancy,' p. 68.

16 This quotation from an Icelandic geographical treatise dated to about 1300 is taken from p. 15 of the Introduction to the Magnusson-Pálsson translation of the *Vinland Sagas*.

Chapter 6

1 The review in question will be found in *Scandinavian Studies*, XXII (November, 1950), 187–8.

2 Quoted from Wahlgren, *Kensington Stone*, p. 5.

3 Ibid.

4 Thalbitzer, *Two Runic Stones*.

5 Wahlgren, *Kensington Stone*, pp. 31–47.

6 Wahlgren, *Kensington Stone*, p. 3. AVM clearly stands for *Ave Maria* ('Hail, Mary'), and inasmuch as Olof Ohman's preserved scrapbook reveals his preoccupation with Theosophy and Eastern religions in general, the AVM may likewise indicate his interest in the secret syllable OM, of which AUM (the U rendered by V in the inscription) is an acceptable 'analytic' rendering.

7 Wahlgren, p. 64, cf pp. 59–69.

8 See photographs in Wahlgren, following p. 82.

9 Wahlgren, p. 183.

10 Page, Review of Robert A. Hall Jr., *The Kensington Rune-Stone Is Genuine* in *Speculum*, 58, no. 3 (July, 1983), 748–51.

11 See William S. Godfrey, 'Vikings in America: Theories and Evidence,' *American Anthropologist*, LVII (Feb. 1955), 35–43.

12 The skeleton that set Longfellow off was Indian, the armor was comprised of ornamental copper medallions, acquired in trade through exchanges with Indians of the Midwest who used copper.

13 See Select Bibliography.

14 See the discussion of this in M. Kaups, 'Observations,' 1970.

15 Wahlgren, *Kensington*, pp. 157–8.

16 Ibid., p. 158.

17 Wallace, 'Points of Controversy,' p. 161.

18 Liestøl in *Minnesota History*, 1968; Page in *Scandinavica*, 1968 (see Select Bibliography).

19 Karlgren in *Scandinavian Studies*, 1967; Kahn in *American–Scandinavian Review*, 1967 (see Select Bibliography).

20 McKusick/Wahlgren, *Biblical Archaeology Review*, 1980; Wahlgren, 'American Runes,' *JEGP*, 1982.

21 Gould on Agrell, *Modern Language Notes*, 1930.

22 Wahlgren, *Kensington*, pp. 70–80, 193–4.

23 Note bibliography in McKusick/Wahlgren, 'Norse Penny Mystery,' 1980.

24 I have personally seen several of these 'mooring holes' in Minnesota – on high ground.

25 Article by Daniel Olson in (Sons of Norway) *Viking* (Oct., 1984), pp. 316–19.

26 I was offered, and accepted, a free review copy sent to a Los Angeles television station, in return for reviewing it over the air with two weeks' notice. Select Bibliography: Skelton.

27 Select Bibliography, Washburn (ed.), *Proceedings*. See 'A $1 Million Forgery?' in *Time*, 4 February 1974, p. 21.

28 *Proceedings*, pp. 134–5.

29 Account in Gösta Holm, 'Nordbor i Amerika före Columbus. Äkta fynd och falska,' *Gardar*, XII (1981), 38–47.

30 Einarsson, *Icelandic Literature*, p. 185.

31 Michlovic/Hughey, 1982.

32 Sherwin, *Viking and Red Man*.

33 Strandwold, *Norse Inscriptions*, p. 28.

34 Wahlgren, 'American Runes,' is mainly devoted to Spirit Pond. See also Haugen, 'Spirit Pond.' Also under Whittall.

35 Zoëga, see under 'Dictionaries.'

36 On Tifinag, see editorial by Glyn Daniel in *Antiquity*, LVIII, no. 221 (March, 1984).

Chapter 7

1 Storm, 'Vinlandsreiserne,' (1887).

2 On Magnus Andersen's voyage see Brøgger/Shetelig, *Viking Ships*, pp. 141ff. It should be pointed out that the Gokstad ship, in a replica of which Andersen sailed, was not a *knörr* or cargo vessel.

3 Tanner, see Select Bibliography.

4 Reman, *Norse Discoveries*, pp. 118ff.

5 Previous publications by the present writer have not attempted to localize Leif's Vínland other than as being somewhere in New England.

6 Originally published as *Landet under Leidarstjernen*, 1960.

7 A. S. Ingstad, *Discovery of a Norse Settlement*, p. 25. A companion volume by Helge Ingstad is projected to furnish historical commentary to supplement the archaeological and scientific contributions that make up the first part. Authors of special treatises in Vol. I beside editor Ingstad herself are Rolf Petré, the late Kristján Eldjárn, Charles J. Bareis and Jon H. Winston, Arne Emil Christensen Jr, Karl E. Henningsmoen, Reidar Nydal, Leif M. Paulsen and Anna M. Rosenqvist. The book is a thoroughly professional account of the work of excavation and subsequent analysis, with detailed site sketches, tables, charts, maps and photographs including some in color. The special subjects include pollen analysis, radio-carbon dating, identification of charcoal finds, and a study of iron objects, slag and ore.

8 A. S. Ingstad, pp. 327ff.

9 A. S. Ingstad, pp. 195–6.

10 See Gad, Greenland, pp. 77–8. The nomenclature derives from Aage Roussell.

11 H. Bessason, *Icelandic Canadian*, 1965, p. 19, thinks this; Wahlgren, 'Fact and Fancy,' is skeptical. The natural scientist is Reidar Nydal in A. S. Ingstad, *Discovery*, p. 355.

12 Henningsmoen in *Discovery*, p. 293.

13 Henningsmoen, p. 295.

14 McGhee, 'Contact,' pp. 8–9.

15 A. S. Ingstad, *Discovery*, p. 230.

16 *Discovery*, 229–30.

17 *Discovery*, p. 232.

18 Suggestions in McGhee, 'Contact,' pp. 18–19.

19 See in *Scandinavian Studies*, 1965, pp. 377–80.

20 For a translation of this famous story, see Gwyn Jones, *Eirik the Red*, pp. 163–70.

Chapter 8

1 Söderberg, 'Vinland.' See Select Bibliography under 'Largely relating to Vinland.'

2 Haugen in *Proceedings of the Eighth Viking Congress* (1977), Odense, 1981, pp. 3–8.

3 Holm in *Gardar*, XII.

4 Wahlgren, 'Fact and Fancy,' pp. 47ff.

5 Select Bibliography under 'Dictionaries.'

6 Select Bibliography.

7 Jón Árnasson Smyrill ('Hawk'), Bishop of Gardar 1189–1209, is the only bishop known to have been buried in Gardar cathedral. He had learned how to make berry wine from King Sverre of Norway, H. Ingstad, *Landet under Leidarstjernen* (1960), p. 122. This passage appears to have been eliminated from the translated edition of six years later.

8 See discussion in Jones, *Norse Atlantic*, pp. 86–7.

9 Wahlgren, 'Fact and Fancy,' p. 52.

10 McKusick/Wahlgren, 'Norse Penny Mystery.'

11 Colker, 'America Rediscovered', *Speculum* (1979).

12 Lawrence M. Larson, *The King's Mirror*, New York, 1917.

13 On that, see towards the end of this chapter.

14 Åkerlund, see in Select Bibliography.

15 Tornöe, pp. 14–17, 44–5, and Plate IV.

16 On the *kenning* cf Hollander, *Skalds*, pp. 12–15.

17 On speeds, cf Tornöe, pp. 34ff.

18 Anderson, *Vinland Voyage*, p. 202, Morison, *Discovery*, p. x.

19 See Select Bibliography under Ramskou; B. Gelsinger, *Foreign Trade*, pp. 99–133, pp. 118ff.

20 Select Bibliography, under Olsen/Crumlin-Pedersen.

Chapter 9

1 Morison, *Discovery*, p. x.

2 *Erik's Saga*, Chap. 5.

3 The estimates are from Tornöe, p. 38.

4 *Greenlanders' Saga*, Chaps. 3–4.

5 Thórhall Huntsman may have been invented as an inverse pendant to Tyrkr in the other saga, cf Wahlgren, 'Fact and Fancy,' pp. 34, 36–40. The verse translation is from Magnusson and Pálsson, *Vinland Sagas*, p. 97.

6 Anderson, p. 172.

7 Reman, *Norse Voyages*, esp. pp. 60–117.

8 Morison, p. 308.

9 Frank G. Speck, *Penobscot Man*, Philadelphia, 1940, p. 66; cf Reman, pp. 110–11.

Chapter 10

1 See the articles by Schledermann, 1980, 1982.

2 Sir George Strong Nares, *Narrative of a Voyage to the Polar Sea*.

3 Schledermann, 1980, p. 221. Cf McGhee, 'Contact,', p. 21.

4 Allen P. McCartney and D. J. Mack, 'Iron Utilization by Thule Eskimos of Central Canada,' *American Antiquity*, 38 (1973), pp. 328–39.

5 Reman, pp. 118–76, argues (p. 141) that Karlsefni's Straumfjord must lie in an Arctic region, partly because of the large numbers of caribou. Writing in 1949, some years before the Ingstad discoveries, Reman makes a point which may support the idea that Straumfjord lay, not on Hudson Bay as Reman thinks, but at L'Anse aux Meadows. He says: (p. 141) 'The abundance of *grass* at Straumfjord suggests that there was *little or no forest*' (italics mine).

6 Schledermann, personal communication of 9 April 1984.

7 Cf Schledermann, 1980, p. 223; Select Bibliography under Sabo, 'A Possible Thule Carving.'

8 Extensive cartographic discussions in Skelton, et al., *Vinland Map*; in Washburn (ed.), *Proceedings*; in Skelton, *Looking at an Early map*. See also under Björnbo. In *Early Map*, p 7, Skelton warns of 'illusory conclusions' that can be drawn from 'visual judgment' which can often be based on 'accidental coincidences.' Speaking of the blind obstinacy and conservatism of mapmakers in adhering to speculative hypotheses, he mentions the bitterness of explorers who went on

arduous journeys 'in search of such chimeras' (p. 29). Often depicted is the map of the North, including *Grönlandia* and *Skraelinge Land* by the Icelander Sigurdur Stefánsson, *c.* 1590. This contains the Promontorium Winlandiae.

9 An especially valuable discussion is that contained in chap. 5 (pp. 153–82) of Gad, *Greenland.*

10 The shrunken and distorted skeletons, it was subsequently established, had become so through years of dampness and neglect in transportation and storage. Cf Steinert, *Tausend Jahre,* pp. 135ff.

11 The report was made by Jon the Greenlander, cf

Gad, pp. 164, 182. Gad, however, lists also the date 1520. Oleson, pp. 76–7. The Icelandic Bishop Ögmundr, driven off course to Greenland in 1519, claimed to have seen people herding sheep in Greenland, but as this viewing was from a great distance, he may have seen Eskimos pursuing a herd of reindeer.

12 Steinert's shaking presentation is on pp. 244–6 of his *Tausend Jahre.*

13 See J. A. Tuck in *Early Man,* vol. 3, no. 1 (Spring, 1981), pp. 13–14.

Sources of illustrations

Ålborg Museum 46; Antikvarisk-Topografiska-Arkivet 26, 28, 41, 45, 51, 52, 53; Bayeux, Musée de la Tapisserie de Bayeux 35; A. L. Binns 42; Copenhagen, National Museum 4, 6, 7, 8, 17, 18, 19, 20, 21, 22, 38, 43, 49, 59, 64, 65, 66, 67, 85, 86, 87, 88, 89, 93, 94, 95, 96, 97, 98, 99, 100, 101; Dublin, National Museum of Ireland 50; Thomas E. Lee 81, 82; O. Lindman 44; London, British Museum 36; Jørgen Meldgaard 91; Minnesota Historical Society 68; Newfoundland and Labrador Historic Parks and Sites 76; Newport County Chamber of Commerce 69; Oslo, National Gallery 1; Universitetets Oldsaksamling 29, 31, 34, 48, 92; P. Schledermann 9, 10, 11, 12, 13, 14, 15, 16; Stockholm, Royal Academy of Letters, History and Antiquities 28; Statens Historiska Museum 2, 41,

45, 52, 53; M. Stromberg 37; Swedish Tourist Board 54; Uppsala, Museum of Nordic Antiquities, Uppsala University 44; Werner Forman Archive 2; Yale University Press 70.

60, 61, 62, 63 from F. Gad, *The History of Greenland,* Vol. I, 1970

27, 39, 40 from J. Graham-Campbell, *The Viking World,* 1980

74, 77, 78, 79, 80 from A. S. Ingstad, *The Discovery of a Norse Settlement in America,* 1977

3 from H. Ingstad, *Land Under the Pole Star,* 1966

5, 102, 103 from H. J. Rink, *Tales and Traditions of the Eskimo,* 1875

71, 72, 73 from James P. Whittall, 'The Spirit Pond Runestones', *NEARA Bulletin,* 1972.

Select Bibliography

Especially useful for further study are the bibliographies contained in the works listed below under Blegen, *Kensington*; McGhee, 'Contact'; McKusick/Wahlgren, 'Norse Penny'; Oleson, *Early Voyages*; Wahlgren, 'Fact and Fancy'; Wahlgren, *Kensington*. A wealth of material on Greenland is contained in the great series *Meddelelser om Grønland* (*MoG*), Copenhagen, 1878–; for medieval Scandinavia see *Kulturhistorisk Leksikon for nordisk Middelalder*, Copenhagen, 1956– (*KLAM*). Recommended reading is the excellent introduction to the Vínland sagas by the translators, M. Magnusson and H. Pálsson. For the most important list of manuscripts cf *Katalog over den Arnamagnaeanske Håndskrift Samling*. I, II. Copenhagen, 1889–94.

Basic texts

Adam of Bremen. *Adamus Bremensis. Gesta Hammaburgensis Pontificium ecclesiae Codex Havniensis*. Introd. by C. A. Christensen. Publ. in photolithography. Copenhagen, 1949.

Antiqvitates Americanae sive Scriptores Septentrionales Rerum ante-Columbianarum in America... Ed. C. C. Rafn, Copenhagen, 1837.

Ári = *Íslendingabók Ara Fróda. AM 113a and 113b, fol*. Introd. by Jón Jóhannesson. Reykjavík, 1956. For English edition see under 'Hermannsson'.

Bárdarson, Ívar. *Det gamle Grønlands beskrivelse*. Ed. Finnur Jónsson. Copenhagen, 1930.

Bjørnbo, Axel Anthon. 'Cartographia Groenlandica' = *MoG* 48. Copenhagen, 1912, pp. 1–48.

Flateyjarbók. Corpus Codicum Islandicorum Medii Aevi. XIII. The Arnamagnaeanske Manuscript 557 4to Containing inter alia *The History of the First Discovery of America*. Introd. by Dag Strömbäck. Copenhagen, 1940.

Flateyjarbók. Codex Flateyensis. MS No. 1005 in the Old Royal Library of Copenhagen. Introd. by Finnur Jónsson. Copenhagen, 1930.

The Flatey Book and Recently Discovered Vatican Manuscripts Concerning America as Early as the Tenth Century. London, 1906.

Hermannsson, Halldór, ed. *The Book of the Icelanders by Ari Thorgilsson* [transl. of *Íslendingabók Ara Fróda*]. *Islandica* XX (1930).

Íslendinga sögur. I. Ed. Gudni Jónsson. Includes *Íslendingabók, Landnámobók, Kristni saga, Eiríks saga rauda, Groenlendinga saga, Groenlandinga Tháttr*. I. Reykjavík, 1953.

Íslenk fornrit. IV. Includes the *Groenlendingasögur*. Ed. E. O. Sveinsson and Matthías Thórdarson. Reykjavík, 1935.

Sagorna om Vinland. I: *Handskrifterna till Erik den Rödes saga*. With an English summary (Kungl. Vitterhets Historie och Antikvets Akademiens Handlingar, Del 60: 1). Stockholm, 1945.

Saga translations

Gathorne-Hardy, G. M. *The Wineland Sagas. Translated and Discussed*. Oxford, 1921.

Gravier, Maurice. *La saga d'Eric le Rouge. Le récit des Groenlandais. Texte islandais avec introduction, traduction, notes et glossaire*. Paris, 1955.

Haugen, Einar. *Voyages to Vinland. The first American saga newly translated and interpreted*. New York, 1942.

Hermannsson, Halldór. *The Vinland Sagas*. = *Islandica*, XXX. Ithaca, 1944.

Jones, Gwyn. *Eirik the Red and other Sagas*. London, 1961.

Magnusson, Magnus and Pálsson, Hermann, transl. *The Vinland Sagas. The Norse Discovery of America*. London, 1965.

Niedner, Felix. *Grönländer und Färinger Geschichten*. = Thule, Altnordische Dichtung und Prosa, Band 13. Zweite Auflage, Düsseldorf and Cologne, 1929.

Works on Greenland

Bobé, Louis. *Hans Egede. Colonizer and Missionary of Greenland*. Copenhagen, 1952.

Gad, Finn. *The History of Greenland. I. Earliest Times to 1700*. Transl. Ernst Dupont. London, 1970, Montreal, 1971.

Grønlands Historiske Mindesmerker (*GHM*). Vols I–III. Copenhagen, 1838–45.

Holtved, Erik. 'Archaeological Investigations in the Thule District'. = *MoG*, vol. 141, nos 1 and 2. Copenhagen, 1944.

Ingstad, Helge. *Landet under Leidarstjernen. En ferd til Grønlands norrøne bygder*. Oslo, 1960.

——. *Land under the Pole Star. A Voyage to the Norse Settlements of Greenland and the Saga of the People that vanished* (Transl., by Naomi Walford, of the previous item). New York, 1966.

Jensen, Adolf. 'Concerning a change of climate during recent decades in the Arctic and subarctic regions, from Greenland in the West to Eurasia in the East, and contemporary biological and geophysical changes.' = Det. Kgl. Danske Videnskabernes Selskab. *Biologiske Medd*, XIV, no. 8. Copenhagen, 1939.

Jones, Gwyn. *The Norse Atlantic Saga. Being the Norse Voyages of Discovery and Settlement to Iceland, Greenland and America*. London, New York, Toronto, 1964.

Mathiassen, Therkel. Numerous treatises on Eskimo archaeology in the various issues of *MoG*.

Nansen, Fridtjof. *In Northern Mists: Arctic Explorations in Early Times*. 1–2. Transl. Arthur G. Chater. New York. 1911.

Nares, Sir George. *Narrative of a Voyage to the Polar Sea during 1875*. vol. 1, London, 1878.

Nørlund, Poul, and Stenberger, Martin. *Brattahlid* = *MoG*, 88, no. 1. Copenhagen, 1934.

Oleson, Tryggvi J. *Early Voyages and Northern Approaches 1000–1632*. The Canadian Centenary Series. London, New York, 1964.

Rink, Hinrich Johannes. *Tales and Traditions of the Eskimo*, Edinburgh and London, 1875.

Roussel, Aage. 'Sandnes and the Neighbouring

Farms' = *MoG*, 88 no. 2. Copenhagen, 1936.
——. 'Farms and Churches in the Mediaeval Norse Settlements of Greenland' = *MoG*, 89, no. 1. Copenhagen, 1941.

Largely relating to Vínland

Andrews, A. LeRoy. 'Philological Aspects of the "Plants of Wineland the Good".' *Rhodora: Journal of the New England Botanical Club*, XV, no. 170 (Feb., 1913), 28–35.

Babcock, William H. *Early Norse Visits to North America*. Smithsonian Special Collections, LIX, no. 19 (Publication 2138). Washington, 1913.

Bessason, Haraldur. 'New Light on Vinland from the Sagas', *Mosaic*, 1:1 (Winnipeg, Oct., 1967), 52–65.

——. 'Some Notes on Leifr Eiriksson's National Origin and the Sources on Greenland and Vinland,' *The Icelandic Canadian* (Winnipeg, Winter, 1965), 13–20.

Brøgger, A. W. *Vinlandsferdene*. Oslo, 1937.

Fernald, M. L. 'Notes on the Plants of Wineland the Good,' *Rhodora: Journal of the New England Botanical Club*, XII, no. 134 (Feb., 1910), 17–38.

Gini, Corrado. *The Location of Vinland*. Bergen, 1960

Hermannsson, Halldór. *The Northmen in America* (*Islandica*, II). Ithaca, 1909.

——. *The Problem of Wineland* (*Islandica* XXV). Ithaca, 1936.

Hovgaard, William. *The Voyages of the Northmen to North America*. New York, 1914.

Jansson, Valter. *Nordiska Vin-Namn. En ortnamnstyp och dess historia* (Skrifter utgivna av Kungl. Gustaf Adolfs Akademien. 24). Uppsala and Copenhagen, 1951.

Jóhannesson, Jón. 'The Date of the Composition of the Saga of the Greenlanders,' *Saga-Book of the Viking Society for Northern Research*, XVI, Part I, 54–66, London, 1962. (Stresses the priority of the *Greenlanders' Saga*.)

Jónsson, Finnur. 'Erik den Rødes Saga og Vinland, *Norsk historisk tidsskrift udgivet av Den Norske Historiske Forening*, Femte Rekke, Første Bind (Kristiania, 1912), 116–57.

——. 'Opdagelsen af og Rejserne til Vinland,' *Aarbøger for nordisk Oldkyndighed og Historie, udgivne af Det Kongelige Oldskriftselskab*, 1915, pp. 205–21.

Kaups, Matti. 'Some Observations on Vinland,' *Annals of the Association of American Geographers*, 60, no. 3 (Sept. 1970), 603–8.

Lendin, Valdemar. 'Vinlandsproblemet. En översikt över nyare litteratur rörande källorna,' *(Svensk) Historisk Tidskrift*, Andra följden. Fjortonde årgången, Häfte 3 (1951), 322–38.

Pohl, Frederick J. *The Viking Settlements of North America*. New York, 1972.

Reman, Edward. *The Norse Explorations and Discoveries in America*. Berkeley and Los Angeles, 1949.

Skelton, R. A., Thomas E. Marston and George D. Painter. *The Vinland Map and the Tartar Relation*. With a Foreword by Alexander O. Vietor. New Haven and London, 1965.

Söderberg, Sven. 'Vinland,' *Sydsvenska Dabbladet Snällposten*, no. 295 (Malmö, 30 Oct. 1910).

Steensby, H. P. *The Norsemen's Route from Greenland to Wineland*. Copenhagen, 1917.

Storm, Gustav. 'Studier over Vinlandsreiserne, Vinlands Geografi og Ethnologi,' *Aarbøger for nordisk Oldkyndighed og Historie, udgivne af Det Kongelige Oldskriftselskab*. II. Raekke, 2. Bind, 4. Hefte (1887), 292–373.

Swanton, I. R. *The Wineland Voyages* (Smithsonian Miscellaneous Collections, CV, no. 12. Publication 3906). Washington, 1947.

Tanner, Väinö. *De gamla nordbornas Helluland, Markland och Vinland. Ett försök att lokalisera Vinlandsresornas huvudetapper i de isländska sagorna* (*Budkavlen*, XX, no. 1). Åbo, 1941.

Thorarinsson, Sigurdur. 'Några reflexioner med anledning av V. Tanners skrift,' *Ymer. Tidskrift utgiven av Svenska Sällskapet för antropologi och geografi*, LXII, no. 1–2 (1942), 39–46.

Thórdarson, Matthías. *The Vinland Voyages*. American Geographical Society Research Series, no. 18. New York, 1930.

Thorsteinsson, Björn. 'Some Observations on the Discoveries and the Cultural History of the Norsemen,' *Saga Book of the Viking Society for Northern Research*, XVI, Parts 2–3, pp. 173–91. London, 1963.

Tornöe, J. Kr. *Early American History: Norsemen Before Columbus*. Oslo, 1964.

Wahlgren, Erik. 'Further Remarks on Vínland,' *Scandinavian Studies*, XL, no. 1 (Feb., 1968), 26–35.

——. 'Fact and Fancy in the Vinland Sagas,' in E. C. Polomé (ed.), *Old Norse Literature and Mythology: A Symposium*, Austin, 1969, pp. 19–80.

Wallace, Birgitta. 'Viking Hoaxes,' in E. Guralnick (ed.), *Vikings in the West*. Chicago, 1982, pp. 53–76.

Washburn, Wilcomb E. (ed.), *Proceedings of the Vinland Map Conference*. Chicago and London, 1971.

Runic collections

Basic collections of inscriptions include the following:

Danmarks Runeindskrifter. I. *Atlas*. II. *Texte*. Ed. Lis Jacobsen and Erik Moltke, assisted by Anders Baeksted and Karl Martin Nielsen. Copenhagen, 1941–2.

Die einheimischen Denkmäler des Festlandes. Ed. Helmut Arntz and Hans Zeiss. Leipzig, 1939.

Islands Runeindskrifter = Bibliotheca Arnamagnaeana, vol. II. Ed. Anders Baeksted. Hafniae, 1942.

Norges innskrifter med de yngre runer, vols. 1–5. Ed. Magnus Olsen, Oslo, 1941–60.

Page, R. I. *An Introduction to English Runes*. London and New York, 1973.

Runic Inscriptions in Great Britain, Ireland and the Isle of Man. Ed. Magnus Olsen, in *Viking Antiquities in Great Britain and Ireland*, VI, 153–233. Bergen, 1954.

Sveriges runinskrifter. I–XIII (continuing), various editors, in recent years Sven B. F. Jansson.

Runic commentary

Agrell, Sigurd. *Runornas talmystik och dess antika förebild.* Lund, 1927.

Baeksted, Anders. *Målruner og Troldruner. Nationalmuseets Skrifter. Arkaeologisk-Historisk Raekke,* IV. Copenhagen, 1952

Brate, Erik. *Sveriges runinskrifter.* Stockholm, 1928.

Düwel, Klaus. *Runenkunde.* Stuttgart, 1968.

Elliott, Ralph W. V. *Runes, an Introduction.* Manchester and New York, 1959.

Friesen, Otto von. *Runorna* (Nordisk Kultur, VI). Stockholm, Oslo, Copenhagen, 1933.

Gould, Chester Nathan. Review of Sigurd Agrell, *Runornas talmystik,* Lund, 1927, in *Modern Language Notes* (1930), 465–8.

Haugen, Einar. *The Scandinavian Languages.* (Pages 113–227 are the best general discussion of Scandinavian runes and inscriptions available in English). Cambridge (Mass.), 1976.

Jansson, Sven B. F. *The Runes of Sweden.* Transl. by Peter G. Foote. Stockholm, 1962.

Musset, Lucien. *Introduction à la Runologie. Bibliothèque de Philologie Germanique,* XX. Paris, 1965.

Representative literary works

Edda. Die Lieder des Codex Regius nebst verwandten Denkmälern. I. Text. 3. durchgesehene Auflage. Ed. Gustav Neckel. Heidelberg, 1936.

The Elder Edda. A Selection. Translated from the Icelandic by Paul B. Taylor and W. H. Auden. New York, 1970.

The Poetic Edda. Translated with an Introduction and Notes by Henry Adams Bellows. New York, 1957.

The Prose Edda by Snorri Sturluson. Translated from the Icelandic with an Introduction by Arthur Gilchrist Brodeur. New York and London, 1923.

Egil's Saga. Translated with an Introduction by Hermann Pálsson and Paul Edwards. Harmondsworth and New York, 1976.

The Laxdoela Saga. Translated from the Old Icelandic with Introduction and Notes by A. Margaret Arendt.

Njál's Saga. Translated from the Old Icelandic with Introduction and Notes by Carl F. Bayerschmidt and Lee M. Hollander. New York, 1955.

Njal's Saga. Translated with an Introduction by Magnus Magnusson and Hermann Pálsson. Harmondsworth and Baltimore, 1960.

The Saga of Gisli. Translated from the Icelandic by George Johnston with Notes and an Essay . . . by Peter Foote. Toronto, 1963.

Additional works

Arrow-Odd: A Medieval Novel. Translated with an Introduction by Paul Edwards and Hermann Pálsson. New York and London, 1970.

Branston, Brian. *The lost Gods of England.* London, 1957.

Ciklamini, Marlene. *Snorri Sturluson.* Boston, 1978.

Craigie, W. A. *The Icelandic Sagas.* Cambridge, 1933.

Einarsson, Stefán. *A History of Icelandic Literature.* New York, 1957.

Eyrbyggja Saga. Translated from the Old Icelandic by Paul Schach. Introduction and Verse Translations by Lee. M. Hollander. Lincoln, 1959.

Gordon, E. V. *An Introduction to Old Norse.* Second Edition. Revised by A. R. Taylor. Oxford, 1957 (excellent anthology).

Heimskringla. History of the Kings of Norway by Snorri Sturluson. Translated with Introduction and Notes by Lee M. Hollander. Austin, 1964.

Hollander, Lee M. *The Skalds. A Selection of their Poems with Introductions and Notes.* Princeton, 1945.

Leach, Henry Goddard. *A Pageant of Old Scandinavia.* Princeton, 1946 (selected translations of prose and poetry).

Turville-Petre, E. O. G. *Myth and Religion of the North. The Religion of Ancient Scandinavia.* New York, 1964.

——. *Origins of Icelandic Literature.* Oxford, 1953.

Vikings

Arbman, Holger. *The Vikings.* Transl. and ed. with an Introduction by Alan Binns. London and New York, 1961.

Brøndsted, Johannes. *The Vikings.* Transl. by Kalle Skov. Harmondsworth and Baltimore, 1965.

Davidson, H. R. Ellis. *Scandinavian Mythology.* London and New York, 1969.

Graham-Campbell, James. *The Viking World.* Foreword by David M. Wilson. New Haven and New York, 1980.

Guralnick, E. (ed.). *Vikings in the West.* Chicago, 1982. The volume is comprised of papers read at an archaeological conference held at Chicago on 3 April 1982 by Gwyn Jones, T. H. McGovern, H. Ingstad, A. S. Ingstad, R. McGhee and B. Wallace, together with a joint list of illustrations. The article by Wallace (*q.v.*) contains details not previously touched on by her.

Hall, R. A. *Jorvik. Viking Age York.* York, 1982.

Kendrick, T. D. *A History of the Vikings.* London and New York, 1930.

Linklater, Eric. *The Ultimate Viking.* New York, 1955.

Magnusson, Magnus. *Hammer of the North. Myths and Heroes of the Viking Age.* New York and London, 1976

Sawyer, P. H. *The Age of the Vikings.* London, 1967.

L'Anse aux Meadows

Ingstad, Anne Stine. *The Discovery of a Norse Settlement in America. Excavations at L'Anse aux Meadows, Newfoundland, 1961–1968.* With contributions by Charles J. Bareis and John H. Winston, Arne Emil Christensen, Jr., Kari E. Henningsmoen, Kristján Eldjárn, Reidar Nydal, Leif M. Paulssen, Rolf Petré, Anna M. Rosenqvist. Oslo, Bergen, Tromsø, 1977.

Ungava

Lee, Thomas E. 'The Norse Presence in Arctic Ungava,' *American–Scandinavian Review,* 61, no. 3 (Sep., 1973), 242–57. This sums up a series of reports by the late Lee, who was on the faculty of Centre d'Etudes Nordiques, Laval University Quebec, in *Anthropological Journal of Canada*, beginning in 1966.

McGhee, Robert. 'Contact Between Native North Americans and the Medieval Norse: A Review of the Evidence,' *American Antiquity*, 49, no. 1 (1984), 4–26.

McKusick, Marshall. 'Ungava Bay Discoveries Reconsidered,' *Anthropological Journal of Canada*, 18 (1980), 2–8.

The Arctic

Jaubert, Pierre Amédée. *La Geographie d'Édrisi* (Transl. of al-Idrisi, *Nuzhat al-Mushtaq*). Paris, 1840.

Nansen, Fridtjof. See under 'Greenland.'

Rasmussen, Knud. *Across Arctic America: Narrative of the Fifth Thule Expedition*. New York and London, 1927.

Sabo, Deborah and Sabo, George. 'A Possible Thule Carving of a Viking from Baffin Island, N. W. T.,' *Canadian Journal of Archaeology*, 2 (1978), 33–42.

Schledermann, Peter. 'Notes on Norse Finds from the East Coast of Ellesmere Island, N. W. T.,' *Arctic*, 33, no. 3 (Sept., 1980), 454–63.

———. 'Nordbogenstande fra Arktisk Canada,' *Tidsskriftet Grønland*, nos 5–6–7 (1982), 218–225.

———. 'Eskimo and Viking Finds in the High Arctic,' *National Geographic*, 159, no. 5 (May, 1981), 575–601.

Thorén, Ragnar. *Picture Atlas of the Arctic*. Amsterdam, London, New York, 1969.

Wolfe, Michael, O. M. I. 'Norse Archaeology in Greenland Since World War II,' *American–Scandinavian Review* (Winter 1961–2), 380–92.

Navigation

Åkerlund, Harald. 'Åss och beiti-åss,' *Unda Maris 1955–56*, Göteborg, 1956, pp. 30–92.

Anderson, J. R. L. *Vinland Voyage*. New York, 1967.

Brøgger, A. W. and Haakon Shetelig. *The Viking Ships. Their Ancestry and Evolution*. Oslo, 1953.

Gelsinger, Bruce E. 'Lodestone and Sunstone in Medieval Iceland,' *The Mariner's Mirror*, 56, no. 2 (1970), 219–26.

———. *Foreign Trade of the Medieval Icelandic Republic*. (Ph.D dissertation, University of California, Los Angeles). University Microfilms. Ann Arbor, 1969.

Graham-Campbell, James. See above under 'Vikings.'

Morcken, Roald. 'Norse Nautical Units And Distance Measurements,' *Mariner's Mirror*, LIV (1968), 393–401.

Munn, W. A. *Wineland Voyages*, St. John's, Newfoundland, 1914.

Olsen, O. and O. Crumlin-Pedersen. *Five Viking Ships from Roskilde Fjord*. Roskilde, 1978.

Ramskou, Thorkild. 'Solstenen,' *Skalk*, no. 2 (1967), 16–17.

Reman, Edward. See under 'Vinland.'

Tornöe, J. Kr. See under 'Vinland.'

Wallace, Birgitta L. 'Vikings,' *Carnegie Magazine*, 42, no. 2 (1967), 152.

Kensington, Spirit Pond

Andersen, Harry. 'Kensington-stenen, Amerikas runesten,' *Danske Studier* (1949–50), pp. 37–60. In two parts of which A. authored the second: '2. En sproglig undersøgelse,' pp. 52–60. See also under Moltke.

Blegen, Theodore C. *The Kensington Rune Stone. New Light on an Old Riddle*. With a Bibliography by Michael Brook. St Paul, 1968.

Brøndsted, Johannes. 'Problemet om nordboer i Amerika før Columbus,' *Aarbøger for Nordisk Oldkyndighed og Historie, udgivne af Det Kongelige Oldskriftselskab*, 1950 (1951), pp. 1–152. Pages 73–88 contain Karl Martin Nielsen's 'Kensington-stenens runeindskrift.'

[Carley, Kenneth]. 'More on the Rune Stone,' *Minnesota History*, 45, no. 5 (Spring, 1977), pp. 195–9.

[Daniel, Glyn]. Editorial in *Antiquity*, LVIII, no. 222 (Mar., 1984), 1–3.

Flom, George T. 'The Kensington Rune Stone. A Modern Inscription from Douglas County, Minnesota,' *Transactions of the Illinois State Historical Society for the Year 1910* (Springfield, 1912), pp. 105–25.

Hagen, S. N. 'The Kensington Runic Inscription,' *Speculum*, XXV (1950), 321–56.

Hall, Robert A. Jr. *The Kensington Rune-Stone is Genuine. Linguistic, Practical, Methodological Considerations*. Columbia, S. C., 1982.

Haugen, Einar. 'The Rune Stones of Spirit Pond, Maine,' *Visible Language*, VIII, no. 1 (Winter, 1974), 33–64.

Holand, Hjalmar R. *The Kensington Stone*. Ephraim, Wis., 1932.

———. *America, 1355–1364*. New York, 1956. (A long list of Holand's books and articles will be found in Wahlgren, *The Kensington Stone*, pp. 217–18, see below.)

Kahn, David. Review of Mongé/Landsverk, *Norse Medieval Cryptography in Runic Carvings* (Glendale, 1967), in *American–Scandinavian Review*, LVI, no. 1 (Mar., 1968), 82–3.

Karlgren, Hans. Review of Mongé/Landsverk, *Norse Medieval Cryptography in Runic Carvings* (Glendale, 1967), in *Scandinavian Studies*, 40, no. 4 (Nov., 1968), 326–30.

Landsverk, Ole G. *The Discovery of the Kensington Runestone. A Reappraisal*. Glendale, 1961.

———. *Runic Records of the Norsemen in America*. New York, 1974.

———. 'Does Cryptogrammic Analysis Reveal Pre-Columbian Voyages to America?' *Biblical Archaeology Review*, 6, no. 2 (1980), pp. 54–5.

———. 'The Kensington Inscription is Authentic,' *Journal of the New England Antiquities Research Association*, 15, no. 3 (1981), pp. 58–62.

———. 'Runic Cryptography is Alive and Well,' *Anthropological Journal of Canada* (Winter, 1981), pp. 1–3.

Liestøl, Aslak. 'Cryptograms in Runic Carvings. A

Critical Analysis,' *Minnesota History*, 41, no. 1 (Spring, 1968), 34–42.

McKusick, Marshall and Erik Wahlgren. 'Does Cryptogramic Analysis Reveal Pre-Columbian Voyages to America?' Reply to Landsverk. *Biblical Archaeology Review*, 6, no. 2 (1980), pp. 55–6, 58.

Moltke, Erik. 'The Ghost of the Kensington Stone,' *Scandinavian Studies* XXV (Jan., 1953), 1–14.

——. 'Kensington-Stenen, Amerikas runesten,' *Danske Studier* (1949–50), pp. 37–60. In two parts, of which Moltke is the author of the first: '1. En alfabethistorisk undersøgelse,' pp. 37, 52. See also under Andersen.

Mongé, Alf, and Ole G. Landsverk. *Norse Medieval Cryptography in Runic Carvings.* Glendale, 1967.

New England Antiquities Research Association. *The Spirit Pond Runestones.* Milford, New Haven, 1972. Contains articles, photographs, maps and sketches by James P. Whittall, Jr., and Donal B. Buchanan; likewise a reprint of a humorous report by Calvin Trilling from *The New Yorker* of 5 Feb. 1972.

Olson, Daniel. 'The Mooring Stone Mystery,' (Sons of Norway) *Viking* (Oct., 1984), pp. 316–19.

Page, R. I. Review of Robert A. Hall, Jr., *The Kensington Rune-Stone is Genuine*, in *Speculum*, 58, no. 3 (July, 1983), 748–51.

Quaife, Milo M. 'The Kensington Myth Once More,' *Michigan History*, XXXI (June, 1947), 129–61.

Steefel, Lawrence D. [Remarks on the bibliography of the Kensington inscription]. *The Minnesota Archaeologist*, XXVII, no. 3 (1965), 97–115.

Strandwold, Olaf. *Norse inscriptions on American Stones.* Weehawken, New Jersey, 1948.

Thalbitzer, William. *Two Runic Stones from Greenland and Minnesota.* Smithsonian Miscellaneous Collections, 116, no. 3 (Publication 4021). Washington, 1951.

Wahlgren, Erik. 'The Runes of Kensington,' *Studies in Honor of Albert Morey Sturtevant*, pp. 59–70. Lawrence, 1952.

——. *The Kensington Stone, a Mystery Solved.* Madison, 1958.

——. 'American Runes: From Kensington to Spirit Pond,' *Journal of English and Germanic Philology*, LXXXI, no. 2 (Apr., 1982), 157–85.

——. Review of Robert A. Hall Jr. *The Kensington Rune-Stone is Genuine*, in *Language*, 59, no. 1 (1983), 231–2.

Whittall, James P. II. 'A "Runic" Amulet,' *Bulletin* of the Early Sites Research Society, 3, no. 1 (Mar., 1975), 1–5. See also under New England Antiquities Research Association.

Dictionaries

Cleasby, Richard and Gudbrand Vigfusson. *An Icelandic–English Dictionary . . .* Oxford, 1874.

Falk, Hjalmar and Alf Torp. *Etymologisk Ordbog over det norske och det danske Sprog.* Kristiania, 1903.

Fritzner, Johan. *Ordbog over det gamle norske sprog. Omarbeidet, forøget og forbedret udg.* 3 vols. *Nytt uforandret opptrykk av 2. utgave.* Oslo, 1954.

Heggstad, Leiv. *Gamalnorsk ordbok med nynorsk tyding.* Oslo, 1930.

Hellquist, Elof. *Svensk etymologisk ordbok.* Tredje

upplagan. I–II. Lund, 1957.

Torp, Alf. *Nynorsk etymologisk ordbok.* Oslo, 1963.

Zoëga, Geir T. *A Concise Dictionary of Old Icelandic.* Oxford, 1967.

Various topics

Almagià, Roberto. 'Cristofero Colombo e i viaggi precolumbiani in America,' *Rendiconti delle Adunanze solenni*, vol. V, fascicole 6 (Rome, 1951), pp. 262–79.

Boland, Charles Michael. *They All Discovered America.* New York, 1961.

Crone, G. R. 'How Authentic is the "Vinland Map"?,' *Encounter* (Feb., 1966), pp. 75–8.

Dicuil. *Liber de Mensura Orbis Terra.* Ed. James F. Kenney. Sources for the Early History of Ireland. New York, 1929.

Enterline, J. *Viking America: the Norse Crossings and their Legacy.* Garden City, 1972.

Fell, Barry. *Saga America.* New York, 1980.

Godfrey, William B., Jr. 'Vikings in America: Theories and Evidence,' *American Anthropologist*, LVII (Feb., 1955), 35–43.

Hallberg, Peter. *The Icelandic Saga.* Translated with Introduction and Notes by Paul Schach. Lincoln, 1962.

Holm, Gösta. 'Nordbor i Amerika före Columbus. Äkta fynd och falska,' *Gardar. Årsbok för Samfundet Sverige-Island i Lund-Malmö*, XII (Lund, 1981), 1–14.

Lindroth, Hjalmar. *Iceland, A Land of Contrasts.* Transl. by Adolph B. Benson. New York, 1937.

McGovern, Thomas. 'The Vinland Adventure. A North American Perspective,' *North American Archaeologist*, 2, no. 4 (1980–81), pp. 285–308.

McKusick, Marshall and Erik Wahlgren. 'The Norse Penny Mystery,' *Archaeology of Eastern North America*, vol. 8 (1980), pp. 1–10.

Mallery, Arlington H. *Lost America: The Story of Iron-Age Civilization in America Prior to Columbus.* Washington, 1951.

Michlovic, Michael G. and Michael W. Hughey. 'Norse Blood and Indian Character: Content, Context and Transformation of Popular Mythology,' *Journal of Ethnic Studies*, 10, no. 3 (1982), 79–94.

Morison, Samuel Eliot. *The European Discovery of America. The Northern Voyages A.D. 500–1600.* Oxford, 1971.

Mowat, Farley. *Westviking. The Ancient Norse in Greenland and North America.* Boston, 1965.

Page, R. I. Review of Alf Mongé and O. E. Landsverk, *Norse Medieval Cryptography in Runic Carvings* (Glendale, 1967). In *Scandinavica*, 7, no. 1 (May, 1968), 70–71.

Quinn, D. B. *North America from Earliest Discovery to First Settlement. The Norse Voyages to 1612.* New York, 1977.

Skelton, R. A., *Looking at an Early Map.* University of Kansas Library Series, Number 17. Lawrence, 1965.

Wallace, Birgitta L. 'Some Points of Controversy,' *The Quest for America* (ed. Geoffrey Ashe), pp. 155–74. London, 1971.

Index